Praise for *Divine Ecosystem*

Randazzo is a master weaver, bringing together metaphor, narrative, autobiography, theology, contemporary culture, and Quaker faith and practice in this lively, new liberal Quaker theology. The ecosystem method makes clear a broader, more complex interdependence of theology that challenges individualized and simplistic theological approaches. These Quaker threads are interwoven with others as diverse as ecotheology, personal narrative, and myriad perspectives and experiences, ensuring that the warp and weft of *Divine Ecosystem* are finely tuned to what is most urgent today. The book crafts a new Quaker theological fabric to add to and make one's own. I am eager to see what Quakers and non-Quakers alike discover of their own theology reflected in this tightly woven tapestry.

—C. Wess Daniels, William R. Rogers Director of Friends Center and Quaker Studies, Guilford College

In *Divine Ecosystem*, Dr. Christy Randazzo weaves together several threads of theological tradition, personal stories, and the urgency of the current moment. What emerges is simultaneously brand-new and deeply rooted in the liberating Jesus Way. Through the metaphor of a tree embedded in its interconnected ecosystem, Randazzo artfully describes the way the Spirit moves, enlivening the community of all life. While this book promises—and delivers—a particularly Quaker theology, *Divine Ecosystem* will be useful and inspiring to those from a variety of traditions who yearn for an embodied theology that speaks to today's issues, including the climate crisis and human belonging in the twenty-first century. More than anything else, this text offers hope grounded in spiritual community, and invites us to stretch and grow toward the Light, bringing forth the seeds of new life as we navigate a new era in the life of the church.

—Cherice Bock, climate policy director, 350PDX; adjunct assistant professor of environmental studies, University of Portland

Christy Randazzo's *Divine Ecosystem* invites us to recognize the *ecosystem* as a grounding metaphor for differing components of Quaker thought, experience, and practice. Weaving together Quaker history and customs, personal stories, sociopolitical analysis, and pop culture references, Randazzo turns things inside out! Instead of engaging theology to understand creation better, we are treated to an expert encounter with creation (through light, trees, vines, rivers, mushrooms, soil, clouds, and more) to understand our theologies better. The book contains not only a profound explication of Quaker theology but also a bold invitation to readers to consider deeply how their own ecological and denominational contexts might combine with and inform emergent ecotheologies.

—Rachel Wheeler, associate professor of theology, University of Portland; author of *Radical Kinship: A Christian Ecospirituality*

DIVINE ECOSYSTEM

DIVINE ECOSYSTEM

A QUAKER THEOLOGY

CHRISTY RANDAZZO

FORTRESS PRESS
Minneapolis

DIVINE ECOSYSTEM
A Quaker Theology

30 29 28 27 26 25   1 2 3 4 5 6 7 8 9

Library of Congress Control Number: 2025935085 (print)

Cover image: Pine Forest Wood Treetops. Long Angle Dramatic Bottom View Up Above. Tall Trees. Blue Sky on Background. - stock photo from Artem Koviazin/Getty Images
Cover design: Ashley Muehlbauer

Print ISBN: 978-1-5064-9695-5
eBook ISBN: 978-1-5064-9696-2

I dedicate this book to my queer and trans family: We are beautiful, we are majestic, we are fabulous, we are loved—most especially by the Divine. We are all conduits of God's grace, compassion, fierceness, and unadulterated joy—that's the *blessing* of being queer.

Regardless of how anyone else feels about it, *we* know that we bring a special beauty to this world. It's God's gift, so no one—no principality, no power, no theology, no religious law, nobody and nothing whatsoever—can take that away from us. Ever.

Morris Antonio Pitts

CONTENTS

ACKNOWLEDGMENTS

I am rooted in my cheery and colorful office, with this north and west view—my library, where I spend all of my working hours. While I spend much of my life in solitude, I am never truly *alone*, as I am rooted in a community that claims me and sees me as family. This book grew from a seed and took root due to the astonishing and gratifying support I've received from all of these branches of my community over the last five years of dreaming this project.

I want to thank Laura Gifford, my fantastic editor at Fortress Press, who remained steadfastly supportive of me during this entire process, especially when I hadn't written a word for this book—in over a year—due to the most overwhelming and oppressive writer's block imaginable. You trust my work: What a fantastic gift that has been! Thank you, truly.

One of the most generous acts of service you can offer a writer is to be willing (and excited!) to read their work from a place of care and love, and to offer that care and love in the form of helpful and honest feedback. I want to thank all of those who dedicated time to read this book before it was published and offered your wisdom as well as your vulnerable honesty. I particularly want to express my gratitude to Janet Demarest, Welling Hall, Joel Thompson, Andrew Glos, Maya Kociba, Katie Breslin, Windy Cooler, Lina Blount, and most especially Dennis Edwards, who has been a friend, mentor, and an inspiration to me for almost two decades now—the truest *mensch*.

To all of my theology/ministry friends (especially Cherice Bock), my co-imaginers of a new world: Thank you for your creativity and passion but most especially for your commitment and love. Y'all have each inspired me, at countless moments and in countless ways, to keep trudging through the quagmire that is committing your life in service to a dream: that we might be able to do our part to build the kin-dom of God amid the rubble of empire. I am absolutely certain that together, we can achieve anything.

To my chosen family: You know who you are and who you are to me. From the depths of my soul, I offer my endless gratitude. You have shown—always—what love means.

To Woven Faith Community: You have become family, in every way imaginable. I love you all and bask in the warmth of the circle of hopeful joy you have wrapped me in these last years—most especially your definite and defiant insistence that God loves queer and trans people completely, intimately, intensely. Whenever I am with any of you, I am home.

My most darling Rebecca, the most precious blessing I have ever received is the honor of being your parent. I see the future in your eyes. You have opened my heart and soul, helping me see possibilities for a new world, a new way of being. You have the strength to overcome every obstacle and the compassion to never lose your humanity in the process. You have doused my heart in hope: Thank you, mija preciosa.

Megan, my most beloved, I will readily admit that living with me has not been an entirely enjoyable experience (to put it *extraordinarily* mildly) during these last months, as I have desperately faced the looming, immovable deadline wall. Your commitment to this beautifully adventurous life we've chosen to live together is the most complete expression of love I have ever received—and I receive it in thousands of little ways, in the small moments that accrue across a lifetime, creating a marriage. Thank you for weaving the trunk and roots of your life together with mine: Of all earthly joys, thou art my choice—today and forever.

Finally, thank *you*, God—my constant companion and the purpose of my existence—from the absolute depths of my heart: You are *everything*.

Convincement Stories

Spa Creek, Severn River, Chesapeake Bay Watershed, Early June 2008

On a beautiful day in early June—a perfect day, really, with a cloudless sky—I was given a vision of the Light of God.

I was standing in the doorway of a church, waiting to enter a planning meeting for that Protestant youth and children's ministry rite of passage—the Vacation Bible School. The sun was streaming through the door, light bouncing off the white everywhere—white walls, white tiles, white ceiling, white stairs—*and then, suddenly . . .*

I was in a grove of trees, hushed, a rectangular forest cathedral with no pews, no rows, no altar, but a tree: bent at two right angles, forming a flat table expanse. Emanating from that table altar was bright light, casting everywhere, drawing me close. I inched forward, and the light came alive, glinting off the green everywhere (so *green*), dancing into vines that slithered and snaked around the altar tree. I *experienced* a presence, and I knew that I was supposed to be *alive*—somehow, following this Light—somewhere: out of all of my previous narratives of church, theology, and God. Roots extended from my feet, embedding themselves in the rich loam understory. Branches snaked off from my arms, towering over me as a second overstory. The light penetrated me, and I felt energy hum from my fingers to my toes. I looked up . . .

And was back in a bright hallway on a perfect early June day. I walked directly to my meeting, sat down, and—in shock—related my experience to my colleagues. We prayed and then spent the next two hours planning daily worship for a camp of fifty children. I went home—silent. I knew that my world had tilted on its axis—so I played with my daughter, made dinner, watched TV, and went to sleep.

This experience was etched deep into my soul, however: Everything I have done since then, whether it was learning about the theology and practice of peacemaking in divided and broken communities, my rooting in Quaker theology, or my turn toward learning (and writing) about ecotheology and theologies of Light, has been done in response to this experience. I now interpret this vision as God calling me toward Friends and toward my theological vocation: It is thus the story of my convincement as a Friend, when I became convinced of the truth of God as the Light Within. This book is a direct consequence of my seeking to understand how to live this vision into being.

Spiritual autobiography with the intent of reflecting on one's life as a means of growing in faith or expressing one's theology—or "journals," as the form is known in Quaker tradition—is a core practice in Christian tradition generally. Augustine, Julian of Norwich, John Woolman, George Fox, and Thomas Merton (among many others) have all written a corpus of spiritual and theological autobiography that still inspires and teaches incarnationally: They relate in story their experience of the Divine, and their response to that experience, with the hopes of aiding others along the way. Due to the experiential nature inherent in Quaker spirituality and theology, these journals have become one of the central means by which Friends pass on their theological thought: relating to a wider framework of embodied ethics the ways they respond to experiences. Quakers thus do theology by experiencing it, living into that experience, reflecting on it, and then "reading" the journals of people in their community, written through their way of life. Friends are, ourselves, *story*.

We particularly learn from the lives of "weighty Friends": those the community has recognized live lives aligned particularly closely with the Quaker way, becoming living journals from whom we all learn. This status in the community is not controlled by any authority. Weight is not earned. Weight is not granted. Weight is *recognized*. Yet, as soon as a Friend is known to declare that they know more than another about the truth of the Divine Presence, they are rapidly reminded that the Quaker way is lived into, and we can only ever truly know our own life, our own experiences. Therefore, this is "*A* Quaker Theology"—it is only one potential expression of the experiences, beliefs, practices, and meaning of the Quaker way. So, consider this my imprimatur to write something known as Quaker theology: not declaring what is capital-*T* True but what is *experienced* and speaking from that place.

This is a theological method that emerges when one focuses on life—as embodied ethic, embodied theology—a *life cycle* through which Quakers experience the reality of the Divine Presence in every fiber of their being, which itself continuously evolves as the Divine continues to reveal themself to us. As we grow, bloom, and hopefully flourish in our lives, our awareness and interpretation of our encounters with the Divine matures and evolves, responding to the certainty of dynamic uncertainty in our lives. Basically, as we change across our lifetimes, the Divine adapts to our evolution, continuing to teach us and reach for us in ways that are relevant to our context in each moment. This is theology about life in relationship, therefore: an ecotheology.

The method is narrative, poetic, metaphorical, constructive—and also systematic, just in a way that suits the Quaker theological landscape. This is my response, my journal, to my experience in 2008 and the theology that emerged, significantly evolving over the last sixteen years. This is an observational *and* researched work, as it emerges from years of immersing myself fully in Quaker community—in the experience of real Quaker faith communities as well as the writings of Friends. As this is Quaker theological method, this is a work of continuing revelation: My thinking about these ideas has changed over time, and the writing I include here reflects that. I have woven into the fabric of this book my writing from across the entire sweep of a sixteen-year time span—my entire life as a Quaker, so far—so you might notice that some sections are written in one style, others in another.

This is intentional: Theology isn't written at some remove from life, as a grand culminating body of work summarizing one's thought at the end of one's life. No! It is written in the flow of life: lived into, reflected on, adapted to—and lived into again. As this is a journal, I have included journal entries from specific points in my life that speak to the story I am telling here. They are labeled with a specific place and a specific time, so that you know when and where I am rooting the story at that moment.

As a result, its methodological structure may not be obvious to you from the very beginning. Like any story, it may need to reveal itself to you as you journey through, and you may need to allow it to do so. At this point, the main thing you need to know is that this is a story, and a method, responding to the question of retaining hope in apocalyptic times. Everything else will be revealed in time.

This is theological method—and.
This is craft—and.
This is construction—and.
This is story—and.

This is experience—and.
This is apocalypse—and.
This is Quaker—and.
This is ecotheology—and.
This is political theology—and
—many more things besides.
This is a life; lived.

Prologue: Promises Made and Kept

Gunpowder River, Chesapeake Bay Watershed, January 3, 2016

I wrote this sermon before the 2016 election and before moving to New Jersey. It serves as an overture, if you will: a summary of the themes of the story I will tell in this book. I delivered it as a sermon, during a time when I was wrestling with Spirit about where they were leading me to go in my life—and in the first flush of the hope of the new year, a year that would bloom into everything that 2016 was in the world, and in my life specifically.

~ ~ ~

The Divine is incarnate and is thus bound and shaped by the limitations and unique beauty of human creaturehood. In Quaker theology, this is called "that of God within" the human person: All of creation is marked by God's presence as a product of their creation. We are capable of being in relationship with God not only because God made us, but also because God desires it to be so. We all share our lives with a constant companion: the spark of the divine within us. This spark calls on us to live into our divine selves, to become, through both faith *and* works, the kind of people who can live into the promise of this intense relationship with God.

This is not unique to Friends, though. The early Christian church spoke about the incarnation bridging the gap between human and divine, bringing humans more fully into the divine life. The Eastern Orthodox church has long termed this process *theosis*, while the Roman Catholic church calls this divinization, and the Wesleyan tradition calls it holiness. The Christian tradition teaches us that we discover who God is by looking toward the human Jesus and that we discover who humans are by looking toward God and God's actions in the world. When we do, we discover something unsettling and surprising: Humans are *not* meant to be powerful.

The Christmas season reminds us of this inescapable truth: God entered the world in the most vulnerable way possible—completely powerless. We sometimes forget the harsh reality of God's birth in the sepia tones of our domesticated vision of the quiet stable. Yet, the ever-existing Incarnate Word of John's Gospel was born to a teenage girl hiding under the crippling social shame of being unmarried and pregnant. Mary the God-bearer came from an oppressed and completely powerless class and race, and was forced to make an incredibly dangerous journey in the midst of an exercise designed to demonstrate the complete dominance and power of her colonial overlords. She was subjected to discrimination based on her class and poverty, and was forced to birth her child in a filthy parking garage without privacy or medical help.

As soon as her child was born—that very night—she was visited by the lowest class of people. Shepherds did the most physically demanding, most unappealing, and most dangerous work of the day, and as a result were forced to live on the margins of society, suffering significant prejudice and discrimination as a result. Therefore, the very first people to visit God, to recognize that God was living among us, were day laborers and sanitation workers. Within days, this oppressed family was forced to flee for their lives to a foreign land due to the fear of impending government-sanctioned violence. (Yes: The Holy Family were Middle Eastern political refugees, and every time that we reject refugees, we are rejecting God—*full stop.*)

God therefore entered the world in the most vulnerable way possible. God took the most profound risks to fulfill the promise of the Messiah. This is not a God of power and glory as we understand it. Is this really what God promised us so long ago? Is this the Savior, the Messiah, who would break us free from sin, death, and oppression? Is this really the model for how God desires us to fulfill our promises? If God was made one of us, and we are thus reciprocally brought into the divine nature, then we are irrevocably shaped by God's nature and must then take very careful notice of what that nature is if we are to live truly *human* lives. This is the key question, then: How are we to make and keep promises in light of the absolute vulnerability of God's promise?

This is the season for making promises, isn't it? How many of y'all made a New Year's resolution this year? How many of y'all have kept your promise? Now, here's the really interesting question: How many of y'all have already broken that promise? I'm sure there are a few! We make these promises in the flush of a new year, a time that seems pregnant with opportunity for birth—and rebirth. Every year, so many of us tell ourselves and our communities that we will exercise more, eat better, serve our community more (or less, as the case may be), yell at our kids less, and the most elusive of all: find contentment with the bountiful blessings that have been so graciously given by God. Yet, how many years have we found ourselves in mid-January quietly laying down the promises we took on with such sound, fury, and fanfare—which, in the end, seemed to signify nothing? We see the hard evidence of our inability to keep our promises—for years—and then proceed to ignore all of it once the new year rolls around again. Why?

Because we actually *are* capable of keeping promises. Thankfully, New Year's Eve is not the final word in human commitment. All of us have made truly significant promises in our lives, such as marriage, parenthood, or friendship: promises that, through the daily challenge of their maintenance, define our lives and give meaning and structure to our identities. We make sacrifices, both significant and seemingly insignificant, in order to keep our word. Through the continual, boring, daily choice to sacrifice, we are transformed into the kind of people who can maintain a promise. In this way, keeping a promise is a discipline that requires continuous effort, often quite strenuous, that is rarely ever rewarded in the short term—and sometimes not even in the long term, at least in a way we can understand as reward. Keeping a promise is something that must be seen as having value in and of itself, done for its own sake, because we refuse to accept that we will ever be the kind of people who cannot keep promises.

This applies even more in the cases where the promise is small, for our inability to keep the small promises undermines our ability to keep the big promises. Now, this doesn't mean that because we struggle to keep our promise to stop hitting snooze "just one more time," we will never be able to hold to our wedding vows. If that were the case, then I'm certain that a good number of us should just take our wedding rings off. Yet, the principle applies when we accept that the big decisions are just a long succession of small decisions made over, and over, and over again. Our commitments to each other are actually these multifaceted collections of daily, tiny, quotidian promises made, kept, and hopefully not broken very often. The promises made that really matter are kept in the quiet moments when it would be far easier to break them—those thoroughly banal times, when it seems like a small deal to ease up in our commitment to becoming the person who fulfills their commitments.

Yet, it is in these quiet—and seemingly invisible—moments that we demonstrate the mark that God's creation has made on our souls. God continually makes promises to the creation. They flow out from God's very essence and are the foundation of our reality. They are the covenants that give the world structure. Through their gradual flowering, we gain the hope needed to sustain us through the pain and sacrifice of waiting: the rainbow, the stars in the sky, the land of milk and honey, the Messiah. It is one truth about God we can be absolutely certain of and depend on: God will always make promises to the creation, which God will always keep, no matter the sacrifices required. Jesus was tempted, in very human ways, in both the desert and the garden, and kept his promise. That's an interesting contradiction, no? Maybe it shows that Jesus can be faithful in all circumstances, perhaps? The lesson here is that if we share in the divine nature of God through the incarnation, we also have the capacity to keep our promises, in times lean *and* fat, chaotic *and* boring, in the significant *and* the banal.

God shows humility by shedding power, safety, and economic security, and shows commitment by continuously shedding the same. God shows determination by continually holding to God's promise to Noah to never again destroy the creation, even when we seem hell-bent on doing it ourselves. God shows courage by being vulnerable in the face of what seems like certain danger. God shows a willingness to take risks by engaging in the extremely vulnerable work of embracing humans—both despite and because of the risk involved. Finally, God shows a willingness to have hope. God knows how often humans fail to uphold their promises by either breaking them or by failing to even make them in the first place. In the terms of the market, humans are very risky investments. Yet, by making such risky promises, God demonstrates a profound willingness to have hope in humanity.

How can we respond to the unbelievable—and seemingly foolish—hope God continually shows in us? We must reflect our divine nature and have hope as well. We must accept that to be truly human is to live into the promise God made to us at creation, when God created us in the divine image. If God hopes, we must hope—and never lose hope. I admit, this sounds both impossible and impossibly naive. The world is not lacking in plenty of good reasons to lose hope. Yet, hope must be our last reserve of strength, our final defense in the face of impending defeat. We must show an intense stubbornness and absolutely refuse to concede hope, no matter the circumstances.

We must consider hope to be our most precious possession—always.

CHAPTER ONE

Quaker Theological Method

Ecosystem Stories

Lower Delaware River Watershed, Late March 2024

The tree right outside my window—a star magnolia—is budding a rambunctious spray of white circles, each thin petal shivering in the wind.

This is deeply disturbing to me.

You see, I tell time by the trees outside my window. As the trees cycle through the rhythms of the year, I note the passage of time by the actions of the leaves and flowers: the tiniest shoots of leaves and the buds of flowers in early spring, the glory of their verdant summer canopies, the vibrant autumn colors of transformation and death, floating to the ground, and finally the stoic, stark beauty of winter. Of the trees that I can see outside the windows of my office, my favorites are three: the aforementioned star magnolia, its cousin the sweetbay magnolia, and my dear survivor, a Japanese (kousa) dogwood.

I've worked from home for years, and during the day, when everyone else in the house is out in the world, these trees are my constant companions. At this point, I feel a close kinship with each of them individually. For example, I've celebrated my easy familiarity with the sweetbay magnolia, the tree closest to my windows (and thus the one I constantly see throughout my day), by marking its outline along my left forearm in that most permanent of decorations: the tattoo. The sweetbay helps me know when winter is almost over, for the last of its leaves finally falls in late winter, soon before the first leaves of the new cycle begin to grow. The star magnolia then gets in on the action, signaling the beginning of spring in late March/early April with the opening of the first white splashes of color on what is generally the bleak and stark canvas of early spring on the lower Delaware. Finally, the dogwood begins to spread its broad white petals, signaling the beginning of the second half of spring.

This dogwood is a survivor because it labored under the weight—and shadow, literally—of a massive cedar tree that took root, years ago, not two feet away. This cedar eventually grew far too large for its location and began to die. The dogwood was forced to adapt to this, eventually becoming stooped and bent over from its branches constantly stretching out to find whatever light could stream through the branches of its massive neighbor. When the cedar finally began to suffer the consequences of its overgrowth—branches shriveling, growing brittle, and falling down—the dogwood took full advantage, sprouting entirely new branches, rapidly stretching to reach the light. These trees are teachers: I've learned that yes, you will suffer potentially deadly consequences if you grow larger than your available resources, and I've also been reminded of the necessity to always strive to persevere, even in the face of the most distant of odds.

These trees are family, literally rooted in this same particular patch of ground where I am myself rooted (metaphorically, at least). Their rhythms and mine coexist, meaning that any shift in their rhythms disturbs me on a deeper level, akin to kinship, with a pain that cuts close to my heart. I feel helpless in the face of something as massive as global climate change, incapable of doing anything to stop it—or even *pause* it. However global these changes are, though, these trees are experiencing these changes in this particular time, rooted in this particular space. That means that I can experience similar changes in the rhythms of life to the trees as long as I allow myself to feel them.

These changes are really happening, and on a global scale. For example, these last few years have been the warmest years in the modern temperature record, which dates all the way back to 1850, when such records began to be kept.[1] At first blush, admittedly, the actual numbers don't appear alarming: The average global temperature in 2023, for example, was 1.18°C (2.12°F) above the twentieth century's average temperature of 13.9°C (57.0°F). It's only when you see the trends that the danger begins to emerge: The warmest years in the temperature record all occurred during the last decade (2014–2024). That means that every year, for at least the past ten, the global average temperature

---

1. NOAA National Centers for Environmental Information, "2023 Was the Warmest Year in the Modern Temperature Record," Climate.gov, January 17, 2024, https://www.climate.gov/news-features/featured-images/2023-was-warmest-year-modern-temperature-record#:~:text=Details,decade%2520(2014%E2%80%932023).

has been record breaking. Literally. A recent report, published in 2021 by the Bulletin of the American Meteorological Society, even ranked New Jersey as the state with the highest average increase in temperature in the entire United States.[2] As *The New Jersey Herald* notes, average temperatures for each of the four seasons have increased dramatically: "Autumns warmed up by 2.47 degrees, winters by 2.98 degrees, springs by 2.10 degrees and summers by 2.34," while the averages for the other states were, notably, at least a degree less for each season.[3]

Again, differences of a few degrees might not *seem* dangerous; I mean, how many of us shift the thermostat in our home two degrees and actually notice a significant difference? Yet, this is where a focus on specific context helps us see the immense impact that these tiny shifts have on larger ecosystems. First, I recommend that you take a second to look at a map of New Jersey, the state in which I live.

As you can see, New Jersey is officially a peninsula, surrounded by water on three sides: The Atlantic Ocean runs along the entire eastern coast of the state; the Delaware River runs parallel to the west, along the entirety of the New Jersey–Pennsylvania border; and finally, the Delaware Bay wraps around the southern coast. This only leaves the small northern land border with New York State.

Water defines the state, mainly through its seemingly ubiquitous abundance. Numerous rivers crisscross New Jersey, while the Delaware and Raritan Canal in Central Jersey still connects the Delaware River to the Raritan River. (When it was built in the nineteenth century, the D&R Canal effectively provided a water highway between Philadelphia and New York, and aided significantly in New Jersey's development as an industrial powerhouse during the Industrial Revolution.) Despite the state's significant population density (the highest population density in the country!), wetland areas dominate massive chunks of the landscape, from the Meadowlands and Great Swamp in North Jersey, to the Pinelands (also known as the Pine Barrens) in South Jersey—a

2. Jessica Blunden and T. Boyer, eds., "State of the Climate in 2020," *Bulletin of the American Meteorological Society* 102, no. 8 (2021), https://ametsoc.net/sotc2020/State_of_the_Climate_in_2020_LowRes96.pdf.

3. Bruce Scruton, "'We Are All in Trouble.' New Jersey Tops List of States Warming Up the Fastest," *New Jersey Herald*, August 30, 2021, https://www.njherald.com/story/news/2021/08/30/nj-weather-tops-list-of-states-global-warming/5615695001/.

massive (1.1 million acres) wilderness area, the largest wilderness area along the Eastern Seaboard of the United States. The sandy soils of the Pine Barrens have created a unique ecosystem that is part wild forest and part wetland, a drowned landscape that is often easier to traverse by boat than by land. Nearly two-thirds of the overall land area of the state is coastal plain, a generally flat landscape whose northern border runs in a relatively straight line from the mouth of New York harbor in the east to Trenton in the west. Finally, the famous Jersey Shore—all 137 miles of it—both is an invaluable economic engine for the state through summer tourism and serves as a central pillar of New Jersey culture and identity.

No water, no New Jersey. Too much water, no New Jersey.

All of this water, coupled with the flat plain dominating the entire southern half of the state, means that New Jersey is *significantly* threatened by the impacts of climate change on water, whether that be a rise in sea levels or an increase in the number and severity of storms. Some models suggest that if sea levels along the New Jersey coastline continue to rise at the current rate, it is up to 66 percent likely that sea levels will rise one foot by 2030 and two feet by 2050.[4] I invite you to consider what impact a two-foot rise in sea levels will have on a state dominated by a low coastal plain, whose interior is riddled with a dizzying number of rivers, streams, and creeks. How would all of this extra water affect tide levels? What about the shoreline? What happens when an already wet state encounters one of these superstorms that are occurring these days with frightening regularity? New Jerseyans already know one answer to that question. It was delivered with brutal effectiveness in 2012, when Superstorm Sandy (a category 3 Atlantic hurricane) hit the Jersey Shore with the energy of an explosive round: It not only killed ten people, but it also destroyed boardwalks up and down the Shore and flooded massive sections of North Jersey—while completely remaking miles of coastline.

In this sense, therefore, climate change is similar to driving on a highway: Small, seemingly imperceptible shifts—a slight turn of the wheel or a tiny increase in global temperature—make significant impacts, especially as they play out over time. Yet, every year it seems that time shifts, slowly but

---

4. New Jersey Climate Change Resource Center, "Sea Level Rise in New Jersey: Projections and Impacts," Rutgers University, May 2020, https://njclimateresourcecenter.rutgers.edu/climate_change_101/sea-level-rise-in-new-jersey-projections-and-impacts/#:~:text=For%20example%2C%20according%20to%20a,feet%20between%202000%20and%202050.

continuously, toward an earlier arrival of spring, and my tree family is directly in the path of these changes. I am at a loss for words to describe this level of terror other than *existential.*

I recognize this intense level of fear, for it's the same terror I would feel as a child whenever I was faced with the potential of the sheer, mind-numbing terror of thermonuclear war with the USSR and its allies. Just like learning to live with the constant drumbeat of the Cold War, and my inability to do anything to resolve it as a child, it is maddening to be forced to realize that while one might be able to make some—likely tiny—impact on this global crisis, one person alone is powerless to adjust the course of these incomprehensibly *huge* changes. I can attest, with absolute certainty, that it's not healthy—on any level but especially mentally—to spend your entire life living with the threat of global catastrophe.

I am not alone in feeling what has been termed *climate anxiety.* Not an actual, diagnosable illness, climate anxiety is instead a constellation of emotional and physical responses—drawn from depression, anxiety, and stress disorders—that have as their root the existential fear that massive areas of the world will soon be unlivable. I appreciated the succinct definition offered by a recent study: "Climate change anxiety, defined as a chronic fear of environmental doom."[5]

Doom! This is not a word thrown around lightly. And so, climate anxiety is itself something not to take lightly or dismiss, for it is inextricably linked to the absolute, literal, fundamental foundation of our existence: the earth's ability to provide life. Despite the Mars-fueled fever dreams of tech billionaires, the earth is our *only* home now, and will likely remain so for an extremely long time. If the soil becomes bitter, the water sour, and the air brown and acrid, what life will survive? Will we be able to live lives worth living? This goes *far* beyond the spiritual practice of meditating on one's own death. While pondering one's own death can train one in disciplining one's ego (an unalloyed good, in my opinion), pondering the end of life itself (as we know it) always struck me as a far more traumatic experience.

How, then, am I to respond? The obvious actions are the things anyone can do: shrink my carbon footprint, reduce my trash volume, recycle, petition

5. Lukas Schwab et al., "Climate Change Related Depression, Anxiety and Stress Symptoms Perceived by Medical Students," *International Journal of Environmental Research and Public Health* 19, no. 15 (2022): 9142.

my government to pass climate-friendly policies—and then vote based on how the government responds, and so on. Yet, I can attest from personal experience that working from home, installing solar panels, and eating vegetarian—all combined—cannot make your climate anxiety go away, because they aren't tackling the problem at its most fundamental root: The stories we tell ourselves that allow us to accept the deep and oft-irrevocable damage we do to the creation around us, and the structures that enable us the power to do such damage in the first place. We know that we can't recycle our way out of the mess we've made for ourselves, yet when the stories we tell valorize the human above the rest of creation, and frame "good" mainly based on serving individual *human* self-interest, the only response we have is on the individual level, serving human needs first.

If I am to help my tree companions, therefore, I must become so rooted to their context, *this specific context*, with all of its quirks and variety and rhythms and beauty, that my ties to this place root themselves deep within my body and soul. I must feel this context from my companions' perspectives. I need to feel the same shifts in climate. I need to breathe the same smoke from wildfires in Canada—or the Pine Barrens, as the case may be. I must embed this soil in my fingernails and help plants take root that will themselves root countless new communities of life. In other words, I must cease to see myself as an individual separate from my companions and instead recognize that we are in a close and intimate relationship: I am quite certain that the sweetbay and I have exchanged oxygen and carbon dioxide many, many times. Therefore, I am not only metaphorically bound up in the same community as these wise and beautiful companions, but am also bound on a material level that is easily measured by the tools of science. Fundamentally: I must acknowledge that I am *already* in such a tightly bound relationship, and as such I must reject the dangerously comforting lies of infinite economic growth and human ownership of the world.

We are thus bound up in an ecosystem, my wise old companions and me. Yet, that ecosystem is itself only a tiny shard in the mosaic of innumerable ecosystems that combine to comprise the ecosystem of the entire Earth: the biosphere, or ecosphere, as it's also known. It is only when I root myself, embed myself, somewhere *particular* that I truly see the interconnectedness of the entire creation: It is only at *that* point I can recognize how vulnerable I truly am to forces far, *far* out of my control.

Vulnerability tears any illusions of human independence to shreds rather quickly. Let's imagine together for a minute. How safe are you in your current situation—truly safe? How healthy are you? When you tell your body to do something, does it tend to respond the way you were expecting it to? Do you feel those pangs of fear in those last few days before your next paycheck, praying that the sometimes random chaos of life doesn't find you until the check finally clears? Now, imagine a wrecking ball swinging through the architecture of your life: Some things might escape unharmed, but nothing would be unaffected. This can happen to *anyone*, at *any time*. Forget this intense and overpowering truth at your peril: The foundational reality of existence is vulnerability. It's folly to say otherwise. To exist at all requires engaging with this world through our bodies—so deeply vulnerable, so easily harmed, and so difficult to fix once broken.

Intriguingly, this paradox is itself the fundamental bedrock of Christianity: It was only through rejecting the pursuit of power for its own sake, and accepting the absolute vulnerability of the human condition, that God could live a fully human life, with an unwavering commitment to embody the justice, the love, the compassion, the beauty, the joy—especially the joy—that God desires for creation. Jesus lived this life so completely that it resulted in his death at the hands of the state—the principalities and powers, the structures that have been created by God to give order and purpose to existence, which have long been warped to an absurd degree.

So, what can I specifically do at this time? I am a theologian, so why not address this situation theologically? Can we heal our planet through healing our ability to think creatively, to allow ourselves to imagine—and construct—new ways and systems of imagining our world and what our place in it could be?[6] If we take a page from the theology of trauma, we are reminded that we heal only when first we accept our inherent vulnerability. You can't heal if you don't first acknowledge that you're capable of being broken. That's what this book is about: offering one way of imagining a new world, a new state of being in the world, that we can create—in response to this crisis, this eschaton (perhaps)—that offers a way to heal the broken narratives of empire, power,

---

6. Serene Jones, *Trauma and Grace: Theology in a Ruptured World* (Westminster John Knox, 2009).

and individual self-interest with stories of hope, compassion for the entire creation, and decentering human will as the compass for all human action.

I have woven a story here that seeks to respond to these challenges with flexibility and creativity; to offer a framework for constructing Quaker theology systematically and comprehensively, while acknowledging that it will be inherently—and necessarily—incomplete; and finally, to root itself in the Christian tradition while being reflected through an intentional and distinctly Quaker perspective—with all of the diversity and ambiguity that come along as a result. This is only one possible way among likely many others. That's the beauty of theology for me: Theology is the conversation between people who are all seeking to hear the voice of God. Therefore, theology is only true to itself when it is a conversation among people faithfully listening—and not simply a collection of monologues recited all at once, in a great cacophony, by people certain of their ownership of the truth. I can only pray that I have listened closely—and faithfully—enough, and that this work reflects that listening.

Ecosystems of Quaker Theology

Climate/Story

There's an old joke, famous among Friends, that goes like this: Ask five Quakers their thoughts on something, and you'll get at least six answers. Quakers are deservedly well-known not only for our insistence on trusting our own perceptions, opinions, and experiences but also for our willingness (and insistence!) to express them when asked. This has led to the most consistently insistent truism about Quaker theology: that it doesn't really exist (not as a distinct tradition, at least), and where it does, it's only in relation to Quaker actions and ethics. Examples of this perception abound, with a profusion both distressing and baffling—at least to this specific Quaker theologian.

This tendency seems most present in the Liberal branch of the Religious Society of Friends, my own theological home. This is particularly pronounced when it comes to the academic study of Quaker theology. I could provide numerous anecdotes that, through their abundance, demonstrate the deep penetration this idea has made in the Liberal Quaker psyche. For example, there was the time when I volunteered to serve a few days in a day shelter and soup kitchen run by a Quaker. After the first day working alongside me, this Friend asked me about my work. Upon hearing that I was preparing to write my first book (and had already earned my doctorate in Quaker theology), the

Friend told me that I had wasted my time on "worldly pursuits" and instead should be applying my talents in a more "Quakerly" way—such as spending my life running a day shelter. *Of course: just like you.*

I disagreed, reminding this person that even the amorphous idea of something being properly Quakerly involved establishing definitions of rightness, goodness, and identity that were themselves built on a vast canon of Quaker theological reflection going back—deep—to the very roots of our community. In other words, you can only say that something is un-Quakerly when you have a definite and specific definition of what *Quakerly* means—thus, his rejection was itself rooted in the thing he was rejecting. This lovely human being then went on to explain my own field back to me, stating a common perception that the only right approaches to the study of Quaker theology are (1) historical, or what we used to believe; (2) sociological, or what our specific beliefs and actions say about our community today; and finally (3) ethical, or the ways that we live out our beliefs in our actions and practices. Notably, the questions that drive my own work—what exactly *do* we believe, what *could* we believe, and what are the structures and systems that inform and shape these beliefs now *and will in the future*—are notably absent in this person's rather limited and obtuse perspective on the construction of Quaker theology.

It might come as a surprise to some Quakers, therefore, that the field of Quaker theology is robust and thriving—but not you, of course, dear reader: You're reading a book on Quaker theology, so you already know what our field can produce. Yet, I must ask: Does it surprise *you* to realize that every. single. time. someone says, "Quakers don't have a theology," they are in fact *making a theological statement*? I hate to be so etymological about it, but as I stated before, one can only reject the existence of something one can define, or at least set a cautious boundary around.

Case in point: If you were to travel back in time and ask me, at different ages, whether I reject spam, you'd likely get the same answer but for *vastly* different reasons. The ten-year-old me would be rejecting Spam, the processed meat in a tin that was served every day at summer camp, whereas the forty*cough*-*something*-me of today would be rejecting the flood of junk in my email inbox. (Well, the adult me still rejects Spam. Just no.) My child self would have absolutely no concept of why some dots on a tiny screen would cause such an annoyed response . . . as opposed to the response of a child living in New York in 1990, being exposed to the phones of today, which would be *pure* science fiction, of course. This modern definition of spam would make absolutely zero sense to someone without the proper awareness and knowledge of the holistic way humans experience the reality of this world, where smartphones exist (and sometimes rule our lives). Think of the vast gulf that exists across the thirty years' distance between these two versions of me. The child-me is perfectly capable of reading every word in a definition of junk email, of understanding that it is in fact a potentially intelligible sentence: *and still* would not understand the sentence in any way whatsoever. Of course this is true: In 1990, people only used hand computers *that* powerful in science fiction.

Theology is analogous to any other language: It has rules (both explicit and implicit), vocabulary unique to it, and a culture deeply integrated with it. It will shift and develop organically, through use and engagement by individuals seeking to mold the language to suit their requirements. Languages have internal variance, often significant enough to create dialects that are noticeably different, yet still rest on the same foundational rules of the original language (e.g., the multiple Spanish, French, and English creole dialects of the Caribbean). When the variance grows significant enough, different languages can develop, creating families, in which the newly separate languages are still similar enough to be at least somewhat mutually understandable, even if their foundational rules differ (e.g., the mutual intelligibility of Scandinavian languages).

When applied to theology, this framework suggests some helpful ways to imagine the work of comparative theological methodology: Theologies from some traditions are similar enough to require only small shifts, or translations, to be mutually intelligible, whereas others are vastly different and would require significant translation in order to allow for mutual engagement. An obvious example of different "languages" would be an attempt between Christian and Buddhist theologians to come to a mutual understanding of the concept of salvation. The fundamental rules of these two theological languages are vastly different, and this gulf makes the translation process a complex one, requiring the development of several steps and procedures in order to ensure that "speakers" are actually mutually intelligible.

In other words, even when two people are certain that they share a language as well as a common context around which to experience that language, they might discover that they are having fundamentally different conversations about fundamentally different definitions of a word. So, when I say that

"Quakers don't have a theology" is a theological statement, I am using a definition of *theology* as basic and simple as possible: *theo-logy*, coming from the Greek roots of *theos* (God or Divine) and *logos* (writing, wisdom, w/Word). Thus, words about God.[7] Claiming that Quakers do not have a theology involves declaring your own boundaries and definitions of the word *theology* strongly enough that you are capable of explaining to other people what you mean by that. You are not only defining *theology*, however, as you are also now required to define what you mean by *Quaker*, which will involve at least establishing some very basic framework to define the term. You might follow the most common tactic among Quakers for defining theology: make a long list of things that we do not believe in or practice, before turning to a discussion of the work that we do. Do you see what you've done there?

Flowers/Testimony

You've engaged in the work of theology: Congratulations! By marking boundaries around beliefs and practices that do not reflect who you are, and then declaring what practices and behaviors frame and give meaning and purpose to your life, you've actually offered a holistic (if wildly incomplete) claim to what you understand Quaker theology to be: more focused on action than on belief, perhaps. This theological statement declares that Quakers express their faith through their actions. Even before one dives into the theological import of the specific frameworks and beliefs one rejects, and the actions one accepts, one already knows that Quakers emphasize the vital importance of living as if this specific moment—and what one does in this moment—matters more than focusing on preparing oneself for some afterlife, hopefully far in the future. Think of the potentially profound implications rippling through your life! If your fundamental principles include the declaration that Quakers demonstrate their faith through a life focused toward peacemaking—because the Divine Presence exists in all people—there's a rather high likelihood that your context is going to be drastically different from those engaged in defense and intelligence work. Now trace the definition of *peace* through your different contexts: I'd bet that they are quite different from each other. Same word, different languages.

---

7. Sallie McFague, *Life Abundant: Rethinking Theology and Economy for a Planet in Peril* (Fortress, 2001), 39.

Bodies/Experience

Back to the question: What *is* Quaker theology, exactly? Specifically, what are the most distinguishing—and most foundational—elements of Quaker theology, especially in the Liberal branch of the global community of the Religious Society of Friends?[8] One oft-cited formulation, involving four main characteristics (experience as primary, faith relevant to the age, an openness to new Light, and progressivism) emerges first in the work of Martin Davie and is expanded on in the work of British sociologist and influential Quaker scholar Pink Dandelion.[9] These characteristics rest on a "rationalist modernist approach" that accommodates critical approaches to the Bible as well as an openness to evolutionary theory that is not bound to any prior commitments to Scripture or tradition. Coupled with the Liberal Quaker emphasis on prioritizing religious experience with an insistence on progressive revelation (each Divine revelation carries more authority than the last), this encouraged Liberal Quakerism to welcome and encourage change and dynamic movement.

This definition offers a direct rebuttal to the notion of Quaker theology's nonexistence, as it claims that the Liberal Quaker perspective has a definite shape and *tradition*: specific and distinct theological elements, among which include, as Rhiannon Grant interprets this passage, "the primacy of experience, change through time (both that faith needs to be relevant to the modern world and that religious progress is being made), and the centrality of the Inner Light."[10] This framework does echo the emphasis, in the negative/positive framework mentioned above, on personal experience in the present tense, yet seems to assume that the Liberal Quaker rooting in embodied practice and

8. Liberal Quakerism, as a distinct and definable branch of worldwide Quakerism, has its roots in the application of liberal theology within Quaker thought in the late nineteenth century. Quakerism at that point was still mainly located within the United Kingdom and countries at one time connected to the British Empire, most particularly the United States. Due to the history of settlement patterns of Quakers in the United States and the subsequent impact of time, geographical distance, and a variety of other theological and cultural influences, Quakerism in the United States became quite diversified, leading to distinct and divergent branches with marked differences in theology and practice. These include several broad categories: Liberal, Conservative, Pastoral, Evangelical, and Pentecostal.

9. Martin Davie, *British Quaker Theology Since 1895* (Edwin Mellen, 1997); Pink Dandelion, *An Introduction to Quakerism* (Cambridge University Press, 2007), 134.

10. Rhiannon Grant, *Theology from Listening: Finding the Core of Liberal Quaker Theological Thought*, Brill Quaker Studies 3.2 (Brill, 2020), 8.

action (*testimony*) goes without saying as the background context within which this theologizing occurs. The four-part framework centers on delineating the locus of authority in Liberal Quaker theology as defined by time and the modernist faith in the inherent value of "progress": As the Divine is continuously revealing themself in new ways, responding to the changes in the times, humans must also always be open to adapting their faith, beliefs, and practices in response to the movement of the Divine. In this sense, authority lies with the present and serves it, but the future always insists on reminding us of our obligations to the horizon.

Yet, as Grant herself notes in her work analyzing the current state of Liberal Quaker theology, based on the words, language, phrasings, and methods of Liberal Quakers themselves, this definition still misses the role that historical voices—certain ones, from certain contexts—play in the construction of Quaker theology more generally and Liberal Quaker theology more specifically. Grant engages in a survey of notable examples of Liberal Quaker theologizing, at multiple levels and definitions of authority, including (1) the writings of corporate bodies of Friends, which could be said to be jointly owned by the community producing the document; (2) the writings of individual Liberal Quakers that have come to be influential to succeeding generations of Liberal Quakers; and finally, (3) the writings of Liberal Quaker academic theologians that seek to construct an explicitly "Liberal Quaker theology" from within the community itself, using the community's own tools alongside the tools of the discipline of academic theology.[11] The challenge with the authority of the third level lies with the discipline of academic theology itself and the level of authority each individual Quaker is willing to grant it.

After doing the absolutely necessary work of examining this widely diverse range of Liberal Quaker theological writing, Grant comes to some conclusions:

1. Liberal Quaker theology can be described as a "single diverse and developing tradition," developed within—and serving the needs of—the community of Liberal Quakers, with a shared core of central themes.
2. The center of Liberal Quaker theology is the belief that direct, unmediated contact with the Divine is possible and available to everyone, through the practice of Meeting for Worship as well as

11. Grant, *Theology from Listening*, 14.

the presence and action of the Inner Light. This enables Quakers to access Divine guidance on both the individual and corporate level, allowing Quakers to develop a specific decision-making process based on this expectation of Divine guidance.

3. The tradition is fundamentally flexible and creative: "Any given core item of the theology can be challenged from within the tradition, but the effect of that challenge is to nuance rather than to break down the central theological understanding. Individual Quakers are in dialogue with, if not always in exact agreement with, certain core principles."[12]

Effectively, there is a definable Liberal Quaker theological tradition, which shares a common set of beliefs and practices, embraces flexibility and adaptability as fundamental components of the tradition, and has been informed by the writings and ideas of certain thinkers and texts that have come to be seen as influential for the tradition. In a very real sense, Grant is telling a story of a theological tradition that is both coherent and holistic: It makes internal sense and can inform every aspect of a person's life and context.

Let's now return to the conversation that began this section: the Quaker outreach services provider who told me that spending my life writing Quaker theology was a worldly pursuit that was not "Quakerly"—that is, not following the established frameworks of rightness, goodness, and identity that are seen as most representative of a Quaker approach to belief and action. Following Grant's definition, however, my work absolutely fits the ambiguous boundaries of Quakerliness, for I engage in the necessary task of continuing the development of Quaker theology from within the tradition and in dialogue with the current context of the world.

Leaves/Interpretation

Yet, this tradition is itself only discernible once one understands the perspective and approach of the tradition using the tradition's own context: In other words, what happens when a Liberal Quaker seeks to engage in theological dialogue with the wider Quaker tradition? Are the traditions mutually intelligible? What about the wider Christian theological tradition? Are the terminology, frameworks, and context that inform Liberal Quaker theology

12. Grant, *Theology from Listening*, 14.

translatable to theological languages other than its own? The wider Christian theological tradition has not engaged with the Liberal Quaker tradition in any consistent or systematic way.[13] This is the case for many reasons—from the tiny size of our community to the fundamentally different way we approach authority when engaging with theological sources. Perhaps the most important reason, though, is that for the vast majority of its history the Quaker tradition has resisted efforts to define itself according to any theological framework other than its own. Instead, Quakers have consistently chosen a complex interplay of narrative and metaphorical approaches that depend on an insider knowledge of the meaning of the specific metaphors, symbols, stories, and language Quakers use to understand—and explain—their experiences to themselves. Compared to other theological traditions that construct their theology using a more precise delineation of authority, or primacy, among theological sources (such as the primacy of the Christian Bible in many Protestant traditions, or church tradition among the Roman Catholic and Eastern Orthodox communities), Quakers have generally avoided systematic frameworks built on any form of hierarchy among theological sources.

Instead, Liberal Quakers have developed what Dandelion has referred to as the "Quaker double-culture": The "Liberal belief culture" is a "culture of silence" in relation to specific formulations of belief, particularly due to the powerful caution around seeing theology as an effective tool to use to describe *experience*—that most authoritative of sources for Liberal Quaker theology. Matters of belief are thus individualized due to the sheer gauntlet of attitudes and actions one must navigate in order to engage in communal conversations about belief.[14] Yet, the Liberal Quaker approach to behavior—the embodied action and practice of expressing one's beliefs through one's behavior and approach to the world—is the opposite in that it is communal, discussed consistently and at great depth, with definitive boundaries—what Dandelion terms a behavioral creed.

In this way, belief exists only as it is embodied and is policed only in terms of its practical expression in one's life. To know a Liberal Quaker's beliefs is to

13. Christy Randazzo, "An Ever-Branching River: The Beautiful Watersheds of the Quaker Theological Ecosystem," *Quaker Studies* 29, no. 1 (2025).

14. Pink Dandelion, "The Creation of Coherence: The 'Quaker Double Culture' and the 'Absolute Perhaps,'" in *The Quaker Condition: The Sociology of a Liberal Religion*, ed. Pink Dandelion and Peter Collins (Cambridge Scholars, 2008), 27.

see how they live, for one is likely to struggle to know a Liberal Quaker's beliefs from their words alone. In this way, one could conceivably define the word *divine* in any number of different ways, as long as those ways lead to actions that adhere to the behavioral creed . . . and can be seen as adhering, according to the behavioral standards understood by the community—whether the community is a specific meeting, a Quaker institutional body, or even the larger Quaker communal culture.[15]

This silence to systematization has often been a productive one for the *tradition*, allowing it to evolve and effectively respond to changes within the tradition as well as cultural and political pressures outside it. An entire culture of religious hybridity not only has been allowed to take root in Liberal Quakerism (particularly in recent decades) but has been encouraged—and flourished—as the dominance of orthopraxy (right action) has consumed all of the theological air (so to speak). Therefore, it has become Liberal Quaker orthodoxy that Liberal Quakers don't have orthodoxy. The innumerable complexities of this approach have been well-explored in many previous publications, including my own—this is well-trod territory in the field of Quaker studies.[16] At this stage, it's mainly important to know that Liberal Quakers have crafted a complex theological method, an understanding of *reason* that Liberal Quakers employ as a matter of daily life and decision-making, which has allowed for some of the—in my opinion—most interesting expressions of theological hybridity I've ever come across.[17]

It also reflects the vital role that listening plays in Quaker belief, practice, and identity. Quakers place a significant importance on listening to God first

---

15. Dandelion, "Creation of Coherence," 28.

16. One representative example is an article I wrote exploring the ways that religious hybridity affected the thinking of Korean Quaker Ham Sok-Heon (1901–1989) as he developed a hybrid reconciliation theology that incorporated every aspect of the complex and multifaceted religious landscape of Korea, with a particular focus on aspects of religious culture that would speak to both North and South Koreans, aiding in an eventual reunification. Ham found that the inherent flexibility of Liberal Quaker theology fit well alongside Buddhism and Confucian beliefs—two religious communities that have had much practice in existing alongside each other in Korea. Christy Randazzo, "The Complex Hybridity of Ham Sok-Heon," *Quaker Religious Thought* 129 (2017): 18–24.

17. Christy Randazzo and David Russell, "The Inner Light and the Light of God: Islamic and Quaker Mysticism in Dialogue," in *Quakers and Mysticism: Comparative and Syncretic Approaches to Spirituality*, ed. Jon R. Kershner (Palgrave Macmillan, 2019), 161–80.

and speaking only (especially during Meeting for Worship) if they feel led to by the Spirit of God. Or, admittedly, if they can overcome their fear of falling afoul of the rather rigid codes and patterns (i.e., *liturgy*) of Liberal Quaker unprogrammed waiting worship.[18] (Yes: As liturgy is really just prescribed forms and rituals of public worship in a religious community, and as Liberal Quakers *absolutely* have prescriptions and proscriptions for their worship form, then Liberal Quakers have a liturgy.[19])

This approach to time insists on a continuous present when it comes to formulations of belief, such that what is believed can only ever be said to be adhering to the individual themselves, and then only in that specific moment. As Quakers must always be aware of the potential for the Divine to reveal themself in new and surprising ways, this experience in turn demands a reimagination of theological categories and a reassessment of theological definitions. This is only as long as belief doesn't run afoul of the categories, definitions, and assumptions communally defined and communally managed by the Quaker community—however that presents itself, of course.

Seeds/Hope

The ambiguity and flexibility inherent in the construction of Quaker theology challenges the traditional assumptions of Christian theology, particularly assumptions of the absolute authority of the canonical Christian *Scriptures*. The difficulty this presents to Quakers seeking to engage in dialogue with the wider Christian theological world cannot be understated. This situation has ensured that this wider community is generally ignorant of the theological tools that have evolved within the Quaker tradition, and has hampered attempts to develop dialogue between Quaker theologians and theologians from other Christian traditions. Quakers are often seen to be speaking a different language, with vastly different assumptions, rules, boundaries, and expectations. Yet *experience* is a theological source as well, and the abundant reservoir of resources present within the Quaker theological tradition—especially with relation to peacemaking, ecological sustainability, and egalitarian theologies—are a rich resource that could greatly benefit the wider Christian theological community, providing valuable alternative approaches to

18. Dandelion, "Creation of Coherence," 33.

19. Pink Dandelion, *The Liturgies of Quakerism* (Ashgate, 2005).

numerous issues of pressing importance. With a little translation, this holistic approach to adapting oneself to the totalizing influence of the Liberal Quaker worldview can actually be made to be mutually intelligible with the theological language of other religious and theological traditions, especially Christian ones.

Fruit/Doctrine

Quaker theology has heavily depended on naturalistic metaphors to explain the Quaker understanding of the relationship, and interrelationship, between the Divine and the created order, whether that involves the particular (such as the "seed" of Christ placed in the specific person), or the comprehensively cosmological (such as the "Light" emanating from God into all people). This reflects a long-standing Quaker concern to see the action and presence of the Divine in the current reality, concerned with the health and thriving of creation while it is still alive. Through its project of expanding the vision of what the Divine is and does, Liberal Quaker theology has placed an even greater emphasis on developing metaphorical language for the Divine. This approach speaks to the Quaker experience of interdependence with a Divine entirely present within its creation, and an openness to expanding the metaphorical palette of the experience-termed-Divine to include other traditions as well.[20]

Quakers recognize the transcendence of God beyond creation as an inherent aspect of what could be considered divinity; yet, due to their emphasis on the epistemological primacy of direct religious experience of the Divine, Quakers stress the immanence of God within the creation to a much greater degree. This stress on immanency colors their view of the Christian anthropological categories, causing them to place greater emphasis on anthropological theories of interdependence, immanence within the creation, and intimate love of the creation. This emphasis on immanence, coupled with a deliberately conceptual experiential theology, influences the types of models of God that Quakers find most compelling.[21] The Quaker construction of an intimately incarnate Christ and the universal immanence of the Holy Spirit are models rooted in metaphor, deliberately left open to reinterpretation and reevaluation.

---

20. Christy Randazzo, "'The Divine Light of Creation': Liberal Quaker Metaphors of Divine/Creation Interdependence," in *Quakers, Creation Care and Sustainability*, ed. Cherice Bock and Stephen Potthoff, Quakers and the Disciplines Series 6 (Full Media Services, 2019), 96–114.

21. Sallie McFague, *Models of God: Theology for an Ecological, Nuclear Age* (Fortress, 1987).

Liberal Quakerism, in particular, expresses an interchangeability between Christ and Spirit in its language, due to the insistence that God takes the form of Spirit: whether the Spirit of Christ, or the Spirit of a universal consciousness, or any number of Spirit-inflected imaginaries from the diverse religious communities whose internal stories often inform Liberal Quakers as much as Quakerism itself. The imprecision around the language delineating Spirit from Christ is reflective of the insistence on founding theology on the base of experience.

The theology of the Holy Spirit, pneumatology, is also not developed in much detail in Quaker theology.[22] Instead, what is defined as Spirit is most often assumed to be the same as what is defined as the Light. This partly reflects the lack of a sustained constructive theological development of the Holy Spirit in Quakerism. It also reflects a Quaker emphasis on Pneumo-presentism (the continuous presence of the Holy Spirit), with an amorphous Spirit representing the divine that is immanently present throughout creation. This Spirit can be understood as the Holy Spirit incarnated in the creation, and thus inherently the form of God that Quakers oftentimes mean when they refer to the mystical experience of connecting with the Light Within/ Inner Light.

While Friends recognize that the Spirit is always present, they also accept that humans are not always able to fully comprehend and recognize this presence in the busyness of daily existence. Quakers argue that gathering together in worship is essential, therefore, to reconnect with (the) Spirit in mystical union, orienting their lives accordingly. The experience of unity in meeting also serves to remind Friends in a very palpable way that the Spirit brings all of creation into unity with God.

This metaphorical approach to the construction of models of God finds its most complete expression, therefore, in the construction of its main metaphor: that of the Light. The framing and meaning of the metaphor has changed over time, however, with both the Inward Light (which guides humans to a closer relationship with the Divine) and the Inner Light (the Divine presence panentheistically interpenetrating creation, existing in a relationship of interdependence with the creation) present within Quaker theologies of Light. It should be noted, however, that these should be considered points

22. Christy Randazzo, "Liberal Quaker Pneumatology," in *The Quaker World*, ed. Wess Daniels and Rhiannon Grant (Routledge, 2022), 240–47.

along a spectrum: Aspects of both "the Light as Divine guide" as well as "the Light as Divine/human interdependence" are present in all periods of Quaker theological history.

I'd argue that the theology of Light serves as a form of theological ocean for Quakers, in that it creates the somewhat illusory impression of the commonality of one unified theological language for what are actually an incredibly diverse scattering of theological islands: While some of the islands form chains stemming from the same foundational ocean floor, there are actually vast trenches separating some island groups from the others, as if they were actually rooted to entirely different continental plates.

The one common thread unifying all of them is the understanding that *Light* signifies the interaction of the Divine with the human: the greatest possible divine immanence within the creation, an incarnation that infuses every particle of the creation. Debate exists about the implications of this: Some claim that this leads to an inherent goodness and sacredness of the entire creation (including humanity), while others insist on chastening that view, acknowledging the human potential for both evil and good.[23] In this construction, the Light is active in the process of human transformation, striving to guide humanity toward a greater awareness of the Divine presence as well as the ethical consequences of that presence. The Light as God's presence within the human person is seen as an incarnate presence that has the capacity to bring the human person into greater levels of relationship with God.

The Ecosystem Method: A Summary

Watersheds

Any border is already an inherently liminal space, a place that is not *one* place but several at once. A border draped across constantly moving water? Doubly so. One of my favorite maps was drawn by cartographer and geologist Harold Fisk in 1944 for a US Army Corps of Engineer report on the "meander belt," the wide, flat expanse of the Mississippi alluvial plain across which the lower part of the river has danced, wriggled—and yes, meandered—since long before the states of Louisiana, Mississippi, Arkansas, and Tennessee were artificially scored into the landscape. Fisk achieved something quite remarkable: By

23. Christy Randazzo, *Liberal Quaker Reconciliation Theology*, Brill Research Perspectives in Quaker Studies (Brill, 2020).

charting each successive shimmy and slide across the plain, assigning each course a unique color, and then overlaying those individual images on top of each other, he created a map both extraordinarily informative and astonishingly beautiful. There is something *true* about this beauty in that it tells the story of a river alive in such depth and clarity that it reveals the insanity and uselessness of the concept of definitive borders in the face of the river's demand for freedom and creativity and *change*. As Heraclitus so famously reminds us, one never steps in the same river twice, as both the person *and* the river are constantly changing.

The official definition of watershed, from the National Oceanic and Atmospheric Administration, is "a land area that channels rainfall and snowmelt to creeks, streams, and rivers, and eventually to outflow points such as reservoirs, bays, and the ocean."[24] Smaller watersheds are considered part of larger watershed systems. This is particularly clear when you look at maps of watersheds—and most especially so with the Mississippi River watershed. It's vast, draining southward through an inverted pyramid between the Appalachian Mountains in the east and the Rocky Mountains in the west, along river courses mighty in their own right. These blue veins carry lifeblood from capillary creeks to river veins, connecting the landscape in a dizzying maze of bends and twists that is ever shifting. Rivers are constantly creating themselves as they flow across a landscape, uncovering and covering land in equal measure.

This is not metaphorical. Darby Creek is a rivulet beginning at the base of the same cliffs that would shelter the Continental Army in the harsh winter of 1777–78, when they made Valley Forge their camp, a few miles northwest of Philadelphia. During the eighteenth century, the mouth of Darby Creek flowed around Mud Island, located across the Delaware from the town of Woodbury, New Jersey. Over the years, the mouth shifted westward, and Mud Island eventually ceased to be an island, instead becoming the same spit of land jutting into the Delaware on which Philadelphia International Airport now sits.

Just a few miles upriver sits Petty Island, a river island that has been claimed by many governments and even a few multinational corporations—most recently the Citgo Oil Company, which at one stage was managed and

24. NOAA, "What Is a Watershed?," National Ocean Service, June 16, 2024, https://oceanservice.noaa.gov/facts/watershed.html.

owned by the government of Venezuela. Of course, no one stopped to ask any of the beings who lived on that island whether they were OK with making their home the site of a massive oil storage facility. The land is now owned by the state of New Jersey and protected as a nature preserve. I love that outcome, of course, but who gave anyone the right to own the island—and thus treat it however they desired—in the first place?

In watersheds, human definitions, boundaries, and political geographies are swept aside in the face of water's overwhelming power: Anyone who has ever encountered a flash flood will attest to the fact that if water really wants to go somewhere, it will, regardless of the concrete and steel edifices erected to contain it. Even when the water seems to be calm, flowing gently downstream, the Delaware River watershed easily demonstrates the arbitrariness of lines on maps drawn by humans, as it paradoxically affirms human-derived boundaries while simultaneously dismissing them. Does the Delaware River watershed define the boundaries of the states of Pennsylvania, New Jersey, and Delaware? Yes . . . and very much no.

As I said earlier, New Jersey is defined by water, yet this water is as much salt as it is fresh. The Delaware River both unites South Jersey to southeast Pennsylvania (basically the Philadelphia metropolitan area) and paradoxically is the physical border between the two states. The weather patterns that shape the climate around my house are the exact same patterns as those in Philadelphia, yet the rules that define how I respond to that climate are made in Trenton (the New Jersey state capital) in conversation with people from rather different water cultures from me, while just across the river the rules are made by people in Harrisburg (the Pennsylvania state capital), which is itself built alongside the Susquehanna River, one of the main sources of the massive Chesapeake Bay watershed. Life in the Delaware River watershed is therefore lived at multiple levels of existence at once, with a complex mélange of interweaving and conflicting identities, communities, and *narratives* all working together to create the *context* of life in this specific place at this specific time.

Imagine a large tree rooted next to a riverbank. The tree is bound up in numerous ecosystems far larger than itself, from the ecosystems surrounding the immediate area of the tree, to the ecosystem of the grove itself, to the ecosystem of the watershed within which it is rooted, and so on, in ever-widening circles, all the way out to the global ecosphere. Yet, the tree is still rooted in one specific location, within one watershed, and is directly affected by the climate and soils of that watershed, and the impact those both have on the body of the tree—the *stories* that define and shape that tree's experience of reality.

Yet, this tree is itself an *ecosystem*, in an inextricable relationship with practically innumerable other elements, both living and nonliving. The abiotic (nonliving) elements are the inherited traits and preexisting factors that constitute the *climate* surrounding the tree, the *soil* within which it is rooted, and the processes of *evolution* that cause the ecosystem to continue to adapt to a dynamic world. The climate and soils of each watershed frame what tree ecosystems are capable of thriving there: However awesome it would be, I simply cannot grow coffee beans in my backyard.

The biotic (living) elements deal with the tree's function and capacity to remain alive and to produce new growth. These are all experienced through the *body* of the tree—*roots* that embed the tree within a specific location, and the *stem* (trunk and branches) of the tree, which gives the tree structure and strength. This experience is interpreted in the *leaves* of the tree through the process of photosynthesis, which converts the energy of light into food that sustains the tree. The tree reproduces itself through the structure and work of the *flowers* of the tree, which—through the interactions of the ecosystem with the *blossom* itself and the *pollen* inside—offer a face to the world, engaging in the intimate work of fertilization. The fertilized flower will eventually become the *fruit* of the tree, or what the tree produces as a mobile object for continuing the life of the tree species, in relationship with the other beings in its ecosystem. Embedded in the structure of the fruit are the *seeds*, which, when planted in fertile soil, offer hope for a potential future. Each of these elements are inextricably related to one another: Without any one of these elements, the life within the tree will eventually fade away.

We are each individual trees, rooted within a grove straddling both sides of the river, bound together in ways unrecognizable to all those who see division where they instead should see community. It's not a border—New Jersey here and Pennsylvania over there—it's one river on which we all depend—and through which our lives are woven. If you seek to locate division, you shall find it. If you seek to experience community, you shall experience it by the bucketload.

The foundational theological idea presented in this book, therefore, is that the fundamental elements of the Quaker theological method work together as a community, all contributing their own perspective to the experience of engaging theologically in the world as a Quaker, in an infinitely complex interweaving of relationships and encounters between every element. I've already provided one example of this method in action: the structure of this chapter so far. Keen-eyed readers will notice that each of the section headings in this chapter have included two words: the first a naturalistic metaphor, the second a theological term. Here's a list of them all, to help give you a sense of the patterns among the terms:

Climate/Story
Bodies/Experience
Leaves/Interpretation
Flowers/Testimony
Fruit/Doctrine
Seeds/Hope

Each heading includes an example of a theological term that element relates to, where the Quaker theological approach of *seeds*, for example, exists in the same space as hope: aware of the immanent presence of profound change, always happening *now*, yet offering hope for a future time when justice rolls down like waters and righteousness like an ever-flowing stream. A seed—that small piece of the future, held in a continuous stasis state of potential life—can hold the promise of new life for years, carried around by wind and water and creatures and fire until it is ready to open itself to the hope that is planting: being rooted in specific soil, with the vulnerability to change inherent in being stuck somewhere specific. Seeds carry the promise of a future. *Apocalypse*, in Greek, simply means "revealing" (or "revelation") a future reality—it needn't inherently mean the end of the world. Thus, seeds offer hope for a future in the face of the uncertainty and vulnerability of being alive. *Seeds*, for Quakers, is therefore an eschatology of hope: both tied together, with neither speaking without the other responding.

In this way, Quaker theology is conversational, where the conversation itself—the engrossing and immersive dance at the intersections of experience, thought, ethics, action, where these elements all interweave—is *itself* the system used to construct theology. From the perspective of Quaker theology, the oft-rigid definitions of systematic theology are an imposition on the field. A system is a system, though, regardless of whether it (1) approaches the central questions of systematics with the intent of rooting in the Christian Bible or church tradition and then advancing through to a simple, logical, rational *doctrine*, or instead (2) roots itself in the ambiguity inherent in the direct *experience* of Spirit and the way of being that emerges as a result.

This perspective plays itself out through the five other elements. Just like the complex and innumerable interactions that combine to make the unique climate of a particular location, *climate* is the narrative context, the sum total of all background and foundational elements that ground the experience of Spirit in a cohesive and holistic story. Akin to a tree, our *bodies* root us in our experience of the world and give meaning to the diverse and unique ways that our bodies are shaped as we each listen—and respond to—the experience of engaging Spirit's wisdom coursing through our veins (or xylem and phloem—the names for the parts of the vascular system in plants, if we're holding closely to the natural metaphor here). *Leaves* are the location where we use specific processes and methods in the *interpretation*—and thus transformation—of the energy of Light's Divine Revelation into resources we can use to exist, survive, and thrive. *Flowers* is the physical embodiment of our interactions with the world, with the *blossom* being the framework of practices and stories that inform and shape Quaker *testimony* (a form of embodied virtue ethics), and *pollen* being the specific forms and expressions of testimony that can fertilize both our own lives and those we encounter when living into these particular testimonies. Finally, *fruit* is the bodies/beliefs/*doctrines* that emerge after our lives are fertilized by *testimony* and which can serve as mobile carriers of the *seeds* of Quaker hope, thus completing the circle. I'll expand on these definitions as I address each element in turn.

In a very real sense, therefore, these elements are in an inextricable relationship, in which each part informs each other in ways seen and unseen, understood and incomprehensible, systematic and seemingly random. The Quaker *ecosystem* is thus a unique theological language, with specific, fundamental elements that form its basic building blocks but which nonetheless also offer the potential of infinite variety: akin to the four letters of genetic code or even the universe of potential inherent within the framework of the letters used in a language. Quakers feel free to play with these fundamentals, bringing them together in often surprising, creative, and complex ways. This language is marked by flexibility, creativity, adaptation—a sense of flow, perhaps—and is highly dependent on metaphor, ambiguity, and even paradox. This language is nonhierarchical, rejecting assumed structures, outcomes, languages, and beliefs; yet, paradoxically, also rests entirely on structures of behavior that themselves rest firmly on the twin foundations of Quaker theology: "that of God within" and "Let your life speak," where the second only exists because of the first, while the first is only truly embodied through the experience of living into the second.

I began this chapter with a story: a reflection on the climate crisis and its specific impacts on my own particular context, read through the dual theological lenses of eschatology (the recognition of profound change for the entire creation, with a sense of the impending end of the world as we know it) and hope (the faith that a future is always possible). The metaphor of seeds captures the uneasy relationship between these two emotions of fear and hope, as seeds have no guarantee of rooting and creating new life—many forced to lie dormant, dying before their potential is realized—but are also each equally vessels of hope for the future. A seed can carry the potential of life even up into space, and—if planted and grown—has the potential to create an entire new network of relationships among both the abiotic (nonliving) and biotic (living) elements of an ecosystem. Yet, embedded within this story/narrative is every one of the other five elements: *metaphors* about the *experience* of being rooted in a specific place (physically and spiritually); *listening* to the *doctrines* and *beliefs* that emerge from being rooted in that specific place, *interpreting* this experience through one's own *context* and *narrative*; and finally, *experiencing* the kind of *embodied ethics* and *testimony* about the kind of life that this situation will demand.

Next, I explored the Quaker theological tradition: its existence or nonexistence, its main components, its processes and frameworks, and the theological teaching—and way of life—that emerge as a result of incorporating the teachings and practices of this tradition when immersed in the global context of the climate crisis. Each section demonstrates aspects of others. For example, the Climate/Story section builds on a story I experienced when in the midst of the context of being in the company of another Friend and discovering that our translations (or interpretations, as all translation is itself an interpretation) of the Quaker testimony did not align: Mine celebrated the work of theology (and the doctrines that emerge) as central to the Quaker testimony, whereas the other translation did not. Again: same language, different translations.

I actually built this section off previous work I've done imagining ecological metaphors for Quaker theology, the testimonies that emerge from living into these metaphors, and the words about God that could help translate this experience into language understandable by others in both the Quaker theological community and the wider Christian theological world.[25] I've been exploring these themes, individually, in separate publications, since I began writing theology for—and within—the Quaker community. This work brings all of these elements into explicit dialogue and argues that they are actually the main components of the Quaker (particularly Liberal Quaker) theological method.

It must be noted that the Quaker tradition has never itself assigned a name for this method. As can be seen from the definitions provided above for Liberal Quakerism, Liberal Quakers seem to focus a great deal of attention on the *what, why, when*, and even *who* of theology but offer few specifics on the *how*. My aim with this book is to offer a potential framework for the *how*, the specific elements of the method of Quaker theological construction. Reflecting the inherent metaphorical framing of Quaker theological thought, the dynamic ambiguity of the relationships between these six elements, and the fundamentally ecological nature of the panentheistic interdependence theology at the very heart of Quaker theology—the Inward Light, "that of God within"—I propose that Quakers adopt a metaphor that speaks to all of these elements: the ecosystem.

As ecosystems are themselves spaces where specific elements engage in a continuously dynamic interplay (and thus demonstrate how the mechanistic explanations of science often overlook the import of the serendipitous and infinitely complex ways that these elements engage—*a fundamental tenet of modern ecological science, actually*), the metaphor of ecosystem can provide a powerful framework on which to develop a constructive theology that is dynamic *and* stable, concurrently *and* paradoxically.

The use of the language of *ecology*—as opposed to simply *nature/natural*—is necessary, as it specifically engages with the interdependence fundamental to Quaker theology.[26] For example, Quaker theology insists that the Light is not simply a *natural* metaphor, which could imply simply a human experience

---

25. Randazzo, "'Divine Light of Creation'"; Cherice Bock and Christy Randazzo, *Quakers, Ecology, and the Light*, Brill Research Perspectives in Quaker Studies (Brill, 2023); Randazzo, "Christian AND Universalist?: Charting Liberal Quaker Theological Developments Through the Swarthmore Lectures," *Quaker Religious Thought* 131 (2018), article 4.

26. Cherice Bock, "Quakers and Creation Care: Potentials and Pitfalls for an Ecotheology of Friends," in Bock and Potthoff, *Quakers, Creation Care and Sustainability*, 69–95.

of the Divine present within the creation. The Light is instead an *ecological* metaphor, as both the metaphorical theology of Light and ecology explore the interwoven, interdependent relationships between distinct elements of an environment or context.

One specific use of Quaker denominational distinctives is present in the format of the chapters themselves: queries. Reflecting the Quaker tradition of using queries to challenge Quakers to discern how their actions and beliefs reflect traditional Quaker teachings, chapters—and sections within the chapters—will include queries in the titles. Also, reflecting the emphasis on metaphor in both Quaker theology and ecotheology, I demonstrate how one can bring these two traditions together using ecological metaphors as metaphorical framing devices and explanatory terms. All metaphors stem from, and are rooted within, the main metaphorical image of a bounded ecosystem.

Of particular note is the benefit that ecotheology could gain from engaging in dialogue with Quaker interdependence and panentheistic metaphorical theologies, aspects that are core to the ecotheological tradition. This could provide a mutually beneficial dialogue in which ecotheology provides the comprehensive theological framework Quakers currently lack, while Quakers expand the metaphorical palette ecotheology uses to expand its visions of the Divine. This includes the use of universalist metaphors of the Divine—especially important given the rise of Christians skeptical of the (often) exclusivist truth claims of many Christian theologies. This book therefore presents an intriguing case study to ecotheology, both demonstrating how ecotheology concepts are applicable in a broad way to other denominational communities and providing a framework on which to build constructive theologies for those communities that marry ecotheology and denominational distinctives. Here's an overview of my argument.

Climate/Story

In chapter 2, I explore the *climate* of Quaker theology: the combined forces of story, context, and place that inform the environment within which a Quaker theological approach takes root, thrives, and evolves as it interacts with the other elements of the environment. I first lay out two of the narratives that have emerged from my own specific location. The first is the colonialist narrative of the "sovereign individual" that emerged from the various liberal, rationalist, and individualist threads of the eighteenth-century Enlightenment and saw a full flowering in the ideas debated during the latter half of the eighteenth century in Independence Hall in Philadelphia. The second is the narrative of the person as *communal*, interdependent with creation and the Divine, and rooted in a specific context, as reflected in the story of the lower Delaware River as watershed—with which I began this chapter.

This approach reflects the emphasis of Quaker narrative theology on using the biographies (journals) of individual Quakers as theological resources. I am intentionally making the choice to root this work in my own context first: not as an attempt to demonstrate that my story is inherently valuable, but actually to demonstrate that each Quaker can only experience the Divine through their own narratives, context, and place. This is an inherent paradox rooted within Quaker theology: Each Quaker can only ever speak from their own experience, yet if this experience is in conversation with the community of Friends, the individual story can serve as a lens through which each Quaker can find universal truths, applicable for their own experience living the Quaker way.

Bodies/Experience

In chapter 3, I develop the concept of experience in Quaker theology, addressing two main frameworks into which Quaker conceptions of community can be placed: huge, systemic communities (*roots and fungus*), and contextual communities (*trunks*). I use these metaphors because they reflect the ways that experiences in universal communities root Quakers in relationships with others, giving a sense of who they are as created beings from a Divine Being, and the ways that specific frameworks of the Quaker community (cultures) give structure and meaning to the experience of Quakers in specific contexts. Reflecting the Quaker tradition of using the lives of Quakers and others whom Quakers have deemed embody key Quaker values and perspectives, I will highlight the life, actions, and beliefs of several Quakers connecting them to cultures, for which their work and life can be instructive.

Leaves/Interpretation

In chapter 4, I propose a framework for developing Quaker doctrine. As Quakers are a tradition with a marked skepticism of doctrine, or the concretizing of Quaker belief into any permanent form (such as a creed or dogma), I explore definitions of doctrine that permit Quaker belief to be definable but to also be flexible and dynamic concurrently. As I envision doctrine as a dynamic, life-giving process in which Quakers synthesize meaning from their experience of the Divine Light, I frame this chapter using the ecological metaphor of *leaves*: the place where the plant *interprets* and synthesizes the energy of Light. Reflecting my emphasis in this book on translating Quaker theological terms and concepts into the frameworks and language of Christian theology, I explore the ways that Quaker theological interpretation exists in dialogue with the Wesleyan quadrilateral. In contrast to traditional Christian understandings of the quadrilateral, this rooting in Quaker interpretation will inevitably require looking first through the lens of the experience quarter of the quadrilateral.

I apply this conceptual framework to an examination of continuing revelation, the main doctrinal approach of Quakers, born from the intersection of an emphasis on the continuous evolution inherent within human experience of the Divine and an insistence that every person has the equal potential to experience the Divine. I examine the impact that continuing revelation has on the authority Quakers grant to theological ideas and texts (both Christian Scripture and the narratives of Quaker lives) and how Quakers develop belief and navigate the accepted fundamental beliefs of Quakers in light of their potential to evolve in light of experience.

Flowers/Testimony

In chapter 5, I outline the foundational elements of the Quaker concept of *testimony*, using the ecological metaphor of *flowers*: Testimony can be the framework that Quakers use to show their way of life to the world, as well as the necessary element to ensure that the Quaker tradition remains vital and continues to exist in future generations. This chapter examines this concept in two ways: as testimony (a comprehensive term encompassing Quaker action in the world) and as testimonies (specific ways that testimony manifests in Quaker action and being).

Fruit/Doctrine

In chapter 6, I gather up the threads laid out throughout the work previously and weave an argument for the actual doctrines that would emerge once the theological method developed in previous chapters is applied to some of the traditional Christian systematic categories as well as other theological categories strongly emphasized in Quaker tradition. As these are the products of the theological ecosystem and as such would be the most portable aspects of this process, I apply the metaphor of fruit to this chapter. Much of this work will build on my own previous work in Quaker constructive theology, as I've explored each of these areas in various formats previously. This is the first time I bring all these concepts together into one cohesive and comprehensive chapter.

Seeds/Hope

In chapter 7, I come full circle: I begin this book with an eschatological narrative and end it by developing a framework for planting these theological constructs into existing Quaker communities, as well as in developing new communities that might seek to use this theological model as a framework for developing their own beliefs and practices. Hence the use of the ecological model of seeds for this chapter. This reflects traditional Quaker use of seed as a metaphor for the existence of the Divine within the person, waiting to be planted within the person's soul. This language is itself reminiscent of biblical use of seed metaphors, particularly in relation to the reign of God, the ways in which the Divine will transform the earth. This includes an overview of ways this theological method and model addresses the ongoing divisions among Quakers, in Christianity, and in the world. This reflects both the overarching Quaker concern for peacemaking and the emphasis Liberal Friends place on developing diverse communities of openness and inclusion.

CHAPTER TWO

Climate/Story

What Are the Stories We Tell About the Divine, the Creation, and Ourselves?

The produce of the earth is a gift from our gracious creator to the inhabitants, and to impoverish the earth now to support outward greatness appears to be an injury to the succeeding age.

—John Woolman, 1772

The world is charged with the grandeur of God.
It will flame out, like shining from shook foil

—Gerard Manley Hopkins, "God's Grandeur"

The Quakers believe that God, or spirituality, is in every human being. *The divinity is called "the Light."* The Light is in everyone, although it burns more brightly in some than in others. It must be looked after and nourished.

—Mary A. Holmes

The Air We Breathe, the Soil We Root In

Context is everything, especially when it comes to winemaking.

The climate and the soil—the abiotic (nonliving) elements that form the foundation within which life roots, and the rhythms (wind, rain, frost, swelter) within which life cycles—are essential to the creation of distinct varietals of wine. Specificity is the key here: Should one feel so compelled, each and every distinct element of wine could be emphasized and highlighted, in order to approach as closely as possible the complete uniqueness of each grape.

Admittedly, there is the sepia-toned romantic mythology of Nana lifting her skirt to dance through grapes in a large wooden tub, and then there is the fermented grape byproduct—an agricultural and industrial process involving massive metal vats and miles of piping, sloshing in the hold of a tanker ship, an artificial lake being transported across the southern sea to a bag, in a box, in a liquor store near you. So, what we imagine as *wine*—the mythical elixir of truth and the Dionysian abandon of the feast, the market dynamics of collectible bottles worth millions, the dreams of champagne and celebration, the solid workhorse of some imaginary nineteenth-century peasant picnic—all of these are the *narratives*, the stories we tell that give meaning, context, and purpose to things, that turn a grape product into *wine*.

The work of narrative is interwoven with the work of (micro)climate in the creation of wine: The story's power compels people to invest time, energy, and resources into locating the correct place to grow a vineyard. First, there's the act of planting the vines themselves, waiting the many years before they mature enough to produce grapes worthy of processing. Second, there's the act of working through several harvests before the winemaker knows what all of the specific elements of this patch of ground will combine into when poured into the barrel. Finally, there's the act of inaction—wine resting in the bottle as it slowly ages, for many years, sometimes—and then, ah! The wine dances with abandon as it slides into the glass. Few things capture that paradoxical mix of the mundane and the mythic quite like wine.

The first time I learned this lesson was from an unlikely source: the rom-com *French Kiss*. This 1995 movie, directed by Lawrence Kasdan, stars Meg Ryan as a jilted fiancée who travels to France in hot pursuit of the boyfriend who has just fallen head over heels in lust with a beguiling French woman—he's ensorcelled, really. Kevin Kline plays the French thief whose story becomes inextricably entwined with Ryan's in a series of twisted-knot plot improbabilities that make sense only in the universe of romantic comedies. Sometime during the odyssey of errors and travel that Ryan's character must endure, Kline's character is forced to return home to his family's vineyard—because all French men have family vineyards, of course—with Ryan in tow.

In a demonstration of how Kline is slowly beginning to fall for Ryan, he decides to share his past with Ryan, here taking the form of a school project he's still deeply proud of: a cabinet filled with vials of every flower, soil, fruit, and plant that surround his family's vineyard and that are all somehow present in the wine produced. Kline demonstrates this to Ryan by having her take a sip of wine and then smell a few vials. He finally asks her to take another sip while paying close attention to the smell and taste of the wine itself. The effect is immediate: Ryan takes the sip and almost immediately her eyes widen as she recognizes the flavor and smell of every vial in the wine itself.

In that moment, two stories come into focus for our heroine: She is deeply connected to the specific soil and climate of that place and its flavors in this specific sip, and she is connected to the communal myth of *wine*—that complex mix of heritage, culture, poetry, aficionados and sommeliers, summer barbecues and outdoor parties. Remove either element—the context or the narrative—and that specific moment does not carry nearly as much power. And powerful it was, for it is in that moment that Ryan begins to accept that she is falling for this man. Of course, it doesn't hurt that the audience has been drenched in the mythic power of wine for most of the film by the point this scene arrives, so we are as primed to swoon as Ryan.

The stories that serve as the climate and soil of our lives, the ones that are so pervasive that they are the literal bedrock on which our understanding of the nature of reality is built, are the stories that we address in this chapter. These stories are powerful because they define what it means to be human, at its most fundamental. These are the stories that are so pervasive that they somehow disappear, such that we don't realize their impact on *everything* because they have extended their influence *everywhere*. The answers they give about the nature of human existence, the meaning and boundaries of the term and concept of *person*, the relationship among the individual, the communal, and the Divine: Each, in turn, affects the climate and soil of Liberal Quaker theology and is affected by them in turn. In this sense, these stories are the landscape on which society is built.

I can understand what it means to exist only through my own experience, as it is literally impossible to experience the world exactly as another experiences it. Yet, there is universality in the human experience: I am certain that if I asked you to remember a particularly humiliating experience but not tell me the story, I could easily empathize with your feelings at that moment without needing to know any details whatsoever, because humiliation has an unmistakable feel, and when you feel it, you *know*. We move through the world, living our lives at multiple, context-specific levels, all at once, each element something that you share with humanity, but each aspect individuated to such a degree that only you will experience *being* in the exact way that you do—*ever*.

For example, we are all interrelated in the community of *humanity*: My experience of the world is far more similar to other humans than it is to the experience of my dog Maggie, despite the fact that we live together. Expand the community wider, and now we can say that my experience of the world is more similar to Maggie's than the insects that annoy both of us. Yet again, my experience of the world is more similar to these insects buzzing around me (as I type this) than it would be to the massive colony of bacteria that resides inside of me. (Well, all of us—how else do you think your digestive system worked?) That I experience anything means that I share the experience of being alive with everything else alive in the biosphere. Finally, the fact that I exist in any form whatsoever means that I share existence with everything else that *is*: rocks, planets, gases, life, elements, and so on. At each level of existence the definition of *being* adapts to the scale of the relationships: The experience of being that is shared among all living things is necessarily less specific than the shared experience of being for all humans. The definition of that shared experience of being keeps becoming more particular, more complex, the closer I get to the community of one—my individual self—that is my own unique, particular experience of being.

This might sound akin to the hierarchical taxonomic ranks of classification (domain, kingdom, phylum, class, order, family, genus, species) fundamental to classifying life in biology. In one sense, I could read these ontological levels through the lens of taxonomic rank and create a classification for myself. If I established the levels of being a certain way, this taxonomy could emerge for me: domain *existence*, kingdom *creation*, phylum *life*, class *earth*, order *human*, family *queer/white/North American/etc.*, genus *theologian*, species *Christy Randazzo*. Shift the levels of classification a bit, change the terms, and different taxonomies would emerge. At one level, this is entirely accurate, as my experience of being is fundamentally shaped by my roots in each of these communities/levels of being: I experience being as both an individual *and* as one among many others, in many communities.

A note of caution is due here: The metaphor of taxonomic rank works as long as you don't allow the assumptions of hierarchy that are inherent within the biological concept of taxonomic rank to fundamentally frame your application of the metaphor of taxonomy; assumptions of priority, or primacy, could get smuggled in unintentionally. These different communities to which I belong—and the stories that are essential to them—are not of greater value or importance than any other communities and stories, regardless of whether they are the (macro)community of the biosphere or the (micro)community of my family.

Similarly, I am not stating that I am my *own* species, so much as to say the consequence of the inherent uniqueness of human individuality is that each, individual person can claim absolute uniqueness: There's never been and never will be another me. I am the only me—in all of my fundamental contextuality—to have ever existed. The light of the sun hits each of us—the innumerable, living windowpanes of earth, our family home—creating the raucous kaleidoscope of abundance that is creation, reflecting through each pane in ways unique and astonishingly beautiful.

The Watershed of the Divine Ecosystem

Individuality River

The Sovereign Individual in Liberal Enlightenment Theology

In 1776, Thomas Jefferson penned the Declaration of Independence of the newly minted United States of America. The second sentence of his document declared, "We hold these truths to be self-evident, that all men are created equal, that they are endowed by their Creator with certain unalienable Rights, that among these are Life, Liberty, and the Pursuit of Happiness." With these words (and the rest of the second paragraph of the declaration), Jefferson indelibly imprinted into our American scripture the liberal concept of the sovereign individual, and the existence of a set of universal human rights, by declaring these former colonies united into a nascent nation, based on these foundational principles. You must admit that the power of these words lies with their undeniable beauty and magnificence, at least in part.

Yet, what truly elevates that entire paragraph into something essential to the American character is the vision Jefferson eloquently and efficiently paints of a new age: a radical new vision of the nature of the relationship between individual people and their community, especially regarding governance and economics. Jefferson's words helped inspire an entire coastline of communities—geographically distant and culturally disparate—to unite and thus to engage in the extraordinarily risky endeavor of declaring war on the military behemoth that was Great Britain. The words carried such weight because so many of Jefferson's countrymen did in fact hold these truths to be very self-evident.

These words did not carry intellectual and cultural weight in North America alone, however; they spoke to the European consciousness with such force that they inspired the French population to declare *Liberté, égalité, fraternité* ("Liberty, equality, fraternity"—gotta love cognates) the national motto of France. Jefferson's words had (and have) power because they speak directly to the dominant state of being of Western culture: the ontology of liberalism. Liberalism is used herein to mean the belief in the primacy of the individual person as the agent of social life, including a focus on individual liberty and rights. This ontology informs nearly every aspect of Western society, including modern science, jurisprudence, and political theory, as well as Christian theology. This ontology is so dominant, in fact, that society rarely critically examines this core assumption: one that is seriously flawed—at least from the perspective of Christian theology.

The roots of the ontology of liberalism lay in the European Enlightenment of the seventeenth and eighteenth centuries. This includes the Enlightenment insistence on the primacy of reason as the factor determining what constitutes a human person, as well as on the concomitant corollary that the seat of reason lay in the autonomous, sovereign individual. I think, therefore I am—in other words. This monadic, independent individual shared with all of humankind the state of being human, yet reason freed the individual from any fundamental tethers with other humans; each person was thus a country unto one's own and a law unto oneself, free to either choose to contract with other humans into a society or instead to remain entirely separate. Both the notion of a personal relationship with Jesus and the myth of the self-made man find their roots in this ontology, as do both "liberal" Christian civil rights movements and "conservative" Christian fundamentalism.[1] The final

---

1. Battle argues that the "personal Jesus" is in fact not Christian: "It is common to hear many preach that one must have a personal relationship with Jesus as Lord and Savior. . . . This homiletic way of articulating relationship with God, however, is individualistic and unintelligible to the way that Jesus taught us how to pray. . . . It is with this communal connection between spiritual formation and daily life that . . . no such individualistic understanding works outside of a communal understanding of spirituality." Michael Battle, *Blessed Are the Peacemakers: A Christian Spirituality of Nonviolence* (Mercer University Press, 2004), 41.

product of such thought can be seen in the marriage of materialism, self-reliance, and individuality with a "personal savior" that is the prosperity gospel movement.

The human person in liberal thought is rational, universal in their response to different circumstances, yet individualistic in their relationships to those around them. Community in liberal thought is contractual, impermanent, and passive with regard to the individual. The most integral right for the liberal human is freedom: that is, the freedom to determine one's own path, place in society, and even identity. This liberty can be understood to radiate in a sphere—of indeterminate size—around the human, protecting their exercise of freedom from the intrusion of others. The only limit on their freedom is when their exercise of freedom impedes another human from exercising their own rights; until that point, however, the individual is said to be sovereign over their actions.

Liberalism recognizes that human individuals gain many benefits from interaction with other humans—such as love and companionship—while survival often depends on others. For liberalism, however, community is not required for human existence; the human individual could exist alone, if their needs for sustenance and physical and mental health could somehow be provided for. This narrative is what I call the "myth of the sovereign individual," where *myth* is understood to be a foundational narrative, not something inherently false. Liberalism bolsters this narrative by using scientific rationalism as its main hermeneutical tool. The myth is rooted in sixteenth-century Renaissance humanism, yet it developed into a theoretical framework during the Age of Enlightenment in Europe. It eventually came to dominate Western thought during the Enlightenment, influencing Western political theory as well as Protestant theology. This framework has shaped the modern understanding of rights, liberty, and democratic process. (I wonder, however, whether liberalism will always be incomplete without a foundation in a communal narrative—despite the admittedly massive benefits of the language of individual rights. My gut says yes.)

The language of rights has its roots in the Enlightenment, which was also known as the Age of Reason. The dominant hermeneutic for most intellectual thought during this period was, as the name suggests, reason. The awareness of the individual's rights to autonomy and self-preservation can be traced to seventeenth-century Dutch polymath Hugo Grotius, although traces of the ideas he espoused can be found in the work of sixteenth-century Roman Catholic theologian Francisco de Vitoria.[2] Intellectual inquiry was influenced by an optimism about the human ability to examine the world—including God, of course—rationally. Ironically, mysticism and mystical theology were also experiencing a flowering during this period. The power of these individual and communal mystical experiences, combined with the Protestant emphasis on individual biblical interpretation and the denial of church-mediated salvation, led to an abundance of new religious groups and sects, each declaring its own right to exist.

This abundance of different groups all claiming some part of "Truth" inevitably led to conflict, for many of these claims were mutually exclusive. In England, the Elizabethan Compromise led to a particularly fecund diversity of religious thought, especially with Puritanism. The situation forced many of the thinkers of the day to seek some form of compromise, while also agreeing on the importance of a few fundamental truths as a minimum necessity for the religious life. Furthermore, the universal activity of the Divine and the clearness of the necessary truths made a theology of toleration imperative.

The liberals saw a correlation between reason and the truth that the mystics gained from Divine Revelation: Since reason was common to all people, similar to the common potential for divine revelation, reason was capable of ascertaining truth separate from tradition and an external authority.[3] Some of these overlaps include the relationship between reason (as defined by the liberals) and the Light Within described by the Puritan mystics and spiritualists, an emphasis on determining which fundamental truths are considered basic and core for religious belief, a stress on toleration and comprehension, a vision of the religious life as having moral *fruits*, and finally, an ambivalence toward time, with negative attitudes about the past and an optimism for the future. At this point, however, the liberals did not discount divine revelation, instead granting it a place beside human reason, capable of speaking to truth in a different manner.

The shift toward reason and away from revelation began when intractable conflicts arose over the truth of different revelations and their interpretations. This was especially notable during the English Civil War (1642–51) and its

2. Roger Ruston, *Human Rights and the Image of God* (SCM, 2004), 194.

3. Jerald C. Bauer, "Puritan Mysticism and the Development of Liberalism," *Church History* 19, no. 3 (1950): 154.

immediate aftermath. Revelation was increasingly seen as unreliable and unstable. Reason emerged as the best alternative, as it "admitted a natural light in man which was universal," laid down basic moral principles that could be discerned by all people, maintained the necessity of individualism, and yet avoided the controversies and instability of divine revelation.[4] Liberalism thus laid a foundation for a stable political society.

The problems with this theory became obvious over time. For one, it was devoid of any spiritual content and had very little to say about evil as a spiritual reality. It also ignored the necessity for human community, meaning that it was—in the end—incapable of meeting the greatest demands of its age and was vulnerable to the passions unleashed by the evangelical revival in the nineteenth century. Arguably, therefore, this marriage between Protestant individuality and liberal rationality froze Protestant moral development. Without a tradition or community in which to root morals, Protestants were left vulnerable to whatever moralities happened to pertain in their cultures.[5] Thus, being Christian often simply became a way to indicate what society regarded as decent.[6]

The transitoriness of the essential content of liberal Christianity was rooted in the weak bond between person and the community. Liberalism offers the illusion that absolute independence is achievable, wherein one exists without any relationship to others. Ironically, this is quite an irrational idea, for who has ever existed without first being conceived within a community of two people, then born and raised within the community of an entire society? Even accepting the very basic conception of community espoused by liberalism, where "community occurs wherever commonly embraced ideas and ends are consciously and intellectually sustained," ideas cannot be embraced without first having been imparted by another, nor can reason be known to be reasonable without some engagement with another.[7] Liberalism attempted

4. Bauer, "Puritan Mysticism and the Development of Liberalism," 161.

5. Stanley Hauerwas, *The Hauerwas Reader*, ed. John Berkman and Michael Cartwright (Duke University Press, 2001), 227.

6. At the end of the nineteenth century, this tendency to meld Christian morality and cultural mores would see full expression in the cultural morality of the Victorian era.

7. Morton Schoolman, "The Moral Sentiments of Neoliberalism," *Political Theory* 15, no. 2 (1987): 205.

to resolve this issue by espousing theories of communities where sovereign individuals mutually coexisted. Thus, community was seen as a necessary evil. The "necessary" was grudgingly granted, yet the "evil" remained, with liberalism always wary that community would somehow stifle individual liberty.[8]

The liberal aversion to communal life was so extreme that some branches of liberalism began to view the individual in atomistic terms, as Craig Calhoun explains:

> Because the nature of each thing—or person—was held to be self-contained (and not a matter of reflection of some ideal order of forms), a kind of atomism became more common. Extreme versions added a conception of contracts of association underpinning communal or social life itself. The hitherto, primarily religious, idea of personal commitment made plausible the notion that membership in society and subjection to authority both depended on consent. . . . This is a distinctively modern claim focused on the subject as simultaneously particular and universalized, and above all as independent.[9]

A person was thus only a member of human society if they chose to be so, and could elect at any time to decide to remove their consent—and their person—from society. Any understanding of humans as interrelated was thus thrust aside. The application of reason to the created order led to a rapid development of the physical sciences, which in turn led to the development of the machine model of creation, in which all living things—including humans—could be broken down to their constituent parts.[10] Liberals could not see or physically

---

8. Den Uyl and Rasmussen expresses this point in response to Charles Taylor's communitarian theories: "Thus, it is in terms of finding a solution to liberalism's problem that the political priority of individual rights arises, and it is in terms of these rights that an ethical framework for a political order, understood as a civil association, is provided. Accordingly, Taylor fails to consider the possibility that something can have value to each of us as a function of our relationship with each other without thereby having to be an end for us. What belongs to us as a whole may only be the securing of the conditions or framework for the pursuit of goods (ends). Those goods we pursue might be the object of some enterprise, but the condition or framework for them is not, in itself, one such good." Douglas J. Den Uyl and Douglas B. Rasmussen, "The Myth of Atomism," *The Review of Metaphysics* 59, no. 4 (2006): 855.

9. Craig Calhoun, "Morality, Identity, and Historical Explanation: Charles Taylor on the Sources of the Self," *Sociological Theory* 9, no. 2 (1991): 247.

10. Sallie McFague, *The Body of God: An Ecological Theology* (Fortress, 1993), 15.

examine the bonds that wove humans together, so they were thus seen to be nonexistent, immaterial, and unnecessary.[11]

This atomism led to a compartmentalized view of the world, in which life could be entirely separated into compartments, including politics, morality, religion, and economics. Religion could be separated from politics, politics from economics, and morality was bifurcated. Following in Martin Luther's footsteps, both liberalism and Protestantism taught that there existed a public and private morality: You aren't allowed to kill someone, but the state can—as long as they follow the rules, of course. The just war theories of Grotius follow this stream. This emphasis on compartmentalized individualism also led to a situation where property (economic life)—the result of the individual's free effort—was seen as inviolate. To restrict one's property would be to restrict their liberty. The accumulation of wealth was no longer seen as immoral or even amoral; it was actually a moral duty, as it demonstrated the individual's industriousness and served as an example to society of the value of free economic activity.

When considered in light of the absolutely mind-bogglingly-massive wealth inequality in our world, where handfuls of people hold a vast majority of global wealth, it tastes bitter and poisonous. Yet, liberalism is not devoid of moral content. The development of individual rights has been one of liberalism's great legacies, aiding in the liberation of many oppressed populations and giving hope and dignity to people who have been dehumanized by economic inequalities and the lack of political autonomy. Yet, many of these same populations have also been dehumanized by liberal societies, raising the question whether using the language of rights amounts to using the tools of liberalism to solve the problems of liberalism.[12]

Alasdair MacIntyre critiques liberalism on just these grounds. He recognizes that rights have a necessary corollary in justice, in which an infringement

---

11. Brinton argues that science was not alone in rejecting organic interconnection, but religion joined in: "Protestantism did away with organic interrelatedness and brought in an almost mechanistic individualism. No surprise that mechanistic science emerged at the same time. Imputed righteousness and its divine transactional character were the only path to salvation, only one person at a time, and not granting the person any say in the matter." Howard H. Brinton, *Friends for 300 Years: The History and Beliefs of the Society of Friends Since George Fox Started the Quaker Movement* (Sowers, 1972), 45.

12. The examples abound.

of one's rights necessitates a call for justice. He notes, however, that while liberalism speaks of universal human rights that apply to all people in all settings, liberalism fails to present a corresponding "universal account of justice," in which justice applies to all people in all settings.[13] In the hypocrisy noted above, liberalism seems to be willing to be universal in demanding rights, yet strangely individualistic and contextual in developing a framework within which those rights will be applied. The challenge of this double standard, for Christians, lies with its baggage: In using the language of rights, the liberal assumption of the atomized individual as primary can take over, while the Christian emphasis on the common good can easily be laid aside.

Within this context, the concept of any "right to health care" (just to note one recent argument roiling the US political landscape) would be a completely foreign notion to the billions of people worldwide who reside in crushing poverty: Rights have meaning only when someone actually has access to them—and a government capable of enforcing them. This disconnect has led some health professionals, for example, to question whether a Universal Declaration of Human Rights can even begin to be a useful tool for social change.[14] Additionally, feminist theory questions whether liberal ethical theory is applicable with respect to the "moral aspects of the concern and sympathy which people feel for particular others," leading some to conclude that liberal moral theory, with its focus on the individual in isolation, may actually be irrelevant to daily life.[15]

The danger of separating individual autonomy from universal rights is the strengthening of one at the expense of the other, in which universal rights becomes such a weak and meaningless concept that it has little defense against

13. Ruston, *Human Rights and the Image of God*, 13.

14. Solomon R. Benatar, Abdallah S. Daar, and Peter A. Singer, "Global Health Ethics: The Rationale for Mutual Caring," *International Affairs* 79, no. 1 (2003): 107.

15. Held says, in full: "Standard ethics has neglected the moral aspects of the concern and sympathy which people actually feel for particular others, and what moral experience in this intermediate realm suggests for an adequate morality. The region of 'particular others' is a distinct domain, where what can be seen to be artificial and problematic are the very egoistic 'self' and the universal 'all others' of standard moral theory. In the domain of particular others, the self is already constituted to an important degree by relations with others, and these relations may be much more salient and significant than the interests of any individual self in isolation." Virginia Held, "Feminist Transformations of Moral Theory," *Philosophy and Phenomenological Research* 50, supplement (1990): 338.

rampant individual autonomy. Two notable examples include the segregation societies of the United States and South Africa. The very similar policies of segregation and apartheid stem from the same liberal root: the complete misappropriation of the language of rights to the detriment of anyone who isn't legally and culturally understood to be "white."[16] This phenomenon is noticeable in the appeals to rights language used by white/European-descent people in the United States and South Africa. White segregationists in the United States spoke of states' rights, cultural heritage, and free speech, while white Afrikaners in South Africa spoke of "good neighborliness" and the right of each color to exist in its own camp without intrusion by the other—hence the use of the term "Bantu homelands" for the poor and remote areas that Blacks were exiled to during apartheid.[17] Thus, liberalism's blindness to cultural context tips the delicate balance between fostering individual autonomy and protecting universal virtues. Often the power of self-interest results in some individuals being granted more autonomy than others, while any sense of universal virtues begins to mirror the virtues that best reflect the norms and mores of their culture.[18]

Allan Boesak bluntly calls racism sin, and then links racism, capitalistic Protestantism, and apartheid by stating that, to many Blacks, racism is the fruit of the Reformed tradition.[19] Howard Thurman makes a similar link with racism, white Protestant Christianity, and segregation, in which the white conscience was insulated from feeling any sense of wrongdoing due to the dramatic fragmentation that compartmentalization had wrought in white Christianity.[20]

It would appear, therefore, that what can destroy liberalism's grand ideals lies hidden at the very root of those ideals and even of liberalism itself. The

---

16. R. Drew Smith, "Ecclesiastical Racism and the Politics of Confession," in *Race and Reconciliation in South Africa: A Multicultural Dialogue in Comparative Perspective*, ed. William E. Van Vugt and G. Daan Cloete (Lexington Books, 2000), 61.

17. Echoes of this policy can be found a century earlier in the use of the term *reservation* by the US government to denote the poor, remote, and often infertile tracts granted to Indigenous peoples.

18. Shades of George Orwell's *Animal Farm*, perhaps, where all are equal, but some more than others?

19. Allan Boesak, *Black and Reformed: Apartheid, Liberation, and the Calvinist Tradition* (Orbis Books, 1986), 86.

20. Howard Thurman, *Jesus and the Disinherited* (Abingdon-Cokesbury, 1949), 44.

racial conflicts in South Africa demonstrate the societal challenges that result from this compartmentalization:

> That, in turn, arose out of liberalism's assimilationist underpinnings, in terms of which people of "inferior" cultures could be incorporated into the white societal ethos only when they had attained the "civilized values" of the West. . . . What liberals did not comprehend, however, was that the black failure to become "civilised" was due not to any innate inability, but rather because the great majority of blacks did not see acculturation to white, Western norms as something that was desirable in any case.[21]

This language is that of empire, in which the country views its actions as justified, as its military, economic, or political might "proves" its claim to divine sanction to occupy its new promised land.[22]

The result in many countries with liberal governmental systems has been moral blindness, in which the liberal-democratic process has been praised as the only system that would guarantee freedom: that most important virtue of liberalism. The nineteenth-century American policy of Manifest Destiny is just one example of this imperial thinking. Admittedly, if one follows the logic of liberal imperialism, such a system appears to make sense—if a system prioritizes individual choice over other concerns, freedom is best protected and fostered only in a system where people are free to make choices. Yet, this has not proven to be the case for vast populations of liberal states. This situation results in such a limited definition of freedom that freedom is often available only to a small minority, while the rest—both the "truly disadvantaged" (the powerless and the destitute), as well as all those who somehow(?) "chose" their plight (addicts, sex workers, and the homeless)—are left powerless.[23]

This compartmentalized dispersal and defense of freedom and rights is seemingly endemic to liberalism. For all of liberalism's positive virtues and—at many times—selfless and heroic defense of the poor and powerless, liberalism

---

21. David Thomas, *Christ Divided: Liberalism, Ecumenism, and Race in South Africa* (Unisa, 2002), 150.

22. Jack Nelson-Pallmeyer, *Saving Christianity from Empire* (Continuum, 2005), 130.

23. Paul Farmer, *Pathologies of Power: Health, Human Rights, and the New War on the Poor* (University of California Press, 2005), 6.

seems hampered by its untenable, yet admittedly idealistic, foundation. This weakness can only serve to make the failures of liberalism that much more disheartening. Failures they are, alas, and unavoidable, for individualism in its pure, idealistic form is simply illogical. One can be free from human interdependence only by standing on someone else's back—who is guaranteed to be poor. Liberal culture can thus be granted the ability to swim in the sea of choice and freedom only by having resources that permit choice and freedom. To be blunt, it's difficult to spend time deciding what hair color defines you when you're hungry and dodging bullets.[24]

The problem with applying liberal thought to issues of climate change and ecological collapse, in particular, lies with the lack of insistency on the necessity of action: Individualist liberalism, with its focus on rights, is utterly ridiculous when faced with the immeasurable complexity of ecosystems. Humans have constructed legal systems that grant them the *right* to destroy ecosystems. What this means in reality, however, is that humans have granted themselves the *right* of annihilation—without taking a second to consider whether any other creature might have something to say about it. Thus, liberalism is left without a significant intellectual and spiritual foundation when a common appeal to survival must be made to an individual society based on a culture of violence. Until we are faced with the insistent necessity of action in the form of immediate, personal impact, our efforts will be deontological, in dutiful service to the principles of universal right—*human* rights exclusively, of course.

Friendly Individualism

In many ways, the Delaware Valley is seen as a heartland for Quakers. In 1681, King Charles II extended a land grant of a massive parcel of land along the western shore of the lower Delaware River to Friend William Penn for the purpose of repaying a debt Charles owed to Penn's father, Admiral William Penn.

---

24. Gutiérrez makes a very similar point with regard to the Latin American situation: "A structural analysis better suited to Latin American reality has led certain Christians to speak of the 'rights of the poor' and to interpret the defense of human rights under this new formality. The adjustment is not merely a matter of words. This alternative language represents a critical approach to the laissez-faire, liberal doctrine to the effect that our society enjoys an equality that in fact does not exist. This new formulation likewise seeks constantly to remind us of what is really at stake in the defense of human rights: the misery and spoilation of the poorest of the poor, the conflictive character of Latin American life and society, and the biblical roots of the defense of the poor." Farmer, *Pathologies of Power*, 142.

The king named it Pennsylvania ("Penn's Woods") in honor of the admiral, and the colony of Pennsylvania was born. William Penn had been a member of the Religious Society of Friends for some time before the land grant and had in fact been involved in an effort by Quakers to purchase the land along the eastern shore of the Delaware River in 1677, to establish a proprietary colony named West Jersey. Three years prior, Quakers purchased land along the Atlantic coast—today's Jersey Shore—to create the colony of East Jersey. By 1702, the government of Queen Anne had seized claim to both East and West Jersey, joining them together into the place we now know as New Jersey.

While New Jersey was eventually taken from Quaker control, Pennsylvania remained so until deep in the eighteenth century. The period of Quaker control of Pennsylvania left indelible marks, from settlement patterns defined by Penn's treaties with the Lenni Lenape people (the actual owners of the land) to the culture—and laws—of religious tolerance, which eventually expanded into a generally pluralistic culture of tolerance for cultural, religious, and ethnic diversity. This tolerance has its roots in Quaker theology and its foundational idea that all people have the potential to possess the Divine spark, or presence, within themselves. Among the various ripple effects of this idea is the understanding that the individual has inherent value and worth. When this idea was coupled with the critique of class inherent in the idea that all are equally worthy in the eyes of God, it led to an egalitarian culture that dovetailed well with the development of democracy as the preferred political framework for the nascent United States of America.

This middle approach was reflected geographically in Pennsylvania's nickname of "Keystone State" (as it was the keystone that held New England and the South together), and politically in the culture of the Delaware Valley, which to this day is still seen as a place of toleration and inclusion.[25] The combination of Philadelphia as middle place geographically for the American colonies, and middle place culturally between the slave society of the South and Puritan New England, led to the choice of Philadelphia as the location for the First and Second Continental Congresses, the capital of the United States until 1785, and the location of the drafting—and ratification—of the Constitution in 1789. Quakers provided the political and cultural ground for the development of the peculiarly American framework of the sovereign

---

25. Colin Woodard, *American Nations: A History of the Eleven Rival Regional Cultures of North America* (Penguin Books, 2011).

individual, and the literal ground on which the foundational ideas of the new republic were developed.

The Quaker tradition generally, and the Liberal expression of it particularly, emphasizes the central role of the individual: The individual's experience is seen as central to Quaker theological method, while each individual is seen as equally capable as any other of learning to hear the Divine voice and offering that message to the community. The Liberal tradition got its name from the Liberal movement in Christianity during the late 1800s, which, with its focus on reason and the use of scientific methods in biblical interpretation, is itself a descendant of the Enlightenment. As Liberal Quakerism developed, it continued to place significant emphasis on the individual's own experience, and on the individual's capacity to use reason to interpret the meaning and purpose of that experience.

This stress on the individual has resulted in an environment of radical openness to new revelations of God, such that one can claim belonging in Liberal Quakerism, can engage in the work of the meeting community, and can be elevated to a position of leadership within Liberal Quaker institutions all while potentially holding any of a mélange of diverse, and sometimes contradictory, theological beliefs. In other words, the ontology of the sovereign individual is rooted in Quaker thought and is still expressed in many of the core beliefs of Liberal Quakers.

Community River

> The paradox of being human is that each of us is at once an individual, a separate being in our own right, and at the same time intrinsically and inextricably bound up and interconnected with other individuals—other aba-ntu. *There is an invisible circuit of connection between us all: activating the flow of humanity, of love, of creative or spiritual power between human beings.* This connection is Ubuntu. It is not a static state though, energy flows from respect for self to respect for others, which in turn regenerates respect for self. But the greatest challenge for Ubuntu is when I do not find it in the other when the other is trapped in a vicious downward spiral of self-destruction and self-hatred, feeding hatred and destruction of others. Do I see anything of myself in that other? If not, what am I blind to in myself? How do I energise my sense of Ubuntu—the flow of

> love and energy from myself to that other person? Can I continue to respect myself if I do not strive to do that? Can I respect myself if I affirm another person who is doing evil to others, perhaps also to me?
>
> —Jennifer Kinghorn

Liberal, atomistic individualism is not the only way to imagine the relationship among human persons, the creation, and the Divine. Numerous other traditions exist—including Christian—that instead argue for a communal humanity, where each individual person is actually bound up in a relationship of interdependence with others and with the Divine. Generally referred to as *interdependence theologies*, they assume a high degree of interdependence among all aspects of the creation, such that, as the *ubuntu* theology of South Africa argues, the human person makes sense only in the context of relationship with others.[26] Quakers understand the human person to be in an inextricably interdependent relationship with the Divine through the presence of the Light Within in all of creation. This interdependence is explained in numerous ways across the Quaker theological landscape, including both the *ubuntu* theology of South African Friends and the Quaker ecological tradition emerging from the witness of John Woolman, a Quaker from the New Jersey side of the lower Delaware Valley. (Notably, this is yet another theological tie to the specific context of the Delaware River watershed.)

Much of my own work has been in this area, demonstrating the overlaps and similarities among various Christian interdependence theologies, including links with Quaker interdependence theology. I argue that the metaphor of Light—the foundational metaphor for the continuous Divine presence in Quaker theology—is the best place to begin to construct a Quaker interdependence theology as well as serve as the cornerstone for future Quaker ecotheology.[27] In each of those books, I demonstrate that Quaker interdependence theology is actually a dialect of a larger language family of Christian interdependence theology, with similar foundational assumptions—even if, at times, the look and feel of the religious languages might vary considerably.

---

26. Desmond Tutu, *No Future Without Forgiveness* (Image Books, Doubleday, 2000).

27. Randazzo, *Liberal Quaker Reconciliation Theology*; Bock and Randazzo, *Quakers, Ecology, and the Light*.

This work is itself rooted deep within Liberal Quaker theology, however. Rufus Jones—arguably the most influential thinker during the early period of Liberal Quakerism—wrote extensively about the mystical tradition in Christianity, seeking to demonstrate that Quaker spirituality emerged from within this wider mystical tradition. Jones also stressed the need to root the new-at-the-time Liberal Quaker tradition in mystical spirituality as a response to the rapid changes occurring in the world (and in Quakerism!) at the beginning of the twentieth century.

While Quaker scholars have since taken issue with Jones's argument about the foundational role mystical spirituality had on shaping the spirituality and theology of early Friends—basically, Jones overstated his case—it is difficult to overstate the impact that Jones had on shaping Liberal Quaker theology and ontology. Regardless of whether his argument was correct in the sense of historical accuracy, his framing of Liberal Quakerism as a mystical religion rang true among early Liberal Friends, meaning that mysticism—and an ontology of communal interdependence—is considered a bedrock of Liberal Quaker faith and practice.

Interdependence Theologies

Christian interdependence theology claims that human beings are created by God as inherently social and relational, made to be in relationship with each other and with God. As social beings, therefore, human beings cannot exist without those three elements (self, others, and God), nor outside them. It is in relation to persons and personal community that the concept of God is formed.[28] One cannot speak of God without implying community as well as person, for neither community nor person exists without God or each other. Each person is therefore inextricably linked with both God *and* with every other person, for while God's existence is not dependent on community or persons, the individual person cannot really be said to exist without relation to her community—or to God. The community lives within the person, and the person within the community, with Jesus Christ as the force that gives it purpose and meaning.

This framework of interdependence sets the paradigm for the existence of creation, therefore, where creation is interdependent with itself. This can only occur due to the communal nature of the creation. Through the incarnation of Christ, all of humanity is created to be interdependent on both God and on

28. Randazzo, *Liberal Quaker Reconciliation Theology*, 32.

other people. Both Christ and the Holy Spirit are active in bringing humanity into a full experience of the life of God. This occurs through a process of theosis, where the transcendent God immanently interpenetrates the entirety of creation, sanctifying it. The Spirit acts in concert with Christ, unifying all pieces of the sanctified creation into one, holy, communal person.

Forces of division and difference act violently, by undermining the interdependence of the divine/human and human/human relationship, thus undermining the fabric of existence. Ecotheology insists that the Divine is continuously acting to repair the damage caused by these forces of violence, however, reasserting the fundamental interdependence of all existence. This demands a vision of the human person that is communal, in which through the actions and being of God each individual person is already reconciled to God, as well as to the entirety of the creation itself. God therefore bridges the Divine/human divide through the interpenetration of the Divine throughout the entirety of the creation.

The consequences of interdependence do not only affect human relationships and the inevitable necessity for continuous peacemaking and reconciliation, therefore; this interdependence demands an awareness of ecological interdependence as well as an ethic—and resultant practices—of ecological care. The emphasis on the marriage of the practices of building just and interdependent human communities with a theology of Divine/human interdependence strongly reflects the same marriage in Quaker practice and theology, and thus deserves some exploration as we note where Christian interdependence theologies can help inform a Quaker ecotheology.

While this is a rich theological tradition, with a variety of perspectives to highlight, the work of twentieth-century German theologian and ethicist (and famous Nazi resister) Dietrich Bonhoeffer helps provide a vision of communal interdependence that aligns well with Quaker theology, especially with his focus on the inherently social nature of the human person. Bonhoeffer stresses that this social nature means that humans are created by God to be in relationship with each other and with God. Thus, the reconciliation of relationship among humans, and between humans and God, is a fundamental necessity for human flourishing.

To explain the concept of divine/human interdependence, Bonhoeffer borrowed the concept of "I-Thou" from fellow German philosopher Martin Buber—who also happened to be Jewish, a fact that was most certainly not lost on Bonhoeffer. The I-Thou relationship stands in contrast to the I-It relationship. The first is a holistic relationship of mutualism between two beings sharing a connection to each other based around love: being for the other.[29] The I-It relationship, by contrast, rejects the authentic, personal encounter between two existent beings and instead has the two beings treat each other as objects to be used, degrading the true dialogic encounter of I-Thou into a monologue with the self. The relationship between the complete human that is "I" and the complete human that is "thou" can exist only if both rest in a state of being truly real. If either fails to be this, then they simply become an object—an it—that exists simply to hold whatever meaning someone desires to ascribe to it.

Bonhoeffer calls this state of being an "open-I," where the "I" is not a consistent being and is not rooted in anything stable or meaningful.[30] The "closed-I," on the other hand, is actually the more integrated, interdependent person. The person is whole and can interact with the other without completely losing the self in the process. The closed-I is also more able to see God, both in themselves and in the other: For as they see themselves and are integrated in themselves, they can see God in themselves. As they do not have any fear of the other, they can also see God in the other. It is through the web of relationships between integrated persons that the collective person, and thus the collective God, exists.

Bonhoeffer presents a vision of individual humans as social beings who are actually composed of three parts or elements: God, person, and community, which Bonhoeffer refers to as the basic ontic relations of social being as a whole. As social beings, therefore, humans cannot exist without those three elements, nor outside them. It is in relation to persons and personal community that the concept of God is formed. If persons cannot exist without God or community, and community cannot exist without persons and God, then the church is crucial in some sense for Jesus as well. As Bonhoeffer claims, "The social significance of Christ is decisive. . . . He is only present in the Church, that is, where the Christian community is united for brotherly-sisterly love through preaching and the Lord's supper."[31] Bonhoeffer presents here the classic Protestant "marks of the church," as defined by John Calvin:

---

29. Martin Buber, *I and Thou* (T&T Clark, 1987), 24–25.

30. Dietrich Bonhoeffer, *A Testament to Freedom*, ed. Geffrey B. Kelly and E. Barton Nelson (HarperOne, 1995), 68.

31. Bonhoeffer, *Testament to Freedom*, 57.

preaching of the word of God and the proper administration of the sacraments. According to Bonhoeffer, the daily life and practice of the church are essential for Jesus to be present, and for humans to be able to experience—and recognize—God and God's work. Bonhoeffer is stating here that God can be experienced only in a communal way, through the daily interactions of individuals in community, worshipping God. This framework of interdependence sets the paradigm for the existence of creation, therefore, in which creation is interdependent with itself. This can occur only due to the communal nature of the creation, where through the incarnation of Christ, all of humanity is created to be interdependent on both God and other humans.

An interdependence theology emerging from within Christian theology is the *ubuntu* theology of South Africa—a theology that, as demonstrated by the quote from South African Friend Jennifer Kinghorn that opens this section, has strongly influenced Friends theology as well. *Ubuntu* is a complex construction that is rooted in the ontology of the languages commonly classed as Bantu, where personhood cannot exist outside its contextual relationship to others.[32] The root *-ntu* means both "human being" and the "being" of God, emphasizing a relationship between the Divine and the human. *Ubuntu* says that no person is completely human unless all are free to express their complete humanity. Racism is sin, therefore, as it creates false hierarchies based on physical characteristics among people who were all equally created in the image of an egalitarian God. Instead, *ubuntu* posits a vision of radical human equality in an interdependent relationship with an active, present God.

In sub-Saharan spirituality, God's being and human beings are directly related.[33] Due to this, *ubuntu* has a theological understanding of knowing all beings through the category of personhood, where the humanity of an individual is best expressed in relationships with others. In this way, in *ubuntu* the human person reflects the *imago Dei* of God the Creator.[34] *Ubuntu* theology emphasizes universal interconnection between the creation and a God who is both immanent and transcendent. In *ubuntu* theology, God bridges these

32. Michael Battle, *Ubuntu: I in You and You in Me* (Seabury Books, 2009), 4.

33. Battle, *Ubuntu*, 2–3.

34. Michael Battle, *Reconciliation: The Ubuntu Theology of Desmond Tutu* (Pilgrim, 1997), 144.

paradoxical states of being through a radical, communal interdependence.[35] *Ubuntu* theology is thus rooted in an understanding of God as collective, in which human persons are woven together in an interdependent collective person through the presence of God in each individual human being. The fulfillment of an individual's potential is reliant on the mutual fulfillment of the potential of the rest of creation, linking every individual with the rest of humanity through the presence of God.

God is still a transcendent reality, beyond all comprehension, however. God does not require any revelation or evidence to demonstrate existence, as God is simply existence itself, the ontic core of reality.[36] God is neither bound to create in order to exist nor bound by human will. The Spirit is similarly not bound by any human construction or definition of how the Spirit should or should not act. The liberty of action and will of the Holy Spirit extends to theosis, remaining transcendent even as it is inviting the human soul into its life.[37] The mystical tradition, as represented by the anonymous author of the book *The Cloud of Unknowing*, stresses this state of utter transcendence. The Divine transcendence is immutable and must be accepted as it is, as it is beyond human reasoning.

The Trinity has deep significance in the *ubuntu* vision of God.[38] God, as Trinity, is a union of diverse persons who are paradoxically different and in

---

35. Tutu is the main proponent of *ubuntu* theology, yet theology is by no means the only field in which *ubuntu* is being used as a philosophical construct. *Ubuntu* has been applied to computer science (*ubuntu* is an open source computer operating system, so named due to the cooperative nature of the open-source model of software design), restorative justice concepts, African philosophy, political theory, and foreign policy, as well as political reconciliation. The concept of *ubuntu* underpinned much of the thought around the Truth and Reconciliation Commission in South Africa and has become a common term used in South African public discourse to describe the approach and goals of the ongoing reconciliation project in South Africa. Luke Lingilo Pato contends that Tutu can be seen to reside within an African tradition of using *ubuntu* as a theological construct, including John Mbiti from Kenya, Charles Nyamiti from Tanzania, Kwesi Dickson from Ghana, and Gabriel Setiloane from South Africa. Luke Lungile Pato, "African Theologies," in *Doing Theology in Context: South African Perspectives*, ed. John W. de Gruchy and Charles Villa-Vicencio (Orbis Books, 1994), 156.

36. Battle, *Blessed Are the Peacemakers*, 113.

37. Yves Congar, *I Believe in the Holy Spirit* (Seabury Books, 1983), 89.

38. Charles Villa-Vicencio, "Christianity and Human Rights," *Journal of Law and Religion* 14, no. 2 (1999–2000): 593.

absolute and complete union in an indivisible Godhead. The persons of the Trinity are inextricably related through love, in which the Holy Spirit—the love that is God—is continually emptied from the Creator into the Son and back again. This kenotic reciprocity of emptying applies also to the creation.[39] *Ubuntu* uses an apophatic approach when examining the Trinity, saying little about the interrelationality of the Trinity beyond the impact that the interdependent Trinity has on the creation.

This can serve as a rejection of the dominance model of human relationship inherent in both Western individualism and capitalism. For Western Christians, the loss of communalism as a counterbalance has permitted individualism to run rampant, and has created a situation in which the human person becomes a commodified self, existing simply to serve the economic needs of the competitive market.[40] This commodification creates people who are wholly dependent on the static qualities of rationality and will, ignoring the potential for mystery, irrationality, and indeterminacy to shape what it means to be human. The objectified, rational self is therefore the apex of value.[41] This logical leap permits Western society to interpret the divine blessing of Genesis 1:28 as subduing, controlling, and using the earth, as opposed to acting as God's steward, responsible for caring for the earth.

This emphasis on communality has its challenges, of course: It can allow the community to overpower the individual and strip them of their uniqueness. The solution to this is found, again, in the emphasis on the *imago Dei* in individual people.[42] *Ubuntu* stresses, therefore, that the individual cannot be separated from their community and cannot compose an ethical system or moral framework without taking into account the impact of their choices on others. Yet, the community does not define the person, nor can it decide to stop acknowledging the inherent personhood of the person as a form of exile.[43]

---

39. Battle, *Reconciliation*, 77.

40. Battle, *Blessed Are the Peacemakers*, 216.

41. Battle, *Ubuntu*, 39.

42. Battle, *Reconciliation*, 42.

43. Boesak, *Black and Reformed*, 51.

This interdependence is also a rejection of Western dualisms, particularly the dualism of the "wholly-other" God and a sinful, broken humanity.[44] As God made creation in God's image, the creation must reflect the image of God. In this way, *ubuntu* melds the diverse interconnectivity of humanity with the diverse interconnectivity of the divine Trinity. The result is a human identity in which each unique, finite human is interconnected with all of humanity as well as with the infinite Divine. This interconnectivity is truly interdependent, as human beings possess an innate desire that can be fulfilled only by human community, coupled with a deep relationship to the Divine.

Interconnectedness builds on first seeing the good in others, leading to seeing God in all of creation. This involves acknowledging that while persons may exist whose free will is so twisted that it has turned evil, they cannot disavow the good Spirit that resides within them. In *ubuntu*, there is no gulf between the holy Divine and sinful creation, as God is continually present, at all times and places, in the entirety of creation.[45]

Reflecting the concerns of ecotheology, in *ubuntu* theology sin is separation from others. This separation involves a rejection of the unification that all people experience with each other, in turn separating human beings from God. Sin can be understood to deny the values that give shape and meaning to the community.[46] Sin is living according to one's own individual desires: loyal to self as opposed to the communal God. As the creation reflects God, therefore, to sin is to deny one's place in the community of creation and of God. This vision of sin does not seek to punish a fallen humanity. Instead, *ubuntu* stresses that God desires reunion with the creation, bringing it into the divine life of the Trinity.[47]

Watershed f/Friendship: *Rancocas Creek, Delaware River Watershed, June 29, 2024*

I touched John Woolman's chair, while standing in his house with my f/Friend Cherice Bock and her son, in Mt. Holly, New Jersey, on an astonishingly

---

44. Battle, *Ubuntu*, 53.

45. Battle, *Ubuntu*, 50.

46. James H. Cone, *A Black Theology of Liberation* (Orbis Books, 1990), 104.

47. Battle, *Reconciliation*, 44.

beautiful, cloudless day. Cherice is a fellow Friend/Quaker as well as my close friend—hence f/Friend, a common way of describing the relationship one has with a friend of yours who also happens to be a Friend. (Witty, no?) Cherice is a Friend who is rooted in the Columbia River watershed, along one of its many tributaries, the Willamette River. She is also rooted deeply in the Evangelical Quaker tradition, one of the main rivers in the wider Quaker theological watershed. While all rivers of a watershed are interconnected, the confluences of rivers are the points where specific watercourses actually bump into one another and mix, creating a new river continuously—rivers might dry to a trickle, but they will continue to flow unabated if they're fed, resulting in a river that flows strong, toward the rest of the watershed. Our friendship took root at a theological confluence, and we were making a pilgrimage to one of the sources of our river: John Woolman's life and his reflections on it.

The Quaker community is rather small—a little over 370,000 people worldwide, with nearly half in east and southern Africa, over a third in the Americas, with around 20 percent (about 80,000) in the United States. All rivers in the Quaker theological watershed flow from the common headwaters of early Quaker history, as it evolved from the energetic initial upflowing of water—from the first experiences of the community of seekers who would coalesce into a movement, through the period of relative unity in the eighteenth and early nineteenth centuries now known as the Quietist period. This unity was managed by the community itself, channeling/disciplining the river to run within a set of embankments/rules that emerged from Quaker experience, maintaining a hedge between the flowing river of their community and the "impure" waters that flowed all around them.

One example includes the development of a culture of "plain," where the principle of stripping away distractions between you and the Divine so as hear the voice of the Inward Light more clearly became instead an aesthetic code (including behavior, dress, language, and architecture) that stripped away anything that was deemed inessential: expensive buttons and colors, architectural ornament, flowery language, and so on. Quakers are not of one mind about their perceptions of the Quietist period and its effects on Quaker theology, practice, and community. Early Liberal Friends often viewed these lifeways to be unhelpful and unnecessarily invasive in the lives of individual Friends, while the Conservative Friends community (several thousand strong) continues to live into some of these disciplines, seeing them as essential for maintaining a common Quaker culture and theological tradition.

Both Cherice and I emerge from communities that have laid aside much of this disciplinary embankment, yet we have both found truth in the testimony of John Woolman, a Quaker who lived during the Quietist period. Like all people who serve as prophets for their communities, Woolman's creation theology, abolitionism, and anti-imperialism perfectly embody the concerns of his time (particularly the Quietist concern for listening to the Inward Light through as clear an instrument as possible) while also seeking something new, calling for dramatic change to that same context.

It is impossible to calculate the impact that Woolman's testimony (both the testimony of his life lived into and shaped by his experience, and the testimony of his words—particularly his highly influential journal) has made on Friends living downstream of his specific historical moment. Some communities might express different aspects of his testimony in various ways (which also differ in the extent to which they might acknowledge their roots in the source of Woolman's testimony), but his work is one of the main tributaries feeding into all of the various Quaker theological watersheds.

Quaker theology is communal and can be no other. It is lived in relationship with an entire watershed of creeks, rivers, and tributaries, all merging into each other and then splintering off into new directions as the river shifts and shimmies its way across the landscape, evolving with the changes of time.

The communal nature of Quaker theological construction is thus inherent in at least four different ways. First, when your faith community is tiny, you will inevitably know many of the same people, meaning that every gathering of Friends is also a family reunion. Second, the emphasis on communal governance in Quaker meetings and institutions requires a continuous conversation between Friends about issues as prosaic and contextual as building maintenance, and as esoteric and universal as doctrines about the Divine. Third, the autocephalous nature of Quaker communities (their relative independence from hierarchical authority structures) actually—and seemingly paradoxically—necessitates closer relationships with other individual Friends as well as other Quaker communities. This is because Quakers cannot easily depend on a higher authority to resolve disputes, provide support, and establish the relationship structures necessary to achieve any of the goals each individual Quaker community might have on their own. Fourth and finally, each

Quaker—regardless of their place within the wide spectrum of belief and practice—shares the same historical roots and origin story. In other words, while individual Quakers (and even individual Quaker communities) might not agree on how to interpret and apply the ideas and teachings of John Woolman (as just one example), all Quakers still need to wrestle with him at some level.

In this way, while Cherice and I came to our common beliefs about Quaker ecotheology—and the role of Woolman in shaping that theology—from vastly different sources, as Quaker theologians we were inevitably going to eventually interact with each other sooner or later. There simply aren't that many of us Quaker theologians out there in the world—ecotheologians even less so. We were both always going to need to wrestle with Woolman eventually. We were both always going to need to engage with each other's ideas, writing, and work as well, eventually. Yet, we were also always going to have much in common, as we share the same pool of historical and contemporary Quaker theology. In this community, you either find a way to coexist with other Friends—even those with whom you disagree—or you begin to work together and develop a close working relationship. Cherice and I thus began as colleagues in Friends theology and quickly became friends.

Over the years, we have worked together on a variety of projects, from coauthoring a book on Quaker ecotheology to cochairing the annual Quaker theological conference (the Quaker Theological Discussion Group), along with cofacilitating more workshops, classes, and programs than I can count. We are coworkers and colleagues. We are rivals (sort of) for the same jobs in the Quaker world. We are partners in the communal construction of Quaker theology. We are both deeply committed and passionate environmentalists, working to convince the Quaker community to take Woolman (and the wider Quaker ecotheological tradition) seriously enough that it places ecological concerns at the center of its understanding of its testimony and witness. I cannot pinpoint exactly where—and how—Cherice has affected my theology, as I cannot imagine my theology without Cherice's influence. I have even had people mistake my own writing for Cherice's, and vice versa.

We are also close personal friends, close enough that we speak nearly every day and share with each other intimate, vulnerable details about our lives. We are family to each other, at multiple levels: as Christians, as Quakers, as environmentalists, as theologians—but also as cousins of a sort, in which we both view each other's children as automatically members of our own families, even before we had the chance to *meet* each other's children. Thus, when Cherice and her son traveled to the Delaware Valley during the summer of 2024, it was simply understood that (1) they were going to stay with my family for at least a part of that time, (2) our children would have the opportunity to meet each other, (3) I would care for her son as I would my own child, and (4) we would make a pilgrimage to Woolman's house together. I couldn't imagine having the experience of communing directly with Woolman's artifacts without Cherice—when given the opportunity to touch the chair of your shared hero, who wouldn't want to share that experience with their f/Friend?

I must note, however, that my deep sense of communal belonging with other Friends is not exclusive to Cherice. Every one of my f/Friends has similar relationships with others within the Quaker theological watershed—as do I, with numerous other f/Friends. This dense network of inter-relationality is the hallmark of the Quaker community, emerging from the roots of our community in the close relationships developed between Friends who lived together, worked together, and were incarcerated together. Thus, the Quaker theological watershed is as individual as relationships between close friends, and as communal as the recognition that we all share John Woolman as our ancestor.

Universalism Creek

Early Liberal Quaker theology was explicitly Christian. By the midpoint of the twentieth century, however, universalist ideas began to emerge.[48] These ideas were not rejecting Christianity. Instead, they argued that while Quakerism has a Christian heritage, universalist themes also have deep roots within the tradition and might be a more appropriate basis for modern Liberal Quaker theology and practice. *Universalist* is understood in this sense to mean, as Quaker universalist Ralph Hetherington explains, a "doctrine of universal salvation or redemption."[49] Hetherington argues that in the context of Liberal Quakerism, universalism stems initially from William Penn's claim that the universal presence of the Light of Christ in all people, everywhere, leads to

48. Randazzo, "Christian AND Universalist?"

49. Ralph Hetherington, "A Theology of Quaker Universalism," *Quaker Universalist Fellowship* 5 (1985): 15.

enlightenment and salvation. This then extends to all belief systems, in which the Christian vision of God is not the only true understanding of the nature and framework of God.

Through the first half of the twentieth century, Quakers claimed (some unequivocally) that Liberal Quakerism was synonymous with Christianity.[50] They envisioned Liberal Quakerism as a continuation of the Christianity of the early Friends and as one branch of a worldwide Christianity. They often assumed that the distinctives of Liberal Quaker theology and practice held the same place of importance for early Friends, citing evidence of the existence of such distinctives among early Friends and extrapolating value from such existence. This included a tendency to assume a direct correlation between Christian Liberal Quaker theological beliefs and the rest of Christianity.[51] Early Liberal Quakers also assumed that these were universally held beliefs among Liberal Quakers, and that Quaker communities were not likely to include those who disagreed with "the proper form of Quaker life," nor those who didn't believe in God.[52]

Some Friends even went far enough to claim that Liberal Quakerism was inherently Christian.[53] Notably, this view didn't argue that Quakerism was the only *true* form of Christianity but that it was the *most true*. The implications of this statement for Liberal Quakers who are not Christian are clear: The Light can only ever mean the Light of Christ, the ground of all Quaker experience of God is the experience of Christ, and union with non-Christians, including Liberal Quakers, is not possible if such union is achieved at the expense of proclaiming the truths of Christianity. T. R. Glover was an early proponent of this view, stating in 1912 that the "living Christ," the expression of Jesus residing within the world and each individual believer, had always been acknowledged by the entirety of the Christian church as a proper theological

---

50. R. Duncan. Fairn, *Quakerism: A Faith For Ordinary Men* (Allen & Unwin, 1951), 20.

51. Duncan Fairn argued that Quakerism rooted itself in what he understood to be the core beliefs of Christianity, which excluded some beliefs that others might consider essential, such as substitutionary atonement. Fairn explained this disconnect by claiming that such beliefs were simply not consistent with Christian belief.

52. William E. Wilson, *Our Response to God* (Allen & Unwin, 1935), 74.

53. Hugh Doncaster, *God in Every Man* (Allen & Unwin, 1963), 59.

construct in which to comprehend the work and person of Jesus.[54] Glover argued that the Christian church, both broadly defined and understood, has always been constituted by people who felt drawn to Jesus, and sought to gain a "new life" through aligning their lives and souls with Jesus and gaining union with others through Christ.

This assumption of overlapping synchronicity between Liberal Quakerism and Christianity was critiqued in such a way that the primary value of Liberal Quaker interpretation of Christianity was still paramount. These Christocentric Friends argued that Liberal Quakers presented multiple visions of what it meant to "be Christian": As Christianity was incredibly diverse, the existence of a wide spectrum of Christian belief within Liberal Quakerism therefore made it the most complete expression of Christianity. Quakers could not—and would not—abandon the term *Christian*. Yet, they acknowledged that while Quaker perspectives on essential Christian doctrines and beliefs—since the time of the early Friends—were shared by other Christians, they weren't *all* shared by *all* Christians.[55] Far from abandoning the term, however, Liberal Quakers have the responsibility of reclaiming Christianity as a term encompassing a whole life ethic rooted in Jesus's life.

In response to this perspective, and to an apparent rise of universalist thought in Liberal Quakerism in the second half of the twentieth century, some Quakers opened space for a potential redefinition of the meaning of both Christianity within Liberal Quakerism and of Liberal Quakerism itself. Representing the tension, Duncan Fairn stated in 1951 that Quakerism "is Christian, or it is nothing," though he did acknowledge that there were Quakers who felt excluded by his statement.[56]

Admittedly, some argued that the universalist position within Liberal Quakerism represented a challenging lack of theological specificity. These Friends argued Liberal Quakerism had moved so far from any requirement of Christian belief that membership did not entail any theological commitment other than a "vague, woolly liberalism" manifested in the concept of seeking.[57]

54. T. R. Glover, *The Nature and Purpose of a Christian Society* (Headley Brothers, 1912), 43.

55. Howard E. Collier, *Towards a New Manner of Living* (Swarthmore, 1936), 53.

56. Fairn, *Quakerism*, 20.

57. Doncaster, *God in Every Man*, 25.

While an openness to—and tolerance of—differences in belief was a necessary corrective to the enforced theological monoculture of previous iterations of Quakerism, these Friends argued that such openness (as represented by the acceptance of universalist positions) threatened to dissipate anything vital about Liberal Quakerism into a constant state of syncretism in an effort to gain theological unity.[58]

This Christian-exclusive Quakerism is not a majority view, however. Instead, most Liberal Quakers claim that early Quakers rooted their faith in Jesus Christ as the concrete and personal revelation of God, making Liberal Quakerism—essentially—Christ-centered, with the term *Christ-centered* meaning that Quakers are rooted in the "main orthodox Christian tradition," including giving priority to issues of conversion, evangelization, and holiness.[59] Yet, each of these issues are read through the unique perspective the Quaker tradition provides, allowing Friends to continue their work of reimagining and redefining the boundaries of "Christian" and "Christianity." In this sense, Christ-centered Quakers retained the essential role that Christ—and thus the Christian identity—played in Quaker life, leading Liberal Quakers to attempt to rehabilitate the word.

Despite the dismissals of those advocating for an explicitly Christian Liberal Quakerism, Liberal Quakerism has a tradition of respecting universalism both as a constitutive aspect and as a necessary critique to the Christian heritage of Quakerism.[60] For some, the existence of an alternative theological perspective to Christianity is (and has been) helpful, providing Christianity with a useful dialogue partner.

While not rejecting the vital importance of Christ for Liberal Quakers, some critiques of Christianity offered by universalists and others have significant weight within the tradition and have led Liberal Quakers to consider the

---

58. Doncaster, *God in Every Man*, 55.

59. Maurice A. Creasey, *Bearing, or Friends and the New Reformation* (Friends Home Service, 1969), 72.

60. The Quaker Universalist Group was founded in the United Kingdom in 1979, publishing the first edition of its journal, *The Universalist,* in that same year. The year is notable, as Janet Scott delivered her Swarthmore Lecture arguing for a greater recognition of universalism in Liberal Quakerism in 1980. The existence of a particular group dedicated to Quaker universalism, as well as an active journal, speaks to the existence of an active community of universalists within British Liberal Quakerism at least by 1979, if not earlier.

viability of using the term *Christian* to encapsulate a religious expression that is inherently open to diverse perspectives.[61] This is the same assumption discussed above—from the perspective of Christian-centered Liberal Quakers—of the central importance of Christian ideas and theology in the heritage of Liberal Quakerism. Again, the argument states that, as Quakerism emerged in the overtly Christian environment of seventeenth-century England, and as every early Quaker received a Christian upbringing, the heritage of Liberal Quakerism is unequivocally Christian.[62] In this sense, while Christianity is not conditional for Liberal Friends, it is also not *exclusively* essential, particularly when considered in light of the variety of ideas and concepts that also exist within the kaleidoscopic variety of Liberal Quaker thought.

This acknowledges the potential for a "non-Christian" Quakerism that accepts the heritage of Christianity while also being skeptical toward viewing Christianity as essential for Liberal Quaker thought moving forward. This argument claims that, should Quakers place Quaker distinctives in one circle, and Christianity as Quakers understand it in another circle, the circles might not automatically align.[63] From this perspective, therefore, Quakerism—as it had developed into a practice and an inclusive life ethic—might actually be a more inclusive circle than Christianity, if Christianity is understood to include some of its more restrictive expressions. Pragmatically, therefore, one could easily consider oneself a Liberal Quaker while not claiming a Christian identity as well.

Janet Scott offers a more consistent expression of the universalist perspective, which most completely addresses the critiques offered by Doncaster and others.[64] Scott acknowledges the debate between universalist positions (the Light is within all people regardless of any relationship that they might

61. Henry J. Cadbury, *Quakerism and Early Christianity* (Allen & Unwin, 1957), 27.

62. Cadbury, *Quakerism and Early Christianity*, 6.

63. Cadbury, *Quakerism and Early Christianity*, 28.

64. Carole Dale Spencer notes the importance of Scott's Swarthmore Lecture on the continued development of a more praxological interpretation of Liberal Quakerism, which had begun early in the twentieth century. While previous iterations of this interpretation claimed that the praxis of Quakerism still rested within a Christian construct, Spencer notes that by 1980 Scott did not insist on Christianity as the primary consideration for being a Liberal Quaker. Spencer, "Quakers in Theological Context," in *The Oxford Handbook of Quaker Studies*, ed. Stephen W. Angell and Pink Dandelion (Oxford University Press, 2013), 153.

have with Jesus) and Christian visions of the Inner Light (the Inner Light is synonymous with the Light of Christ), yet dismisses them both, stating that the construct of the Light does not adequately explain the relationship between word and Jesus.[65] Scott also claims that explaining the relationship of God to humans in explicitly Christian terms is dismissive of other religious traditions.[66]

Arguably, Liberal Quakers have—historically—framed the debate between Christianity and universalism as the question, "Is Quakerism Christian?" Scott cites Rachel King in critiquing the argument that the early Friends linked the Light explicitly with Christ as incomplete, as it does not take into account the universalism present within Fox's vision of the Light. Fox was therefore using inherited Christian terminology of incarnation and salvation, as the construct of a universal Light unifying all of humanity does not take the Christian revelation—and its insistence on the specificity of Christ—into account. Scott argues that early Friends were Christian by default; as they were born into a world undergirded by Christian assumptions, the early Friends had little choice but to express their teachings using the language of Christianity.[67]

The debate within Liberal Quakerism between Christianity and universalism incorrectly places the focus on the alignment of Quakerism with Christian belief and doctrine. Instead, Liberal Quakerism should focus on developing a form of life that reflects the existence of God within each person and the necessity to abandon ourselves to God. This would entail a shift in the Quaker hermeneutic from viewing Quaker distinctives through Christianity to viewing Christian theology through the lens of Quaker experience. (This book is a response to this call.) This does not stem from an effort to denigrate any truth resident within Christianity. Instead, this reflects the need to respect "all human experiences of truth" without adhering to any one truth claim out of a sense of obedience to dominant structures of belief.[68]

In this perspective, beliefs about Jesus held by individual Quakers, such as the incarnation, matter little to the corporate experience of Liberal Quakers.

---

65. Janet Scott, *What Canst Thou Say? Towards a Quaker Theology* (Swarthmore, 1980), 8.

66. Scott, *What Canst Thou Say?*, 8.

67. Scott, *What Canst Thou Say?*, 9.

68. Scott, *What Canst Thou Say?*, 27.

Instead, a recognition of the universal presence of God forces humans to acknowledge that God upsets all concepts of human order, and that God calls humanity to release any claims to certainty inherent in theological doctrines. Instead, we are called to live a risky life entirely dependent on the movement of the Light. Christian doctrine, therefore, is just another in a long line of certainties that separate Quakers from the freedom that the Light calls humans to live.

Confluence

A confluence between these two perspectives, therefore, views Quakerism as inherently Christian, yet defines Christianity in universalist terms and avoids making claims of Quaker uniqueness and exceptionalism.[69] This approach acknowledges the existence of universalism within Liberal Quakerism and chooses to engage with that tension by imagining a uniquely Liberal Quaker Christian universalism: another river in the wider watershed of Christian universalism, a strain of Christianity with roots in the very beginning of Christianity itself. This approach acknowledges the reality and benefits of pluralism for Quakers, yet expresses extreme caution toward the corrosive effects that excessive pluralism can have on Quaker distinctives: Quakerism can only make certain truth claims as long as they are emerging from—and resident within—the Quaker faith heritage.[70]

This approach looks skeptically at the claims of other Quakers: that the life of Quakerism was paramount, superseding any actual belief structure inherent to Quakerism, and demanding an absolute tolerance of a variety of spiritual paths within Quakerism.[71] This approach views these other traditions—Jewish, Muslim, Buddhist, etc.—as failing to meet the "previous convictions" of Quakers, and thus place those people outside the admittedly flexible bounds of Liberal Quakerism. These traditions include practices that are considered, by some, to actually be contrary to the Quaker life, such as

---

69. One example of this phenomenon is Alex Wildwood's 1999 lecture, *A Faith to Call Our Own: Quaker Tradition in the Light of Contemporary Movements of the Spirit* (Quaker Home Service, 1999).

70. Christine Trevett, *Previous Convictions and End-of-the-Millenium Quakerism* (Quaker Books, 1997), 45.

71. Trevett, *Previous Convictions*, 86.

rituals of goddess offerings in the meeting house: a very real example that actually violates Quaker beliefs about externals, priesthood, liturgy, and the absolute dependence on God over and above any human ritual expression. If rituals such as these are accepted—in part because they aren't specifically Christian—then would this openness to ritual extend to liturgy, ritual, and sacrament in other Christian traditions? What actually separates Christian communion from offerings to the goddess when the Quaker tradition frowns on *any* ritual that doesn't specifically emerge from within the roots of the tradition itself?

While Friends might respect and gain wisdom from any number of other religious traditions—some of which exist within the wide pluralistic bounds of modern Liberal Quakerism—Quakerism is not synonymous with any of them and should thus be cautious about what practices and concepts are imported from outside the tradition itself.[72] This caution toward the benefits of pluralism and tolerance is necessary, therefore, as the current tolerance and openness in Liberal Quakerism toward other traditions might actually be harming the ability of Quakers to find any sense of unity within the tradition anymore, and may even be contributing to the demise of Liberal Quakerism as a particular religious community.[73] Admittedly, this might sound alarmist. Yet, pluralism is also contributing to an increased secularism in Liberal Quakerism, which has the potential to eventually undermine any religious aspect in Quaker belief and practice.

There is a possible way forward, however. First, we acknowledge the challenges that many Liberal Quakers have with using the words *God* and *Christ*, especially due to the challenging baggage that often accompanies those words, especially for those with traumatic histories in Christian community. Yet, save removing every mention of either word in Liberal Quaker texts, these words are part of the Quaker heritage and must be dealt with in some form.[74] Instead, this challenge can only be resolved through the process of discernment, where Friends seek to determine how to order the whole of life according to the desires that God, or the "Spirit of Christ," has for humanity.

---

72. Trevett, *Previous Convictions*, 91.

73. Christine A. M. Davis, *Minding the Future* (Quaker Books, 2008), 56.

74. Peter J. Eccles, *The Presence in the Midst: Reflections on Discernment* (Quaker Books, 2009), 7.

By acknowledging the Christian heritage of Liberal Quakerism for the sole purpose of determining what form of life God desires—which is building off a Christian foundation without being beholden to non-Quaker framings of Christianity—Liberal Quakers can honor their heritage without clinging to it.

Confluence—Quantum Light

In previous generations, Friends have tended to think of Light as a spiritual metaphor relating to the personal or human community experience of Light: illumination so one can see, heat so one can feel warmth. Considering light ecotheologically, however, broadens the range of ways the metaphor of Light can help people recognize the Light's movement through the entire community of creation, including human dependence on the sustaining power of the Light and humanity's interdependence with other parts of creation, since human beings cannot access the entire spectrum and nourishment the Light provides without assistance from other species.

Energy from light becomes the stuff of life, causing the reactions that build material bodies. Ecotheologically speaking, the Light flows into all beings on this planet, transforming into the body of Christ through human—and other—bodies, the land, and the climate itself: both the abiotic *and* biotic elements of the biosphere. This insight helps articulate a concept Friends have long known and felt: that the Inward Light enlivens and transforms us, and it helps expand our understanding to include other parts of creation.[75] It helps us recognize our utter dependence on God as well as our interdependence with other parts of creation in a way that breaks down dualism and hierarchy while elevating our sense of belonging and interconnectedness with the Light and all creation.

Before we launch into a description of the impact of an ecotheology of Light, however, I need to first define what *Light* actually means, both scientifically and theologically. An ecosystem is defined by the cycling of energy and matter through the physical environment, the living and nonliving parts

75. This understanding of the Light goes back to George Fox, who discusses the "light of Christ," accessible to all, which is the "light of life," and which opened him to a new way of understanding scripture. George Fox, *The Journal of George Fox*, ed. John L. Nickalls (Philadelphia Yearly Meeting of Friends, 1997), 33. In his experience of going "into the paradise of God," after passing "through the flaming sword," he discusses the spiritual and physical transformation and renewal that happened in him, which he attributed to the "power and light of Christ" (27).

of the air, water, climate, and landscape interacting with and shaping one another, with nutrients cycling through the different species in ways that each of them can access. Energy from the sun enters the biosphere (the global, interconnected ecosystem of all life and natural forces on earth) and makes the cycling of nutrients possible. Our global community thus requires continuous input of the sun's light energy to function: The sun is the sustainer of all life on this planet.

Light can come from many sources: stars (including our sun—the star of our solar system), electricity, fire, molten metals, lightning, chemical reactions, and bioluminescent, fluorescent, and phosphorescent life forms. The sun's light, heat, and energy make many of these other types of light on earth possible, through the movement of energy from light waves through the biosphere: Fires burn organic matter that grows because of sunlight, the climate depends on the continuous movement of light energy through the biosphere, and bioluminescence, fluorescence, and phosphorescence require light energy in order to store and then emit energy from an organism in the form of light.[76]

While light is most often understood as that portion of the electromagnetic spectrum visible to human eyes, the radioactive energy of light is far wider, encompassing wavelengths invisible to human eyes (gamma rays, X-rays, ultraviolet, infrared, microwaves, and radio waves) but absolutely crucial to life in the biosphere.[77] Visible light can be dispersed through a prism so we can see the different colors of light as the different wavelengths pass through the shorter and longer parts of the prism at different rates. "White light" becomes a rainbow when dispersed through a prism or through water droplets in the sky—at the correct angle, of course. Various material objects absorb some of light's wavelengths and reflect others, so that the colors those objects appear to be are the light waves being reflected off the object's surface.

Objects can also appear differently when viewed through a transparent intermediary, such as water, some windows, or a lens. For example, straight

---

76. The metaphor is limited in the sense that, of course, other planets have other stars. This does not mean that other gods operate in other places, but that the sun is a useful though imperfect metaphor for explaining our relationship to God and other parts of creation.

77. Some other species can detect ultraviolet or infrared radiation with their eyes, so the definition of light can sometimes expand to include these wavelengths. The term *light* is used in physics to refer to the whole spectrum of electromagnetic wavelengths, whether or not they are visible to the human eye.

objects can appear bent when they are submerged in water as the light travels at a different speed through the water than through the air, a process called refraction. How might we think of light differently if we consider we may be viewing the Inward Light through a prism, perhaps seeing only a portion of the Light's spectrum, or that we may be viewing the Light reflected off another object?

The sun is not something humanity has control over, and while its light, heat, magnetism, and energy are relatively constant, these aspects of the sun's impact do fluctuate in ways we do not currently fully understand, cannot predict, and do not have control over. This tension between a relatively predictable and stable source of life-sustaining heat and energy, and an entity that sometimes sends the massive—and disruptive—surges of electromagnetic radiation known as solar flares hurtling toward earth speaks truth about the Light: It is wild and untamable, the Source and Sustainer, without which none of our lives could exist.

Light appears to have both the properties of a wave and a particle, according to quantum mechanics. A particle of light is called a photon, which appears to travel in a wave pattern at the constant speed of light.[78] Photons do not have mass, but they have velocity; therefore, Einstein's famous theory of relativity, $E = mc^2$ (energy is equal to mass times the speed of light squared), equates light's energy with its velocity, the speed of light. Light is purely energy—and not matter (though it has other properties, such as wavelength and frequency)—but because it has energy, it can transmit that energy into matter. Therefore, energy and matter are the same thing, just in different forms. Similarly, the spiritual Light is not material: Its energy is the source of life.

The implications of energy and matter being the same thing, in different forms, are profound: As human beings, we are light energy temporarily experiencing material form. Thus, we are all just beams of light, with all the paradox, mutability, and dynamism that comes from being made—and sustained—by ever-changing light. The distinction between our own bodies and the light energy that makes it possible for us to exist becomes difficult to define. This applies as well to the rest of the ecosystems that transform light in ways usable for ourselves and for other species. The paradox of energy and matter as both

---

78. 186,000 miles/second, or 299,792,458 meters/second.

the same in essence, and vastly different in expression and function, helps break down assumed binaries between spirit and matter, or hierarchies in which humanity is assumed to be closest to God while other parts of creation are less Godlike. In light of this, doesn't it seem kinda silly to place rigid gender and sexuality expectations on bodies whose existence depends on light—to name just one consequence?

Energy from the sun is also cycled through the ecosystems in which we are embedded, as water, air, and seasons cycle through the climate to maintain a range of livable temperatures. While the sun's light stimulates species' growth and initiates movement of air and water, it is also critical to have times where sunlight is not present. Seasons and rhythms of growth and rest—especially as these are experienced differently as energy cycles through local climates—are essential for ecosystem functioning and species health. Different species intentionally grow in places with more or less light based on their particular needs and preferences, and the work they contribute to the ecosystem. For example, some species live in caves or at the bottom of the ocean, never or rarely being exposed to sunlight. They are still bound up in the interrelationship of light energy, as they are still bound up in relationships with other organisms that communicate energy from the sun into forms they can use. This also applies climatically, where local climatic conditions vary depending on the rhythms of light energy entering ecosystems: the wet and dry seasons of equatorial regions, and the birth-growth-death cycle of deciduous life in areas farther away from the equator.

While a competitive evolutionary model has emphasized "survival of the fittest" since Darwin's work in the late nineteenth century, competition does not explain many of the behaviors and choices species make. Individuals and species do compete with one another for resources at times, but they would not long survive without mutually beneficial symbiotic relationships. More recent depictions of the relationship between the species in an ecosystem envision a web of relations, recognizing that even the predators are eaten by bacteria and fungi after they die, and that the different species rely on one another in a complex and interdependent web rather than a hierarchy. This includes even the ecosystem of our bodies—the flora that live in our gut and make digestion possible, and thus transmit light energy into our bodies.

Our lives are maintained through inputs of energy in the form of food and oxygen. We need plants, fungi, and a whole host of microorganisms in order to continue to live on earth, since we cannot by ourselves transform the sun's rays into energy useful to our bodies. Plants engage in photosynthesis, utilizing carbon dioxide, water, and sunlight to produce oxygen and glucose. Energy from the sun is stored by plants as glucose, and they release oxygen into the air as a byproduct. People and other animals need plants in order to survive: Since we cannot perform photosynthesis, we have no way to access most of the sun's energy on our own. Everything that exists on our planet therefore depends on the energy from our star circulating through this fragile, interdependent biosphere, in which entire food chains depend on the photosynthesis of plants: No plants, no food for herbivores, no food for predator species—no life.

This is true not only for the plants and animals we can see, but also the organisms and processes that occur underground, underwater, and inside our own systems. Fungal networks connect the different species of plants in a healthy forest, helping move nutrients between various species so they can each contribute the nutrients they specialize in and receive other nutrients of which they would otherwise be deficient, as well as helping plants receive necessary nutrients from the soil.[79] Fungi and microorganisms help break down dead organic matter into soil. Algae and microorganisms in the ocean help cycle air and nutrients to keep the ocean ecosystems functioning, which ensures the regulation of the climate, whether that be regional mesoclimates or the microclimates that give such variety and flavor to wine. Our own bodies contain microbiomes with a variety of gut flora such as bacteria and fungi that help break down and process our food and keep us healthy. Some estimate that about half the cells in a human body are actually bacteria.[80] Our bodies are unable to receive the nutrients we need without the aid of these other microscopic species.

This diversity has some significant implications. Each different being requires a different set of conditions—soil, climate, light energy, water, and so on—in its ecosystem in order to flourish: the uniqueness of context. Light

---

79. An excellent popular audience resource on this topic is Peter Wohlleben, *The Hidden Life of Trees: What They Feel, How They Communicate—Discoveries from A Secret World*, trans. Jane Billinghurst (Greystone Books, 2016). For a scholarly perspective, see: Marcel G. A. Van Der Heijden and Thomas R. Horton, "Socialism in Soil? The Importance of Mycorrhizal Fungal Networks for Facilitation in Natural Ecosystems," *Journal of Ecology* 97, no. 6 (2009): 1139–50.

80. R. Sender, S. Fuchs, and R. Milo, "Revised Estimates for the Number of Human and Bacteria Cells in the Body," *PLoS Biology* 14, no. 8 (2016): e1002533, doi.org/10.1371/journal .pbio.1002533.

is not constant, but shifts throughout the day and the year, creating cycles of growth and rest that differ depending on context and the adaptations that life has made to that specific context. Natural light does not occur simply in light and darkness, but in gradients of light and darkness at dawn and dusk, winter and summer. The sun itself is constantly burning, emitting energy and sending it toward the earth, and the planetary community is always receiving that energy and cycling it through the biosphere. Yet, life cannot survive direct, constant, unmediated sunlight: Life needs the atmosphere and the reflective poles to filter and limit the amount of light energy that enters the biosphere. Life must exist in an appropriate context—place and community—to receive a healthy and beneficial level of light, or face the suffering and death that is a consequence of overexposure to—or lack of—light.

Although Light theology equalizes—each person is connected to Light—it has often emphasized individual experience, discernment, and responsibility only to the self. Friends have also encouraged collective discernment, listening to the Light together and learning from that of God in one another, but it has been an ongoing challenge to live out a truly communal following of the Light when we think of the Light as an inward experience that is only personal. While the corporate process of making decisions in Meetings for Worship with a Concern for Business is a communal engagement with the Light, we have also tended to sense the Light's directions in ways we expect, making it difficult for people of a diversity of backgrounds to be able to be full participants in the life of our meetings unless they conform to the dominant group's forms.

Additionally, while Friends have traditionally thought of the Inward Light as something that is within all people, we have not extended the horizon of this Divine Presence to include other creatures. An ecotheology of Light can break down hierarchical dualism by reminding us we are part of an interconnected web of life, each receiving different things from the sun and able to contribute our small part to the ecosystem; none of us can sense and utilize all the Light's gifts on our own. We need others—other people, other species, and other parts of creation.

As we receive the ongoing grace of the gift of life from the sun's light, we also are held and sustained in the Light, without whom we are nothing. While the existence of God does not require the existence of creation, creation would not exist without a Source. Likewise, there are suns with planets that do not sustain life—the existence of a star does not require life, but human and other earthly life require ongoing energy from a star or other energy source. Along with Meister Eckhart, we also recognize that God is no-thing: God is not a thing in the sense of a created entity; God is wholly other and can never be truly and fully known. This is the apophatic aspect of the Uncreated Light. And yet, God is so near that God enlivens each breath we take; our existence is based on God's continuous sustenance and care. This is the kataphatic aspect of God, present with us as the *energeia* that moves through our bodies, communities, and ecosystems.

Recognizing our nothingness paradoxically opens us to our kinship and interconnectedness with the rest of the community of all life. Not only are we completely dependent on God to sustain our lives through the gift of Light, but we are also interdependent with the rest of creation. Like Hildegard, who experienced the word of God as the living Light who not only gave her visions but whom she also believed and experienced to be the "life underpinning creation itself," we can experience the green, life-giving energy that connects God and all creation. We are created to be in community and we must rely on others, working with others to ensure all our needs are met.

Let's consider the role of darkness in an ecotheology of Light. At times, the Bible upholds a very dualistic understanding of Light and darkness, so it is easy to assume darkness symbolizes evil. This is problematic in part because it is used to uphold white supremacy, with white people seen as closer to God on the great chain of being, while those with darker skin are assumed to be further away.

This is also problematic because it seems to forget that light is energy as well. During the night, solar energy is still present, continuously bombarding our atmosphere with energy. In the local ecosystem, the energy received during the day is processed at night through rest and secondary cycles. This rhythm of light and darkness happens each day, and—depending on your location on the earth—relative to the tilt in the earth's axis, which creates the light and dark seasons that are more likely to occur the closer one is to either pole. Similarly, one can argue that as there is no darkness in God, darkness simply *appears* to be the absence of God—the absence of Light. The Light still exists but is not currently present to our awareness. Thinking of light and darkness as a rhythm of presence and absence fits well with the mystics' awareness of the apophatic and kataphatic aspects of God: We know God's Light through its presence, and we can also learn of God through experiencing God's perceived absence. Yes, God isn't absent, but also, yes, at times we cannot directly sense God's presence; regardless, God is present even when we cannot sense their presence.

The rhythm of this seasonal, climatic movement from light to dark offers space for rest at night and dormancy in winter, activity and growth during the day or the summer. Following these daily and seasonal cues can encourage a more sustainable way of life for human bodies and for ecosystem communities. Rather than fearing the dark or considering it evil, a rhythm of light and darkness is consistent with the practice of Sabbath rest. Rhythms of light and darkness can lead to inward contemplation and outward action as well.

The experience of a "dark night of the soul" is common in church history and in the lives of those in our own time: There are times when people have a hard time sensing the Light. When Light is considered good and darkness evil or deficient, times of darkness can feel shameful, scary, and helpless. While these are not easy times, considering darkness as part of a rhythm can open space for learning in a different way: learning about rest and dormancy, about yearning for the Light instead of basking in it, processing what one received in the times when the Light felt close. It may also be possible to learn how to sense the Light through other inward senses. In the literal dark, wandering in the wilderness invokes legitimate fears of predators, cold, and losing the way—but if we travel together, in community, we can stay safe at night.

Passaic River Watershed (New Jersey), Late Autumn 2022

What does this all look like in practice: In other words, how would a Quaker hold multiple communal narratives in tension, and express that stance in a way that reflects their specific context?

I've been an adjunct professor for much of my teaching career, which means that I get hired to teach individual courses for multiple schools—I literally sign a new contract for each course, each semester. This is the specific, individual context for the experience I'm going to relate here. The universal story for the community of adjuncts is one of adaptation, flexibility, open-mindedness—and a continuous reminder of the precariousness of your position. When your options are limited to whatever courses you can find, you become quite adept at teaching a wide variety of subjects, across as many different disciplines as you can make your experience stretch. You learn to quickly grasp the fundamentals of concepts and ideas that could be completely new to you and are often far outside your area of expertise. You are most often teaching introductory classes, to freshmen, who might be taking your class purely to fulfill a requirement: You need to quickly get to the core, the root of the most essential aspects of whatever you are teaching, and build your material up from there. Take any thoughts of your fantasy teaching environment and lay them aside, because the only way to engage these students is to help them connect with the material in ways that make sense to *them*. You need to be able to listen to the story your students tell you about what they understand in the material, what they don't, and why—and then you need to respond in kind. I firmly believe that teaching is a conversation, and if your students can't understand the words you are saying, then you need to learn to translate the words you are using into language that makes sense to them.

This is how I found myself in front of a half-full auditorium trying to explain—for the first time!—the specifics of how the cycle of samsara works in Hinduism, mere weeks after I learned this information myself. Samsara is the name that is most often used for the cyclical process of reincarnation that—along with the karmic cycle—determines what happens to people after death in the numerous expressions of the Jain, Hindu, Buddhist, and Sikh traditions; in other words, the way that a *vast* number of people in the world understand what happens to us after we die—and even what it means "to be."

What can this story already tell you about the specific context of this experience? For one, I've obviously not been raised in any of these traditions, nor was I around enough other people such that I was required to learn about them due to a commonly understood cultural or political expectation. The fact that I had to learn about samsara in order to do my job, and the fact that I had never before learned more than the most basic details about this profoundly important concept, both say a great deal about the communities in which I have lived my life, as well as the particular quirks of my own specific experience.

I teach religious studies and mythology courses at Montclair State University, a public university located in North Jersey, close enough to Manhattan that you can see the entire stretch of the Manhattan skyline from the east side of campus but far enough away that the only reason you can see it is that the campus sits atop a high bluff. Montclair is twenty miles from Columbia University and fifty miles from Princeton University but exists in a *very* different world from either of these schools. Montclair's mission is to provide an affordable education to New Jersey residents. My students have been fresh-faced recent high school graduates, grandparents seeking to fulfill a lifelong dream, single parents trying to make a better life for themselves and their families, and people attending part time because they already have a full-time job.

North Jersey is arguably the most densely populated part of the United States, as well as the most ethnically diverse, and the students in my classrooms reflect that diversity. The largest Hindu temple outside Asia, the BAPS Swaminarayam Mandir, is fifty-six miles away, meaning that there is an *extremely* high likelihood that I will be teaching about the basics of Hinduism to Hindu students. Same goes for Islam, as two of the largest Middle Eastern enclaves—Turkish (Little Istanbul) and Palestinian (Little Ramallah)—in the United States both lie three short miles away, in Paterson. Teaching about the concept of modesty in Islam feels rather different when a hijabi student is sitting, smiling at you, *right there in the front row*.

Anyway, I was wrestling with the challenge of explaining the paradox of the *atman* (the unchanging and eternal sense of "self" in Hinduism) being reincarnated into *jivanatman* (the ever-evolving individual being that actually takes a bodily form, often translated as *soul*) at that specific moment in time, at that specific place, speaking to this kind of audience. Lo and behold, what should enter my brain but the famous saying by Heraclitus, the Greek philosopher who saw harmony in the act of change and the interaction of opposites: "No man ever steps in the same river twice." I've long known this saying, in large part because it's an extremely common idea in the United States, for a variety of historical, cultural, and even geographic reasons, but mainly because Western culture views Greek philosophy as foundational. However, the saying also just rings *true*.

In one sense, I am the same person every time I step into a river, while the river is itself the same: I have lived next to the same river—the Delaware—the entire time I've lived here in South Jersey. Yet, I am also continuously evolving as I age, while the river itself is also continuously evolving as the environment around it shifts and changes. Similarly, while the *atman* is eternal, it resides in a continuously evolving *jivanatman*: thus, both unchanging and dynamic, simultaneously. Suddenly, I could see comprehension begin to dawn on faces across the auditorium: All it took to explain this complex concept (to the non-Hindus in the audience, of course) was finding a way of translating it into language that my students could connect with from their own experience.

The work I do to attempt to understand this concept from a religious tradition significantly different from my own demands a profound level of empathy from me. In this case, it forced me to expand my own intellectual landscape to such an extent that I had that powerful sense of having experienced an epiphany, that elusive feeling that I *got it*, and I could finally understand the paradox of context: Each human will experience the world as an individual, and develop individual beliefs in relation to that experience, beliefs that are themselves a collection of responses to the various communities and communal stories within which we are rooted.

This was arguably inevitable, however: I can't imagine teaching about something as fundamental to a person's sense of *being* as their most essential religious beliefs without having opened myself to allowing these ideas to live in my mind and heart to such an extent that they become old friends. We cannot live with another's ideas without having them impact us and our own beliefs—even if it takes the form of rejection: We are still responding to the idea and are thus being influenced by it. My context made this revelation necessary: I'd be surprised if I were living in this time and place, doing this work, and engaging in these conversations without being influenced at some fundamental level by the ideas I'm teaching. If I were teaching in a different context, I would respond differently, even if the differences seemed minimal.

In fact, I can say this for certain, as I have taught a World Religions course in three very different contexts (different schools, different states, different decades) and have taught it differently each time, responding to each context. Yet, I share enough other communities with other adjuncts that the experience of teaching something in which you lack anything resembling expertise is a universal experience we can all share.

Universals, but in specific, individuated contexts. This is storytelling as well: universal themes expressed in specific, individual ways. We are all just bodies, rooted in our contexts, sharing in the universal experience of human existence.

CHAPTER THREE

Bodies/Experience

How Do We Experience Ourselves and the Divine?

> *You will say, Christ saith this, and the apostles say this; but what canst thou say? Art thou a child of Light and hast walked in the Light, and what thou speakest is it inwardly from God?*
>
> *This opened me so that it cut me to the heart*; and then I saw clearly we were all wrong. So I sat me down in my pew again, and cried bitterly. And I cried in my spirit to the Lord, "We are all thieves, we are all thieves, we have taken the Scriptures in words and know nothing of them in ourselves." . . . I saw it was the truth, and I could not deny it.
>
> —Margaret Fell, 1694

River Leven/Morecambe Bay Watershed, Late June 1652

Margaret Fell experienced an apocalypse in church one Sunday in late June 1652.

St. Mary's Parish, the local Anglican parish church in Ulverston, was located a little over a mile away from her home, Swarthmoor Hall. Fell was the wife of a prominent local judge, Thomas Fell, so she was expected to attend services at St. Mary's due to her role and place in local society. Thomas Fell was of the landed gentry class of Cumbria, then and now a hilly upland area in northern England, filled with vast moors and few people. Margaret Fell was well-known in her community as a woman of power and substance, regardless of her spouse's social position: While Judge Fell owned Swarthmoor Hall, Margaret's place as its head was undisputed.

She was also known to be a spiritual seeker who regularly made efforts to listen to the various preachers, personalities, and prophets who stopped in

Ulverston on their way to somewhere else—and decided to speak. She would often invite them to visit her at Swarthmoor, so it wasn't really surprising when a traveler in strange clothing and a powerful aura—answering to the name George Fox—showed up at her door. He spent the night and visited the church building the next day. As Fell relates it, she was in the steeplehouse with her children, singing with the rest of the congregation, when she saw Fox walk in the door. (*Steeplehouse* is the name early Friends gave to church buildings to separate the building from the people gathered in it: the latter being "the church" and the former just a building, or house—with a steeple.) When the congregation finished singing, Fox approached the priest and asked for permission to speak to the community.

Anglican churches of this time were at the center of village life. In fact, once the Church of England was declared the official state church, after the Tudor religious reforms of the sixteenth century, the local church was drafted into the English state's governance and taxation structure. England was divided into geographical units based on proximity to a local parish church, and that parish was tasked with a wide array of duties that today would fall under a local municipality or town government, including care of roads, tax collection, and care of the poor and indigent. People who lived in the parish were expected to support its work by paying taxes (or tithes) to the parish, and in turn the parish was expected to support the people by serving the function of a one-stop shop for the needs of the village, whether they be spiritual or earthbound.

The parish was also expected to serve as "commons," or public square: As people from the village were expected to attend services with something approaching regularity, Sunday morning was a time when someone could grab the attention of the majority of people in an area, meaning that rectors of these parishes were expected to allow time during the service for speakers. They often just gave community announcements, but sometimes people who wanted to share a message with the community would ask to speak. A traveling preacher standing up during a church service to speak was therefore a common sight.

What transpired when George Fox stood to speak that fateful summer Sunday was decidedly uncommon, however. By the time Fox arrived at Ulverston parish, he had already been preaching his radical message of personal experience of the Divine, unmediated by clergy, for five years and had already gathered a small band of people convinced of the truth of the message.

(Early Quakers said that they were "convinced" when they became Friends, and this is still the word used to describe the process of conversion for Friends, whereas those born into—and raised by—Quaker families came to be called "birthright Friends," as they were members of Quaker communities by "birthright.") Fox had, only a few weeks earlier, experienced a powerful vision while on top of Pendle Hill—about sixty miles southeast of Ulverston—where he saw "a great people in white raiment by a river's side come to the Lord," which Fox understood to be the gathered people he was supposed to share his message with. In other words, Fox knew exactly what he was doing that Sunday morning, why he was doing it, and under whose authority he preached. This was a prophetic voice at the top of his game.

As often happened when Fox preached, he annoyed the priest, who made an effort to silence and remove Fox. Admittedly, this is an entirely reasonable response of a priest to another person taking charge of the service and then skillfully insisting that people had no need of this priest—or his blessed bread—to fully experience the Divine Presence. Imagine someone entering your workplace and loudly telling everyone that your job harms every member of the community—especially their souls! (There's a reason Fox became so familiar with the inside of a jail cell.) However, Fell was so intrigued and moved by his words that she stood, and—with just a glance—commanded the priest to allow Fox to continue speaking. Margaret Fell was fierce: a force to be reckoned with, that's for sure! As Fox spoke, Fell, the avid seeker, realized that she had finally found the message that she would devote her life to: that people not only could interpret the meaning of the Biblical scripture themselves but even could experience the Divine Presence within themselves, unmediated by anyone—or any institution. Fell remembers Fox's words in a form that every Quaker knows by heart: "You will say, Christ saith this, and the apostles say this; but what canst thou say? Art thou a child of Light and hast walked in the Light, and what thou speakest is it inwardly from God?"

She later related the earth-shattering impact this had on her entire outlook on life, in a passage equally famous among Friends: "This opened me so that it cut me to the heart; and then I saw clearly we were all wrong." Fell wasn't simply having a passing brainwave that led her to view the world—and her place in it—from a new perspective. Instead, in an overwhelmingly vulnerable moment, Fell felt the knife of truth—that impossibly sharp edge of realizing that you are encountering something true: fundamentally, foundationally, unavoidably—cut deeply, straight to the core of her being. This is visceral—literally: Fell was so shocked at the revelation that she sat straight down and began to weep bitterly. I can imagine her tottering, as the room spun and the world turned and her entire framework of faith and belief began to crumble and simultaneously re-form in front of her. This is a spiritual enlightenment, an instantaneous mourning for a self—now far gone—who existed in a completely different reality, and the construction of another person, through the act of weaving them into the framework of a new reality: happening all at once, in the lightning crack of a moment of revelation.

Fell didn't even pretend to push back against the revelation, to attempt to blunt its power through the usual human tricks of bluster, denial, retreat into fantasy, justification, or passing blame. This was a reality that Fell experienced as *real* to the same depth of *Truth* as the apostle Thomas had experienced the realness of Jesus's side after the resurrection in John 20. This is the truth of the two lines on a pregnancy test, a child's first step, the first cup of coffee on the morning of a move across the country, the last time you hold the hand of a dying friend and weep out your love for them, the moment that you realize he really did cheat on you—again. These are all apocalypses, for in them we encounter implacable *Truth*.

In these moments, we become pitch pine trees. These are trees spread throughout the Pinelands (commonly known as the Pine Barrens, a massive forest preserve here in South Jersey) that have adapted to the regularity of forest fires in the Barrens through tying their reproductive cycle directly to fires: The seed cones of pitch pine trees need the heat of a fire to open and spread their seeds in the forest. The death of pitch pines is thus woven inextricably into their birth. In the face of the all-consuming fire of a revelation of Truth, our pitch-pine bodies see the old world burn away as the new one takes root in the ashes.

For Fell, this was a realization of a moral failure, accountability for which Fell took bravely, straight on the chin: "We are all thieves, we have taken the Scriptures in words and know nothing of them in ourselves." Everything that Fell understood about the relationship between humanity and the Divine was seen to not only be false, but also a mark of pride, placing human institutions before the Lord by having the church steal the power of the scripture away from the Divine and hoard it. In one fell swoop, Fell had recognized three separate commandments of the ten broken by her and her community for as long as she could remember: stealing, falsehood, and—perhaps most egregiously—placing human understanding and will above God. This was the apocalypse, for Fell: the destruction of a world and the rebirth of another, swimming in an amniotic sea of regret, repentance, anxiety, and the love of God.

Fell had just experienced one of the best-known convincements in Quaker history, and the proof of its truth and power lay with Fell's immediate actions—and their profoundly significant implications. Within a week, the majority of Fell's family, and a significant portion of the folks who lived and worked on Swarthmoor Hall's land, had all become convinced of the Truth of a Divine Presence of immediacy and action. By the very next Sunday, Fell had already begun to take on the role of spiritual mother to a flock of eager children. Despite his best efforts, the rector of Ulverston Parish had failed to unconvince this new community of Friends, and the Quaker movement rapidly thrust its roots into the fertile ground of Swarthmoor Hall.

Fell could also manifest this change in mind to a change in her soul and body, as Fell showed her husband when he arrived home and discovered that his own world had dramatically transformed. Judge Fell was decidedly displeased about this extreme (and extremely rapid) change in his household, and told his wife as much. Fell sat down next to her husband, however, and apparently the power of this new Truth emanated from her in a way that grabbed the judge's complete attention. Fell doesn't describe what this manifestation looked or sounded like, but the effect on Judge Fell was definitive enough: He was struck speechless with amazement and seemed to accept, at the very least, that this Truth was true to his wife and that she now carried an exciting (yet unsettling) new power and certainty. This prominent spokesperson for the conformity of the status quo came home to a wife who—in the space of a *week*—was completely transformed. She was now quite obviously a prophet and minister to a new community of dissenting nonconformists—his entire family! In his own home! Thomas Fell reacted in perhaps the best way possible (at least from the perspective of the nascent Friends movement): He not only allowed the new Quakers among his staff to stay, but he eventually accepted his wife's new mission and allowed her to turn Swarthmoor Hall into a warm incubator for the early years of the Friends movement. Remember: Thomas Fell was a judge, and could therefore have simply had everyone thrown in jail. His patience and forbearance in this moment is truly noteworthy.

In this passage, Fell not only speaks with the certainty of the newly converted, she also speaks with the wisdom of a longtime seeker who has seen prophets come and go and heard innumerable renditions of "prophetic truth" that were neither—at least to her. Fell stresses that she now recognizes both what is true and what is from God, and Fox's message is both. Hearing a message resonating with an obvious divine power, delivered by a prophet? Experiencing a vision of overwhelming physical presence? Having one's world end? Sounds like an apocalypse to me. Stories like the perceived falsehoods she rejected are often told at the level of society, and refer to both to way that the pieces of the structures of the world fit together, and to the tools necessary to experience that reality. In this moment, Fell realized that the story that had guided her entire life was actually fundamentally *wrong*—a wicked lie—and she now needed to accept a brand-new story.

Understanding Fell's context is key to understanding the extent of the changes she brought to the small universe of Swarthmoor Hall and the surrounding parish. She was a woman (gender) who was a member of the landed gentry (class) who could both read and write—quite well, in fact (class and education status), with a particular role to play in her society (social and institutional expectations), and with access to government and legal connections willing to offer protection for her and others connected with her (systems of power, social control, and punishment). Margaret Fell wasn't just married to the status quo; she was herself rooted deep within it, and regardless of her search for something . . . else, she embodied its values and assumptions. The world in which she was rooted and from which she sprouted, had formed her, marked her, with the shape of its assumptions about the ways that these structures of identity—gender, class, national origin, religious community, systems of belief, family status, and many more—fit together and interacted with each other, and the ways that each of these aspects of her specific context shaped the framework of her engagement with society.

This story *was* true for Fell: at least in part, at least at one time in her life. Regardless of whether Fell was ready for a new story—admittedly, all evidence seems to point to that being the case—society (and her place in it) was still *the* story of her life. Until she heard Fox preach and she realized that this story held no weight for her anymore, that is. Instead, she claimed all of the power she possibly could in this new story, because she *knew* that her purpose in life was to plant the seeds of this story in as many hearts as possible: If you'd just experienced the utter annihilation—and subsequent resprouting—of your inner certainties, wouldn't you *also* want to tell some folks about it?

This chapter continues the focus on foundational narratives begun in chapter 2, yet with stories that give framing and meaning to our bodies. These stories address the grand social constructs that many people share, but which each individual person is going to express and interact with differently, depending on both the specificity of their own individual context and the grand societal narratives in which that context exists. The foundational narratives of chapter 2 are the ones that tell the story of reality at the level of the Divine and the meaning of human existence (the climate and soil: Are humans individual entities, or are they social creatures in unique bodies bound together by the Divine Presence?). The foundational narratives of chapter 3, however, address the story of reality at the level of social structures and the ways that those structures shape how we experience hearing the voice of God, through the soil in which we are rooted and the dizzying variety of forms—*bodies*—people can take.

An example of this is the profound shift in Fell's understanding of her role as a woman in a religious community. By attending Anglican worship regularly, with her children, she was at least passively—if not actively, it could be argued—allowing the Anglican view of women as the receivers (not producers) of religious wisdom to shape her faith life. After her revelation, however, Fell immediately took charge of the religious life of her household, even in the face of her husband's initial disapproval. She never attended worship at Ulverston Parish ever again, nor did her children. She rejected every effort of the parish priest—the famous antagonist named "Priest Lampitt" in Quaker communal lore—to make Fell see "reason" and to accede to the authority of the Anglican Church again. The Church of England in seventeenth-century England was the state religion, according its priests a level of power that commanded attention. It wasn't always easy to deal with local priests who decided to bear the full weight of their spiritual *and* political authority on people who failed to conform.

In a witty yet theologically profound way, by claiming the role of spiritual mother Fell directly attacked the foundations of Father Lampitt's authority. It's a masterpiece: a defiant gesture rooted in Fell's own experience that weaves a compelling tale, a vision of a new theological landscape rooted in creation, life, and an egalitarian image of motherhood as a role anyone can participate in, at least in part. This is a worldview woven by the healing and flourishing of life, and undisciplined by the rigid conformity of the patriarchy. Of *course* she upended Judge Fell's place as her husband: She'd already upended everything else.

When read through the dual lens of Quaker theology and ecotheology, we can think of these narratives as answering two questions. One is at the level of *roots*, one of the main structural forms of plants that provides stability and shapes the ways that each specific plant interacts with the *soil* of its environment: What are the stories that root us in specific contexts and shape our connections with the rest of creation around us? The other is at the level of *bodies*, the body of the plant aboveground that interacts with the *climate* of its environment: What are the stories—alive and peaceable—that shape the form that our bodies take, and the ways that these larger forces of identity bend and warp and transform our souls as well as our actual, physical bodies? These stories are the ones that emerge from—and respond to—our daily lives. This is the level of families, schools, the ways we spend our free time, the communities who claim us: the stories, ideals, and beliefs we encounter in our daily lives, which all place their imprint deeply within our bodies and souls.

As *trunks* are the parts of plants that are aboveground and are thus more visibly affected by the conditions of the climate in which they are surrounded and immersed, and as any trunk that seeks to address the climate apocalypse must be deeply familiar with facing the ends of worlds, I am choosing to offer a sketch of two trunks that developed in response to apocalyptic times—the culture of life imagery and imaginary of early Quaker women, and the cultures of peace framework of twentieth century Quaker and peace scholar Elise Boulding.

These are both stories written in lives experienced—and reflected on—primarily through the lens of family, where the family is understood to be the community of those with whom we have the closest, most intimately vulnerable relationships, our (usually) first experience of living in community, the space where we have our first experiences of love, compassion, beauty—as well as of pain, suffering, and ugliness. While political and economic theories, frameworks of sickness and health, and moral tenets are all gigantic forces at play on the level of society, we actually encounter them at the level of daily life: how our *bodies* are shaped by the particular forms of our families.

This chapter tells the broad outlines of these stories, each of which emerges from within Quaker tradition, ecotheology and its metaphorical and narrative tradition, or both. When overlaid on top of each other, a vision emerges of an understanding of experience—the foundation of Quaker theology—as narrative dependent, in which variety in the shape and form of the branches of our identities ensures that we often have different experiences of the same reality: different tree species experiencing the world differently, yet gathered together as one in a community of common stories we all share.

Roots and Fungus, Families of Mushroom and Vine: Where Are We Anchored, and to Whom Are We Connected?

God's love is a mushroom.[1]

Well, more accurately, a mycorrhizal network—the webs of fungi that join trees together through complex, interdependent relationships with tree roots.

This metaphor should gross me out, as I am famously squeamish. If I'm not absolutely certain that the tiny white speck on the corner of the pie crust is not fungus, that pie is not entering my body, come hell or high water. Maybe it's because I have a digestion with the sensitivity of an electron microscope, and have been reminded of the limits of my physical body far more often than I would have ever wanted to. Yet, I am absolutely in love—immersed and enraptured and overwhelmed—with how fungus lives. It's somehow both a high-minded, conceptual/intellectual love and a visceral, "gut" love, the same kind of love I feel deep within my body and soul when I am overwhelmed with the astonishing beauty of creation.

I am fascinated by the mind-boggling complexity of mycorrhizal networks: the symbiotic relationships between the roots of green plants and the networked webs of fungal bodies. Fungi actually evolved a relationship with terrestrial (rooted in earth) plants around the same time that plants began to actually take root in soil—the roots of their relationship are as intertwined in history as they are in the ground: Mycorrhizal fungi actually join their bodies with the bodies of plant roots, directly embedding the fungi in the plant body itself, and vice versa. Mycorrhizal networks are just one of the aspects of the soil rhizosphere: the narrow region of soil in direct relationship with a plant's

---

1. Parts of this section are adapted from two articles: Christy Randazzo, "Let Love Be the First Motion," Political Theology Network, April 19, 2021, https://politicaltheology.com/let-love-be-the-first-motion/; Randazzo, "True Vines and True Branches," Political Theology Network, April 22, 2024, https://politicaltheology.com/true-vines-and-true-branches/.

root structure, within which the complex, interwoven relationships of soil, root microbiome, mycorrhizae, chemicals, water, and air pockets all occur.

What I love about mycorrhizal networks is the ways they bring plants into interdependent relationship with fungi (plant roots feed fungi sugars, while fungi feed plants water and minerals extracted from the soil) and bring plants into relationship with each other through the transmission of biological signals from the roots of one plant—through the mycorrhizal network—to the roots of another. In this way, plants are not only rooted in the soil; they are rooted to each other through these often massive bionetworks: Fungal bodies can actually grow to mammoth proportions, covering entire square miles of soil. Or larger.

What captivates me about this idea is the immediate and profound sense that it shatters my perception of what is real about life. Trees talking to each other through the mycorrhizal internet flattens the boundaries hemming in my sense of the possible. I'm in love, though not specifically with the concept of interconnectivity: I am overwhelmed with the astonishing beauty of life itself and the experience of being alive on a planet where trees texting each other is not only possible but the experience of the vast majority of plants.

Admittedly, not all fungi seek symbiosis—some species are absolutely parasitic, and take from their hosts far more than they give, if they give anything at all. Yet, as with all metaphors, poetry is the intent far more than consistent accuracy, and when I imagine the interdependent relationship between creation and the Divine, I am absolutely limiting the scope of my poetics to mycorrhizae as beneficial symbiosis, not parasitism.

What does it mean for God's love to be a mushroom? Let's first turn to 1 John 3:

> We know love by this, that he laid down his life for us—and we ought to lay down our lives for one another. How does God's love abide in anyone who has the world's goods and sees a brother or sister in need and yet refuses help? Little children, let us love, not in word or speech, but in truth and action. And by this we will know that we are from the truth and will reassure our hearts before him whenever our hearts condemn us; for God is greater than our hearts, and he knows everything. Beloved, if our hearts do not condemn us, we have boldness before God; and we receive from him whatever we ask, because we obey his commandments and do what pleases him. And this is his

> commandment, that we should believe in the name of his Son Jesus Christ and love one another, just as he has commanded us. All who obey his commandments abide in him, and he abides in them. And by this we know that he abides in us, by the Spirit that he has given us. (1 John 3:16–24 NRSV)

A core truth of the English language is that it is inconsistent in its imprecision, sometimes frustratingly so. It's cliché at this point to note that *love* can mean just about anything in English. In light of 1 John 3:16, where love is defined as no less than sacrificing one's life, this imprecision might even become a moral issue: Using the same word to describe both the ultimate act of sacrifice as well as intellectual amazement (mycorrhizal networks are admittedly amazing, to be fair) must surely diminish them both, somehow.

I think that such etymological gatekeeping is far more akin to moral grandstanding than to moral guardianship, as dismissing any sense of love that is not exclusively self-sacrificial misses the gritty and often prosaic daily experience of the symbiosis between human beings. It also misses 1 John's expansive and all-encompassing view of love: in which love not only emerges from God but God so encompasses love that the Divine is themself love, binding all that *is* into interdependent relationship, in which love is the mycorrhizal network linking creation to the Divine—each abiding within the love one has for the other, with everything abiding within God.

In 1 John, love is cosmic: all things at once, all of which are bound together through the Divine (4:7). Love is the underlying reality of creation, as the Divine is the foundation of being. Love is the force of creation, flowing continuously from the Divine to creation, giving it life (4:12). Love is the binding web of creation, linking every element and being in mutual, interdependent relationship (4:13). As we each abide in each other through Divine love, the inherent corollary is that humans are created to be in a loving relationship with all of creation (4:15–16).

While an astonishingly beautiful vision, it also bears the marks of an unflinching awareness of the depths of human sinfulness, gained through the lens of Jesus on the cross. For 1 John, the love undergirding human relationality makes sense only in light of absolute empathy for the other: a care for the other so profound that whenever they are in need, we are willing to give everything we have—yes, even including our lives—simply because that is what one does when God's love abides in one (3:16–17). Thus, this potentially abstract, cosmic love is actually rooted deep in the lived experience of humans, in which one does not simply speak of love but enacts love in embodied actions (3:18).

In this way, the cosmic reality of relationship with God is demonstrated through the earthy mycorrhizal symbiosis of loving acts toward others. Humans are sinful, sure, but God's love allows humans to live in relationship with the Divine life by giving humans a way to express that Divine love in the very human form of acts of love for each other (3:19–22). By following Jesus's example in their lives, humans demonstrate their faith in the Divine. The Divine/human relationship is thus interdependent: Humans reach out to God through their enacted love for others, while the Divine lives within humanity in the form of the Spirit, which gives humans the feeling of love itself (3:23–24).

It is generally acknowledged that the Gospel of John and the author of 1 John were connected by the same narrative tradition, if not the same community of believers who developed a unique Johannine theology. A Quaker perspective on this emphasizes the deep interrelatedness of Jesus, the Divine, and humanity through the abiding of the Divine; the overpowering love of God for the creation; and the sacrifice of Jesus on the cross as the most complete expression of that love. In this way, it can be said that the parable of the good shepherd (John 10:11–18) is the parabolic expression of the teaching stated plainly in 1 John 3:16–24 as an accepted truth of the Christian life. As the good shepherd embodies his complete love for the sheep through his willingness to go so far as to even lay down his life for them, Jesus willingly does likewise for humanity and thus becomes a living embodiment of the love of the Divine for humanity. Thus, as God is love, Jesus is also love, and enacting love in this way is how John teaches us to follow Jesus.

Yet, what does this actually mean?

It is an accepted truism among Friends that the Gospel of John is "the Quaker Gospel," in that much of the foundation of Quaker theology and practice is based on a Johannine vision of God, of the relationship between humanity and the Divine, and the necessity of embodying the Divine love in real, human actions. Quaker theology has long held that—akin to the abiding presence of God in all who love others as God does—the Divine Presence resides within all of humanity, with a cascading ripple of consequences. As all have the ability to connect with "that of God within," hierarchies between humans cease to carry any value: that is, no human is inherently better than any other, no matter their earthly station. Nor, as the inherent corollary, is any human inherently worse than any other.

For the first Quakers, this was often expressed in a rejection of the "divinely ordained" differences between nobility and commoners. Following that line of logic to its conclusion, all divisions between humans must inherently fall away. War is impossible when divisions of enemies and allies cease to exist. Gender hierarchies cease to have any meaning when all humans are equally capable of testifying to the love of God. Anything in any way resembling a Calvinist "elect" is obviously swept away as *elect* and *damned* are meaningless terms in the face of the ubiquitous Divine Presence. The list could go on. Quakers were expected to demonstrate the same respect and love toward every single person. This emphasis on enacting theology through *bodies* created a specifically Quaker tradition of testimony, or the act of doing theology: In this way, their life would be testimony to the world of their commitment to living this life of enacted Divine love.

Yet, as with all ideals, Quakers have often fallen far short of where we might hope to be, where our ideals and theology and ethics all call us to be. Despite our well-burnished reputation as leaders in the movement to abolish slavery, many, many Quakers participated in that original sin whose roots run deep in the foundations of our modern world and still bear the strange fruit of white supremacy and state-sponsored violence. Yes, Quakers were early in our rejection of the system of chattel slavery, but we remain marked by the fact that it took almost two centuries to move all Quaker communities to finally enact this rejection.

It is in the manner that this change occurred that I find hope for us all as we face the evils of white supremacy head-on. See, Quakers were not blind to the cruel irony of being a people who simultaneously claimed that the Divine Presence lay within all while also either holding slaves themselves or supporting the system through their purchases and investments. In this way, history folds back on itself: They were as enmeshed in the chattel slave system as we are enmeshed in the fossil fuel system. Again, in an eerie echo to our current time, the challenge that seventeenth- and eighteenth-century Quakers faced was that it seemed impossible to extricate themselves from what seemed to be a system on which their entire world depended. Quakers were a "peculiar people," but even peculiar people needed to buy cotton and sugar.

What eventually shifted their perspective was a reminder of this teaching at the heart of the Quaker testimony: that God's love encircled all of creation, and this love demanded human action. Noted abolition figures such as Benjamin Lay and John Woolman are often credited with spurring Quakers to live by their ideals, by pursuing a complex web of enacted testimony: actions that spoke to an underlying belief. These actions emerged as a Divine call from deep within that then compelled them to concrete action.

Woolman, for example, refused to wear cotton, to use any product dyed with indigo, or to consume any product made with sugarcane. As a lawyer, he imperiled his own practice by refusing to prepare any wills that would pass on humans as property. More importantly, Woolman did these acts publicly, as both a writer and as a traveling minister. He embodied this testimony in his actions, refusing to allow Quakers to ignore the compulsion of Divine love.

In one notable example, Woolman expressed the Divine call to meet with local Indigenous tribes in Wyalusing, Pennsylvania (likely members of the Susquehannock Tribe), in this way: "Love was the first motion, and then a concern arose to spend some time with the Indians, that I might feel and understand their life and the spirit they live in." God's love moved within him, calling him to a specific act toward specific people, in an effort to demonstrate God's love toward them.

The testimony of the Divine Presence in all eventually made support of the chattel slavery system untenable, and Quakers moved to align their everyday actions with their testimony. This phrase—"Love was the first motion"—has come to embody the Quaker understanding of the incarnation: both the incarnation of God in the person of Jesus, and the Divine presence within each and every human person. It speaks to a mystical experience of the Divine love within, yes. However, it also demands that we respond to this love through actions of love. As 1 John 3:17 states so clearly, "How does God's love abide in anyone who has the world's goods and sees a brother or sister in need and yet refuses help?" How can we stand by and see a brother lying in the street being choked, a sister killed simply because someone else blamed her for his own sexual discomfort, or a young father killed because of a minor administrative offense—and refuse help? Refuse justice? Refuse to enact the love of God?

The simple truth is that we can't. Love is the first motion of our lives, and we are defined by how we respond to that motion. We focus so much attention on the grand gestures and acts of love and forget that it is often in the daily, unremarkable expressions of love—the symbiotic relationships we share with other people and the often unnoticed (but absolutely essential) mycorrhizal symbiosis we share with all of creation, through the mycorrhizal love of God.

How do we embody—or *incarnate*—this interconnected mushroom love? A lawyer, bewildered by Jesus's admonition to love your neighbor as yourself, opens the door for Jesus to answer his question with one of the most challenging teachings of the Gospels: the parable of the good Samaritan, Luke 10:25–37:

> Just then a lawyer stood up to test Jesus. "Teacher," he said, "what must I do to inherit eternal life?" He said to him, "What is written in the law? What do you read there?" He answered, "You shall love the Lord your God with all your heart, and with all your soul, and with all your strength, and with all your mind; and your neighbor as yourself." And he said to him, "You have given the right answer; do this, and you will live."
>
> But wanting to justify himself, he asked Jesus, "And who is my neighbor?" Jesus replied, "A man was going down from Jerusalem to Jericho, and fell into the hands of robbers, who stripped him, beat him, and went away, leaving him half dead. Now by chance a priest was going down that road; and when he saw him, he passed by on the other side. So likewise a Levite, when he came to the place and saw him, passed by on the other side. But a Samaritan while traveling came near him; and when he saw him, he was moved with pity. He went to him and bandaged his wounds, having poured oil and wine on them. Then he put him on his own animal, brought him to an inn, and took care of him. The next day he took out two denarii, gave them to the innkeeper, and said, 'Take care of him; and when I come back, I will repay you whatever more you spend.' Which of these three, do you think, was a neighbor to the man who fell into the hands of the robbers?" He said, "The one who showed him mercy." Jesus said to him, "Go and do likewise." (NRSV)

Upon seeing this traveler and his condition, two successive religious leaders—both a priest and a Levite—leave him alone. They were ritually clean and had taken many pains to get that way. Should the dying body of the traveler—likely on the very edge of death—breathe his last, his dead body would cause them days of inconvenience as they waited the required time period for cleansing. Plus, the Jericho road was one place where you would not want to get stuck after dark. Or alone. Who knows—maybe the "traveler" was actually a decoy, waiting to lure some unsuspecting person into a trap? The Levite and the priest used some intelligent common sense and decided to not risk joining the traveler in his likely fate.

Instead, a Samaritan risked his safety, money, and even his life for the sake of some Hebrew, a member of the people who had persecuted and discriminated against his community for centuries. A modern scenario can be easily imagined—with poor/rich, Black/white, Indigenous/colonizer dichotomies all coming to mind. Either way, the Samaritan insisted on viewing the traveler as family and took care of him accordingly. The text is rather clear on this point: The traveler risked his life, and spent significant amounts of his own resources, committing himself to the continued care of someone he refused to see as a stranger, one to whom he owed nothing.

Why, then, do we so often fail to acknowledge our human identity as members of one family? The outpouring of love and support that often unfurls in response to massive natural disasters dramatically and movingly proves that we understand the concept of one human family and our responsibility to our fellow humans. What troubles me is that we often seem to forget this lesson when we look at our daily lives. Is the Divine only in crises, or does God live in the messy aspects of being a human in a body that needs things? Where is Spirit in the grudges we hold or the anger we harbor against those with whom we disagree on matters of theology? What does it mean to be family with people we are likely to never meet?

Oftentimes, our failures as a family are sins of omission, times when we don't mean to harm someone or ignore their joy, but we just don't see it or recognize it for what it is. Being a member of a family carries certain responsibilities, which can change depending on your role in that family—parent, child, grandparent, auntie, family friend, and so on. Being a member of a human family carries responsibilities that are just as vital to the health of the family as your responsibility of parenthood yet may differ in ways that are inconvenient and uncomfortable. We often look at the Divine family and place expectations on it that are similar to those of our families of birth. Yet, the hierarchy of the traditional, patriarchal family just doesn't apply on the level of the Divine family.

In other words, advanced age doesn't grant you the right to expect the Divine family to accede to your wishes on how things should run. Just as importantly, youth does not release you from the responsibility to respect and learn from the wisdom and traditions of your community. Our equality within the Divine demands a radical awareness of our attitude and actions toward all. For example, we must create spaces for children to take their rightful place as full and complete members of the Divine family. We must reevaluate our views on hierarchy in the gospel and whether Jesus actually agrees with us. Again, what does it mean to be a Divine family?

I have real issues with the common idea that a family is automatically understood to be the "traditional" family: The nuclear family structure of mom, dad, and kids that is actually only a few decades old. I find much more beauty and scriptural basis for viewing the term *family* as a community of beings who are equal to each other, beholden to all, who care about each other through all of the joys and pain of life, with all contributing to the flourishing of the community.

We all carry a reserve of fear within ourselves, which inevitably leads us all to be tempted to limit our involvement in the life of the community. We fear our ignorance—not knowing how to teach, cook, organize a sports team, coordinate an activity, and on. We've trained ourselves to look at participation in our communities as the realm of a dedicated band of experts. We don't want to teach, for example, because we are positive that we aren't scholars, and god forbid we're asked a question we don't know the answer to: Whatever would we do?! We also fear what will happen to the boundaries we have created between us and others when we open our lives to each other: What will people think of me? Will they judge me? Will I be mocked? Will my life become too complicated?

The beauty of a family is that the members of a family are willing to be vulnerable to each other and to learn from their mistakes. Jesus himself stated that unless we had the faith of children—that is, a sense of wonder and a willingness to be foolish and ignorant—we could not inherit the kingdom of God. This fear culminates in its worst symptom: when we refuse to offer loving support and stability to someone in need. Yes: Christianity is built absolutely, utterly, and entirely upon the concept of empathy for other members of the creation family, and what could be more foolish than withholding our love and concern from another member of our family?

Let's return to considering roots—specifically roots in South Jersey.

The Pinelands is an area dominated by sandy soil. The forests in this region are dominated by tall pines, while the understory is crammed full of a variety of scrubs, vines, other nondominant tree species, brambles—life in all of its abundance, in other words. These forest communities are diverse and interwoven, in which the root systems of trees and vines and brambles and flowers and everything green and growing all join together underground, while their bodies often intertwine aboveground, creating a community where benefit and support are often mutual.

Vines are extraordinarily tenacious, as anyone who has wrestled with a patch of honeysuckle can attest. As soon as you are absolutely certain that you have finally cleared all vines from a patch of ground—especially the roots—you should prepare yourself for the inevitable peek of yet another runner snaking along the ground. This is due to the extensive root systems of many vines, in which the roots are both deep and broad, requiring a massive amount of effort to extract.

This is also due to the fact that vines can be unbelievably hungry for expansion and growth, leading to some of the most incredible aspects of vines: their ability to grow long, segmented stem pieces that shoot out along the ground, climb damn near everything, and even curl around the smallest outcropping or branch. Just like a climber scaling a wall for the first time, vines will push stabilizing segments into whatever surface they are crawling along. Once the vines have reached a sunny patch, they will then pour energy into growing clusters of leaves to take advantage.

Lest we forget, vines are as dependent on the sun as virtually every other plant on the planet: There's a reason vines work so hard to push their leaves to the most advantageous location possible. The process of photosynthesis—the biological process in which light energy is converted by the plant into the chemical energy that sustains the life of the plant—depends on a complex interdependent relationship among all parts of the plant: in which energy and resources flow from root to stems to branches and leaves, yes, but also from leaves back to root. The unidirectional nature of Jesus the true vine, feeding the energy of God to an entirely dependent humanity, might make theological sense (in some contexts), but it certainly makes very little biological sense.

Once the vine has reached this stage, if left unchecked, it will begin to starve whatever life it happens to have climbed, its dense canopy of leaves grasping every particle of light possible, leaving little—if any—to reach whatever tree, grass, or bush the vine happens to be using for support. This is neither gentle nor painless: Vines can absolutely conquer entire hillsides, fields, and even highway overpasses. Just look up photos of kudzu vines in the American South, and you will immediately understand what I am describing.

What are vines, therefore? Extraordinarily tenacious organisms capable of overcoming powerful obstacles, with solar panels for leaves that facilitate a complex interplay of interdependent relationships within the plant itself, inextricably embedded into their entire surrounding environment, rooted in ecosystems of often dizzying complexity. In other words, when you take the vine metaphor at its word, the traditional interpretation described above is not only embarrassing in its simplicity but absolutely false to a laughable degree. Continuing our exploration of agricultural metaphors of interdependence in the Gospel of John, let's explore this complex, interdependent world of the understory—the mad jumble of vines, brambles, soil, roots, and plant bodies—with actual vines in mind, in light of the powerful imagery of Jesus as the true vine from John:

> I am the true vine, and my Father is the vinegrower. He removes every branch in me that bears no fruit. Every branch that bears fruit he prunes to make it bear more fruit. You have already been cleansed by the word that I have spoken to you. Abide in me as I abide in you. Just as the branch cannot bear fruit by itself unless it abides in the vine, neither can you unless you abide in me. I am the vine; you are the branches. Those who abide in me and I in them bear much fruit, because apart from me you can do nothing. Whoever does not abide in me is thrown away like a branch and withers; such branches are gathered, thrown into the fire, and burned. If you abide in me and my words abide in you, ask for whatever you wish, and it will be done for you. My Father is glorified by this, that you bear much fruit and become my disciples. (John 15:1–8 NRSVue)

Jesus begins the passage in 15:1 with the declarative confidence so often present in John's Gospel: "I am the vine, and my Father is the vinegrower." These roles establish an unexpected relationship between Jesus and God the Parent, in which the Parent acts and Jesus is acted on. This isn't a relationship of absolute dependence, however. Vines can survive just fine—even thrive!—without any intentional intervention from any external actor.

This also isn't a hierarchical relationship. Jesus the vine consents to pruning, recognizing that a relationship of reciprocity exists between vine and vine grower. The vine grower helps the vine thrive as much as it can by pruning away the literal dead weight. The vine helps the vine grower by producing as much fruit as it can. Fruiting happens only when a plant is healthy enough, so in a very real sense the health of the vine—and thus its capacity to fruit—depends on the grower. This is perichoresis—the nonhierarchical, interdependent dance of the Trinity—viewed through an eco-theological lens.

If hierarchy and absolute dependence aren't present in the Divine interrelationship, therefore, what about the relationship between Jesus (vine) and humanity (branches)? A simple reading of 15:3–7 might indicate that the branches are entirely dependent on the vine for the energy and nutrients necessary to exist and to fruit. This is true: Branches separated from the energy flowing throughout the entire vine will never be capable of producing fruit—let alone survive—and will inevitably die, dry up, and be gathered together for the fire. (It should be noted, however, that this reading ignores the time-honored practice of growing new plants from cuttings, a practice Jesus would almost certainly have been aware of.)

Yet, there's this pesky verb that keeps emerging and complicates this reading: *abide*. In this context, *abide* connotes living with, or residing with (and within), another. This echoes John 14:20, where Jesus sketches out a complex interdependence: Jesus lives in both the Parent *and* humanity, while humanity lives in Jesus. Unspoken, perhaps, is another implication: If Jesus lives in the Parent and also with humanity, then both humanity and the Parent could be said to live in—and with—each other.

Again, this speaks powerfully of a paradoxical interrelationship between Divine and human, one that actually reflects the true interrelationship between leaf, branch, stem, and root—in which the entire plant must work together in order to survive and, hopefully, thrive. Unsurprisingly, this is the actual reality of vines. This is also the reality of the creation, in which each and every atom of the creation is bound together in a complex, interdependent web of relationships, a harmony of life built into the very fabric of the world. While this passage is rooted within the Christian tradition, this vision of an interdependent creation is recognized across the human religious landscape, speaking to the power of its truth.

In other words, this bounty requires active human participation in their relationship with the Divine. Of course, the Divine existed just fine before human existence, whereas if we take Jesus at his word, humanity is absolutely dependent on the Divine energy to give life: The Divine gives and we just receive, God commands and we simply obey. Shouldn't we take Jesus at his entire word, though, and not just the parts that serve our desire to rest in the comforting bosom of a hierarchical authoritarian structure?

What about our responsibility to other branches? If Jesus is a vine, can we really accept a theology that permits us to sit back and take without contributing anything ourselves? Can we permit other branches to die due to sickness, poverty, or our blithe neglect? A vine thrives when all of its branches thrive; if Jesus is a vine, then doesn't that require that we all work, as hard as we can, to ensure that every single branch thrives? If Jesus is a vine, then every part of the entire vine must recognize itself as a part of a whole vine and do all it can to contribute to the whole. From the perspective of actual vines, therefore, couldn't it be said that those who rest certain in their own goodness as Christians, ignoring the rest of the vine, are in actuality the dead branches—the ones gathered for the fire?

I've most often encountered Christians engaging with the metaphor of Jesus as vine in a way that seeks to domesticate its wildness and tame its unruliness, a comforting metaphor of a loving Jesus who channels divine energy in one direction: into the lives of Christians alone, from Jesus the vine out to the human branches. In this vision, Jesus is the one true vine, who asks that we live only and exclusively through him, and only through the specific vision of Jesus present in a particular expression of Christianity; conveniently, of course, this is often whichever expression the person explaining the metaphor hails from.

This exclusivist vision gives license to a Christianity that sees value only in specific forms, on specific branches, and allows Christians in these communities to view this situation as divinely ordained—as normal, as built into the structure of the world, as vines themselves. It is then the shortest possible stroll to every other fruit of Christian exclusivism, especially the destructively acidic harvest of Christian nationalism, in which Christianity is so tiny it can fit neatly within the anemic harvest of a white supremacist political program. Is this result really what the world of this metaphor looks like?!

Actually . . . no, not in the slightest: As we've already established, it couldn't be further from the truth. The world that exists in forests at the level of the soil—both above it (vines and undergrowth) and below (roots and mycorrhizal networks)—is dizzyingly complex and unbelievably rich, holding a shockingly high percentage of the overall biomass of the entire forest. This region is defined far more by relationality than separation. For example, smaller trees are often protected by larger nurse trees—not necessarily from the same family or even the same broad type of tree (evergreen versus deciduous, for example) whose canopies provide shade from too much sunlight, break winds that might uproot these trees when they are most vulnerable, and protect from animals who might feast on the extremely vulnerable shoots just beginning to pop up out of the ground. When the smaller trees eventually grow tall, the nurse tree either dies of old age or simply continues the process of adapting itself to its neighbors that began when the smaller tree began to take root in the soil.

In case the meaning of the metaphor wasn't glaringly obvious already, our human families are a true expression of the Divine family only when we are vulnerable with each other and weave the roots and vines of our lives around the roots and bodies of others in the community. We can survive storms, droughts, floods, predators—almost anything—when we act as if we are all rooted in the same soil and live accordingly. When we isolate our trees, planting them in decorative beds filled with low bushes and some ornamental plants, and we regularly remove plants that take root in these beds—weeds—in an effort to fit a specific vision of appearance or beauty, we emphasize the appearance of individual plants over the potential for the true "state of nature": communal interdependence. Funny thing about weeds: They are, basically, any plant that is considered undesirable for a specific location. We don't refer to dandelions living in forest understories as weeds—they're just . . . forest.

Do trees fall over more easily when they aren't blessed by being embedded in a tightly woven root community instead of forced to deal with (literal) storms—alone? Absolutely! I am certain that we are weaker when we're isolated and alone. Life is not an individual affair: We are bound up in interwoven ecosystems, in which the oxygen we breathe was given to us by the trees surrounding us, while the carbon dioxide we exhale is an offering to the other members of our Divine family: the trees, bushes, vines, and green growing things that are rooted in the soil of the specific corners of our lives. Opening your life to others (regardless of the species, gender, class, skin color, ethnicity, etc.), caring for the vulnerable, and being cared for in turn: These are the marks of a human family rooted in the rich soil of the Divine family.

Viewing our relationships with others through the lens of mushrooms leads to a series of conclusions: We must overcome our fears of vulnerability. We must listen to Jesus's call of radical equality. We must all be willing to sacrifice our comfort and convenience, becoming foolish and vulnerable before our family. Finally, we must see everyone in the community as a part of the same forest and act accordingly.

Trunks: What Are the Stories That Unify Us and Give Our Life Structure and Purpose?

Cultures of Life

As I described earlier, Britain in the seventeenth century was undergoing rapid and revolutionary changes at all levels of society—even the monarchy. When Elizabeth Tudor died in 1603, childless, the Tudor dynasty ended. James Stuart, king of Scotland—and Elizabeth's cousin—succeeded to the English throne, thus beginning the momentous century of Stuart rule and uniting the kingdoms of England and Scotland. This was only the first of numerous political earthquakes to hit Britain and the Stuart family as all hell broke loose during the reign of James's son Charles I. Between his determined belief in the divine right of kings and his singular inability to understand the value of ecclesiastical and political compromise, Charles helped create a perfect storm for revolution. Beginning in 1639, Charles fought a series of wars with his subjects that culminated in both parliaments—English and Scottish—declaring war on Charles in 1642. The resulting conflict, now known as the English Civil War, would last for three years, result in his defeat, and—again, combined with his genius for inflexibility, arrogance, and stupidity—eventually led to the English Parliament executing him in 1649.

The chaos wouldn't end with his death, however, as the newly declared commonwealth government, a republic ruled by Parliament and an executive committee, would not last more than a few years. In 1653, Oliver Cromwell gained enough power to disband Parliament and declare himself "Lord Protector": a monarchy in all but name. Cromwell did not last long in his position as Lord Protector either, as his body did not last past 1658, when he died.

By 1660, a thoroughly exhausted Britain acceded to the calling of Parliament again and the restoration of the monarchy to Charles's son, Charles II.

I offer a summary of the political upheaval in the first half of the seventeenth century to demonstrate how absolutely wild this time was, especially for the millions of people whose lives were convulsed as wave upon wave of profound political, religious, and cultural change crashed on society. As these things tend to go, the decisions made by the powerful—Parliament and the monarchy, for starters—resulted in unexpected consequences.

For example, in 1604 James established a committee of scholars whose task it was to create a common English-language translation of the Bible that was authorized by the monarchy for use in the state church. The committee also attempted to remove the pro-Calvinist leanings of the Geneva Bible, the version most likely to be used by English-speaking people at that time (who weren't Anglican clergy, of course). The committee finished its work in 1611, having created the King James Version (or Authorized Version, as it's also called). James wanted a text around which he could unify his country and his church. What emerged was a cultural juggernaut, whose profound impact on the English language, and everything touched by the English language, is incalculable.

The same goes for Jamestown, the first English colonial enterprise in the Americas—outside the failed Roanoke colony of the previous century—at the mouth of the Chesapeake Bay, in an area of Algonquian territory ruled by the Powhatan Confederacy. What began as a small fort clinging to life on the edge of a continent soon became a force of astonishing power, completely transforming both English society and the Indigenous societies of what is now known as the United States. In 1619, the English unleashed the scourge of English participation in the transatlantic chattel slavery trade, when the first enslaved Africans were forced to disembark on the shores of land that would eventually become the state of Virginia.

Similarly, when Parliament responded to Charles and his desire for absolute power with the calling of voluntary militias in 1642 to fight Charles and his royalist forces, they channeled a powerful democratizing energy that had already been pulsing through the country—but without a leader to guide it or even a direction in which to flow. Once ordinary English people were being dragged into these political conflicts directly, as the soldiers called to fight for (or against) the king and the people over whose land these soldiers marched, it was impossible for anyone who had not been involved in the conflicts before to remain so for long.

Civil wars are by definition universal affairs: Regardless of one's military status, everyone living in a country at war with itself is a combatant. Everyone suffers permanent war wounds—just calling them scars seems to miss the shocking significance of the injuries that civil wars inflict on an entire society. The fundamental question at the core of civil war, as a concept, is existential: What would it be like to experience life as a citizen of your nation? What values and beliefs guide and guard society? What does it mean to have value, worth, autonomy, and purpose in society? Who receives citizenship, and why? What will the legislatures and the courts decide for society, and why? Who benefits, and why? Effectively: What vision of a good society will frame, define, and empower the daily experience of every single individual person in the entire country for the foreseeable future?

The English Civil War most decidedly earns its civil title. It's actually only one in a series of wars from 1639 to 1653, across both Britain and Ireland, with the handsomely direct title "The War of the Three Kingdoms." It says exactly in the title how expansive this conflict was. The "Three Kingdoms" were Ireland, England, and Scotland, for each of which Charles I individually held the crown. That means that every single one of these kingdoms had to be fighting against the king, which in turn means that—effectively—the entire English-speaking world was fighting against itself. People in the kingdoms were simply done with the idea of a king telling them what to believe and do without having any way of raising an objection.

These were people whose faith had been tested and broken and reborn and strengthened. That process so transformed them that many came to radically different answers from the king to the questions of authority, ownership, class, gender, the domestic sphere, family relationships, and the Divine. Many were also soldiers who had personally experienced the horrors of war and came to the conclusion that they were unwilling to add to that violence in any physical way anymore. No one could accuse these people of naivete: They knew that there were people whose deeds were deserving of a violent response, because wars are violent, ugly things that often attract people who crave free reign to do violent, ugly things to other people. This kind of violence and ugliness infects a society when it is used on itself, especially during a civil war. Many early Friends were former soldiers whose time marinated in the stew of their participation in the War of the Three Kingdoms had convinced them that the violence of war was a weapon so dangerous that only God had any right to be handling it. In the eyes of these people, Charles I, whose reactionary and authoritarian response to the challenges and opportunities of the time created the circumstances for an initially rebellious uprising to mature into a full-throated revolution, had lost his claim to the authority to wield war.

What happens when whole populations of people, every one of them injured by the status quo and then by the convulsions of several years of civil war, begin to question the story of reality told by these same societies? Will they begin to see these previous certainties—monarchy, religion, the horizon of opportunity available to common people, to name just a few—collapse and mutate in a shockingly short time frame? Eventually, these same masses of people might begin to feel as if their potential for transforming the world were limitless—and at that time, in that place, they absolutely transformed it. An English folk ballad written during this period captures this mood best: "the world turned upside down."

The energy created by this boiling cauldron fostered and energized the birth and growth of a wide variety of groups emerging from both the yeoman and peasant classes, unified by a sense of disaffection at the world as it was and an overwhelming desire to completely reimagine society at all levels and aspects. These included, among many others, the anarcho-socialist Diggers and their rejection of the concept of privately owned land, as well as the antihierarchical Levellers and their claims of universal human equality. These groups were considerably diverse in their approach and methods, however, both between and within the groups themselves.[2] Some were apolitical and explicitly religious (the pacifist Muggletonians), while others were the mirror opposite (the antinomian Fifth Monarchists), but all were stamped by the apocalyptic furor of their times, acted in response to it, and contributed their own revolutionary energy to that century's frothy turmoil.

Early Quakers were very much of their time, therefore, in being extraordinarily apocalypse focused, fundamentally egalitarian, and antihierarchical. The lockstep unity of message and action of Friends that emerged after the restoration of the monarchy (at least a decade in the future) was in large part a response to that same restoration and a desire to—quite literally—stay

---

2. Christopher Hill, *The World Turned Upside Down: Radical Ideas During the English Revolution* (Penguin, 1984).

alive. It would be enforced by an entire structure of committees responsible for ensuring messaging unity across the world of Quaker publishing and preaching. During the creative time of anarchy that was this first decade or so of the movement, the words of Friends—whether sermons, pamphlets, or books—emerged free and unfettered, in a flood shocking in its overwhelming volume, its astonishing power—and, at least to modern readers—its vituperative vocal violence.

Suffice it to say, while these Friends were certain that God would intervene to help shape this new, modern world being birthed right before their very eyes, the Friends community of the 1640s and 1650s was deeply ambivalent about the form that God's action would take in response to shaping this new world, and thus the form—roles and actions—that human beings should take in response. Many of the men who joined the Quaker movement during the period between the English Civil War and the Restoration of 1660 understood the world to be in the midst of an apocalyptic upheaval inaugurated by God, termed "the Lamb's War." This war was described by Friends' pamphleteers and preachers in significantly violent terms, akin to the violent language one would *expect* when describing a war, holy or otherwise.[3]

It must be noted, however, that Quakers took pains to insist that any actual, physical violence that might emerge during this great upheaval would not be "carnal," in that it was physical violence on humans, perpetrated by humans. Instead, Quakers understood from their reading and interpretation of Revelation that all violence would be performed by God, perpetrated against the spiritual forces of the antichrist and the beast. This freed Friends to foment this revolution with the acid power of their words. Many Friends took on this mission with a vengeance.

Apocalypse encounters people in various ways, however, and an example of that is the imagery of natality and life creation that Quaker women often chose to emphasize instead: images of the Divine as the Creator birthing a new world, where the divine capacity to give birth was reflected in the human

3. Douglas Gwyn, *Apocalypse of the Word: The Life and Message of George Fox* (Friends United, 1986). See also Walter Hjelt Sullivan, "Earth Quaker Action Team: Reclaiming the Lamb's War for Justice and Sustainability in the Twenty-First Century," in *Quakers, Creation Care, and Sustainability*, ed. Cherice Bock and Stephen Potthoff, Quakers and the Disciplines 6 (Friends Association for Higher Education, 2019), 327–44.

roles of Quaker women as mothers birthing this new movement.[4] As we've already seen, Margaret Fell particularly leaned into this maternal framework, expressing her role in the movement as a spiritual mother of this new world. This form of motherhood was not limited to those who had physically given birth but was instead seen more as a societal role built on maternal-ness, an approach to one's life and mission that stressed the responsibilities and capacities inherent in the birth and care of life.[5]

This understanding of motherhood as perspective and role emerged directly from the experience of women, on whose shoulders the responsibilities of care (for children, for elders, and any who needed nursing and healing) and home (cooking, cleaning, procuring supplies, hospitality, and creating the domestic atmosphere) had always rested. During the civil wars, however, the responsibilities of these roles—and as a result, their meaning—shifted dramatically. On a practical level, women have always been responsible for maintaining the continuance of life while men are away fighting as soldiers in war. In the end, crops need to be sown, gardens need to be weeded, food needs to be cooked, houses and people need to be cleaned, vulnerable people (the young, the old, and the sick) need to be cared for. Life continues, and someone needs to be responsible for ensuring that these tasks continue as well. War therefore inherently shifts the meaning of gender in a society, scrambling roles, expectations, rules, and even power dynamics as society convulses from the waves caused by these upheavals to the previous status quo.[6]

Early Quaker women were therefore already reimagining the nature and meaning of their own power and abilities before they had their often earth-shattering experiences of convincement. Yet, once they experienced the leveling empowerment of engaging the Divine Presence in their own bodies and souls, and were led to give testimony about the Divine in mixed-gender groups, where men not only listened to the testimony of women but granted

4. Grace M. Jantzen, "Choose Life! Early Quaker Women and Violence in Modernity," *Quaker Studies* 9, no. 2 (2005): 149.

5. Kristianna Polder, "Margaret Fell, Mother of the New Jerusalem," in *New Critical Studies of Quaker Women, 1650–1800*, ed. Michelle Lise Tarter and Catie Gill (Oxford University Press, 2018), 187.

6. An excellent introduction to this concept is provided in Cynthia Enloe, *Bananas, Beaches, and Bases: Making Feminist Sense of International Politics*, 2nd ed. (University of California Press, 2014).

them authority as a result of the power of their testimony, Quaker women gained a confidence in their own authority that is still bracing in its insistence on being directly rooted in the experience of women and thrilling in its claim to a specific, feminine form and expression of power.

This framework is as indebted to the apocalyptic experience—and Revelation—as the emphasis on violence and death of the Lamb's War. Quaker women seldom failed to take the opportunity to protest the injustices of the world, nor to pass judgement on those who (in their eyes) had failed to truly and deeply listen to the Divine Presence, and thus to respond accordingly in their daily behaviors and expressed beliefs. Images of fires and hellfire and damnation and the dismantling of the current world order run rife through the often barbed, and astonishingly blunt, writings and sermons written and delivered by Quaker women both before the Restoration and in its immediate aftermath.

Quaker women also emphasized the gentleness inherent in the imagery of the Lamb in the Lamb's War framework, including the rejection of physical violence as an option for those fighting this war. This war might be seen as analogous to the Greater Jihad in Islam: an inner, spiritual struggle against forces of evil, violence, and destruction that seeks to first experience the peace of the Divine Presence within, and then to live into the new life available to those who commit everything they are—their very bodies and souls—to surrendering to a form of life that testifies to the power and truth of the Divine Presence. Fighting in the Lamb's War was both the framework of life and the meaning and purpose of life itself.

However, these spiritual mothers placed their emphasis on the creation of the new Jerusalem, and on the hope unleashed by the new life and vitality that early Quaker women experienced during this time, rather than the destruction of the world. In this way, Quaker women directly contradicted the patriarchal visions of docility and submission attached to motherhood—and by extension femininity—by insisting that their role as spiritual mothers was central in building the new society after the Lamb's War had dismantled the old. In this way, they were laying claim to a powerful spiritual and temporal authority directly connected to both the biological natality of women and the gendered assumption of all women as inherently maternal, regardless of their biological ability to birth children.

They also stressed imagery of creation, life, and hope, tied to the universality of the Divine Presence available to all people, everywhere. Ensuring that they did all in their power to enact this vision of new life in a new Jerusalem, early Quaker women understood that this new life depended on their embodiment of a new form of life: built around a profound respect for the value of life and its inherent holiness. In other words, Quaker women were just as committed as Quaker men to living in a way that was guaranteed, in that time and in that place, to lead to severe repercussions, including imprisonment, torture, and death. What's different is the emphasis they placed on what could be termed an entire culture of life, built on principles, responding to the new way of life being offered by the direct experience of the Divine Presence—the underlying divine energy that made life alive.

Cultures of Peace[7]

It's difficult to overstate the impact that World War II had on the societies choked by Nazi occupation. While the words "Nazi occupation" might conjure romantic images of the French Resistance—berets wreathed in a fog of cigarette smoke—the truth was, paradoxically, simultaneously horrifying and prosaic. An occupation by a foreign power is fundamentally disorienting in that it forces the occupied to have their awareness constantly tuned in two directions simultaneously.

For one, the occupied are always aware of the existential threat to their entire world living among them, powerless to defend themselves from the bone-chilling knock on the door in the night. If you're someone who carries the ambivalent blessing/burden of being a member of a category marked for special attention (i.e., discrimination and oppression) based on race, ethnic identity, religious belief, gender, sexuality, physical or mental condition, class, or any of the innumerable ways that "us" can be categorized against "them," you'll know that this awareness becomes so prominent in your mind, body, and soul that it can literally twist and devour you. This is survival: the flood of adrenaline that pummels your body as your focus narrows to a world no larger than a millimeter across, adapted to a constant state of existential dread.

---

7. This section is indebted to Elise Boulding's work as a whole, of course, but most especially these central texts: *The Underside of History: A View of Women Through Time* (Halsted, 1976); *Women in the Twentieth Century World* (Halsted, 1977); *Children's Rights and the Wheel of Life* (Transaction, 1979); *Building a Global Civic Culture: Education for an Interdependent World* (Teachers College Press, 1988); *One Small Plot of Heaven: Reflections on Family Life by a Quaker Sociologist* (Pendle Hill, 1989); *Cultures of Peace: The Hidden Side of History* (Syracuse University Press, 2000).

The occupied are also aware of the ways that the axis of the world seems misaligned, somehow, in which the outlines of your daily life are the same but the world is a bizarre dreamscape: as if you have awoken in another universe that looks like your own but works according to an entirely different set of rules from your own. This is the twisted surreality of becoming second-class people in one's own home, disorienting because it seeps into every facet of daily life, from mail delivery to municipal services to employment to education. A foreign occupation thus destroys the world where this country exists as autonomous and sovereign and births a world where none of this is true.

This has two timelines, both shocking and transformative. The first timeline is the flood of foreign soldiers across the country's borders, the (often) unsuccessful military response by the home country, and the triumphant entry of foreign soldiers in the country's capital in an explosive and frightening show of force and violence. The second timeline is the slow but seemingly inexorable corruption, failure, and crumbling of the structures, concepts, beliefs, and relationships that make the country work and give the society its unique social and cultural flavors. This could begin before the military strikes as disinformation campaigns aimed at undermining faith in the country and everything it represents, disillusioning the populace and planting seeds of doubt and fear. This is all done for the purpose of cutting the people off from any cultural and social beliefs that could give them the courage and moral strength to continue resisting.

Once the populace sees the rapid defeat of its military, has been cut off from its myths, is thoroughly disillusioned by the state of its country, and feels utterly disempowered to change this state of affairs, it is much easier to control. The final goal is to have the country not only accept its defeat but begin to incorporate the occupying nation's beliefs and myths into its own, fallen ones, resulting in a new hybrid identity. Once that happens, the country (the old world) has lost, the occupying power has won, and the new world of this new identity as occupied people is alive and consuming everything. This is an apocalypse, and in World War II, these apocalypses were revealed literally across the entire world.

These occupations are also civil affairs, because the success of an occupation entirely depends on the occupied people accepting their defeat and cooperating with the occupiers in every aspect of their governance. People become collaborators for various reasons, ranging from ideological (they agree with the ideals and intent of the occupying country and want to support it), to apathetic overwhelm (in which people are so overwhelmed by everything that they simply accede, seeking to just live a "normal life"). The occupation also leads to resistance (obviously so!), and people are required to choose sides, often at the behest of a rifle barrel to the temple. Neighbors begin to fear neighbors—people who may have been dear and close friends and even family—and the gentle threads of relationship and obligation weaving the country together come undone. This civil war doesn't end once the occupation does, however, as this slow-moving hurricane has torn the fabric of society apart, and that does not heal easily or quickly—*if* it ever heals.

This is the apocalypse Elise Boulding (1920–2010), Quaker, sociologist, and peace scholar, faced as she saw her home country, Norway, slowly be consumed by the Nazi machine. Boulding was raised in the United States but was born in Norway and spent the first three years of her life there: to Boulding, the United States was home, while Norway was *home*. Seeing her home—the place where many members of her family still lived—infested by the Nazis in 1940 shifted something deep within Boulding's soul, and she became thoroughly and irrevocably committed to the cause of peacemaking everywhere and to the undermining of violence anywhere.

She would eventually become one of the founding scholars of the field of peace studies, focusing the bulk of her life's work on the study of these seemingly intangible threads that, when woven together, make society possible and give people the strength to maintain their faith in nonviolent resistance as an effective response to the threats to their society. As a result of this holistic focus on the entire society, Boulding focused a great deal of her work on understanding the fundamental elements of cultures that foster deep relationships between people, particularly in family life.

The range of topics Elise Boulding addressed in her work is dizzying, including the practice and theory of social change and peacemaking, the political ramifications of family life, and an examination of the unique role that women play in society, bringing skills and perspectives—unique to their experiences as women in society—to the resolution of social problems. Boulding wove the strands of these concerns together as she also wove her family life and research together into the one fabric of her life. She was fascinated by cultures of peace that exist as alternatives of and critiques against what she viewed as the dominant violence culture in Western society. She defined cultures of peace as cultures that promote peaceable diversity holistically, weaving that intent through every aspect of culture: lifeways, belief patterns, values, behaviors, relationships of mutual care and well-being on an institutional level, and an ecological orientation that seeks to ensure that all of creation has what it needs to flourish.

A central tenet of peace studies is that peace is inherently dynamic, as both force and state. Peace as force is peacebuilding, the effort to transform society's response to conflict from coercive and violent to nonviolent and justice seeking. Peace as state is space enough for all communities in society to thrive and feel safe to risk exploring new ways of being community, with new behaviors and perspectives on the way the communities of society relate with each other. She stressed, however—again, reflecting bedrock orthodoxy in the field of peace studies—that conflict is actually inevitable and inherent in the nature of life in society. Often, conflict is the result of differences in needs and arises out of a situation of limited resources. Conflict does not always become violent, however, and in fact it doesn't need to become violent in the first place. The mitigating factor in all conflict is the foundational human need for community and bonding. Peace culture could therefore be a catchall term for all aspects of a culture that lead toward peace.

War/violence culture is often seen as the natural state of culture, unfortunately. It is embedded deeply into our most fundamental beliefs, teachings, and values, warping and twisting them to the extent that we are able to legitimate violence and find ways to blame God for it all. This makes state violence that much easier to justify. Boulding argues that the only way to diminish the power of the war/violence culture is to create valid and viable alternatives through greater recognition of the often hidden peace cultures that have existed and thrived alongside the war culture. She pays particular attention to religious peace cultures, as peace-culture faith communities (such as the Quakers, of course) have been highly influential on peace movements throughout history.

One of the key components of Boulding's work was a reexamination of women as creative agents, specifically in social change and in peacebuilding. She stresses that their knowledge and experience worlds often equip them in particular ways to do the work of peacemaking effectively in ways that men's knowledge and experience worlds do not—at least to the same extent. This emerges from their experiences and the ways that society has limited the scope of women's roles while simultaneously granting them significant power over profoundly important tasks. Many of the tasks women are expected to perform are the same, regardless of the community in which they are rooted. This means that while the definition of a task might differ across cultures (such as food preparation), the task itself is still seen as fundamental to women's role in society for a truly significant percentage of societies worldwide. For example, women who are homemakers can often draw on years of experience managing complex scheduling challenges and negotiating the multiple and overlapping needs of their communities. These women are leaders in their community, in every possible meaning of the term.

Peace cultures often exist in the form of communal groups. These are trust groups, and micro-societies, in which there is mutual respect, some degree of social equality, mutual aid, and regular intergenerational communication. Group practices often celebrate a shared history and communal identity and provide a meaning for life. The group identity and boundaries could be rooted in ethnicity, religious belief, or land: The binding agent is less important than that the group is bound together. It is incorrect, however, and unhelpful, to think of ethnic groups as minority groups, as it assumes a normative majority that is held to be monolithic and in opposition to the minority group. In reality, the majority is itself composed of a number of smaller, ethnic communal groups; the inability to see variety and diversity within the assumed "dominant" culture is itself an aspect of imperialism.

Boulding claimed that the rise of intrastate ethnic conflicts in the latter half of the twentieth century could be directly related to Western colonial nation building, in which disparate ethnicities in an area were brought together into one country for the purpose of serving the colonialist's needs. These ethnic groups often had long-standing conflict-resolution processes that were plowed under and destroyed by the colonial power in its desire to reshape society to reflect the needs and desires of the colonists.

The pace of change in industrial societies can hit Indigenous community groups especially hard, because their entire culture and society is often built around the closeness of personal relationships, and thus their solutions to problems are most useful on the personal and intimate level. This is not unique to Indigenous groups alone, however. Industrial societies, it can be argued, still struggle with the need for close, intimate relationships between people and the necessity of having knowledge of how to leverage these relationships for solving societal problems. Boulding argues that the decentralized and highly personal nature of communal groups can actually be a more effective means of governing a diverse society.

The whole vision Boulding presents of a peace-culture society is admittedly utopian. Boulding stresses that if peace cultures were actually allowed to develop in their entirety, in every single aspect, they could cause massive, rippling changes to society globally, leading to the resolution of all current social ills. This is absolutely an area of critique of her work, as this concept is rooted in an ultimately utopian vision of a future society that is still highly local in its context and focus. This obviously doesn't take into account the irrevocably global nature of the internet and other technologies, betraying its roots in a pre-9/11, security-state world. Her ideas could thus be said to be naive, reflecting an idealized vision of a perfect, interdependent society, composed of an overly complicated network of highly autonomous groups all clamoring for attention and priority.

Boulding might respond to this critique, however, by arguing that for peace cultures, experiments seen as utopian by everyone else are actually practical, achievable, and effective ways to have humans live together nonviolently. They provide numerous, creative alternatives to the dominant violence cultures. Therefore, utopia wouldn't be an epithet of impractical thinking but rather a necessary creative exercise to develop alternatives to dominant—and thus normative—societal structures. She'd also argue that local, preexisting tribal and communal structures are often highly effective agents of revolutionary and participatory change, as these structures are fluid, spontaneous, and responsive. Thus, utopian visions that emphasize local community structures might be the only effective response to the overwhelming power of the dominant structures.

It was at the level of the family that Boulding rooted her work, however, as she viewed the family as in a sense the first peace culture—the foundation on which the rest of her work rests. The characteristics explored below outline what is as much a theory about global peacemaking as it is a Quaker theology of the family. I offer a brief exploration below of the central characteristics of peace cultures in Boulding's thought, which I encourage you to read with the two perspectives (a theory about global peacemaking and a Quaker theology of the family) in mind.

Peace cultures place a high priority on "peaceableness": both a state of being and a pattern of behavior. This is where viewing Boulding through her

Quaker context is helpful in understanding this term, as it can be translated as the character of a person who experiences the presence of God, both in themselves and in others, and responds to this by embodying peacemaking as a way of life—basically testimony but with an orientation toward peace especially. For societies to be able to create the best circumstances possible for peaceableness to embed itself deeply enough in the foundations of society that it's seen as integral to what makes society work, the entire society needs to commit wholeheartedly to peaceableness, weaving it into every aspect of life. Social expectations and pressures train people from birth how to approach violence and conflict, instilling a complex spectrum of personal habits and societal expectations.

Peace cultures are often alternative economic and governmental systems. They critique the valorizing of capitalism and the priority of economic growth. They stress the need to take the quality of family life into account in terms of work. A key aspect of that is the need to recognize what Boulding terms the "hidden economy" as an often unacknowledged economic resource that's devalued by the market system. The hidden economy, including bartering and exchange networks, is often dominated by the unpaid labor of women and children in a multitude of volunteer positions, with the burden of childcare one notable example of the kinds of unpaid, or poorly paid, positions that are actually of foundational significance and importance for the survival of society. This informal economy could possibly, according to Boulding, constitute up to half of a society's productivity and—if fully appreciated—could constitute a valuable resource for societal economic development.

Peace cultures often provide an alternative ecofeminist view of the interdependence of creation, as opposed to capitalism's view of the creation as simply a large bank of exploitable resources. Boulding argues that there exists an inextricable link, in the West, between economic growth and what is termed "development." The result of this link is that science, technology, and capital are the only measurements with which we grade value. This often creates a particularly toxic view, prevalent in the West, of subduing the earth as a means of "improving" it, in which unlimited economic growth is seen as an achievable and worthy goal. Unlimited growth is simply unsustainable, however; it's only the Western mastery of science and technology that has made such economic progress a possibility, and it's only achievable at terrible cost to the health of the creation. While the myths of economics and corporate boardrooms give permission to ignore such costs, peace cultures insist that humans have no right to permit anyone to engage in such destruction—no result can be beneficial enough to outweigh the costs.

Peace cultures often provide an alternative, participatory flow of information, in which every member of society is able to participate. These two-way, participatory information flows are often restricted in cultures of violence, in which information is controlled by hierarchies of elites and authority for the purpose of social control. Keeping information in the public domain is thus an essential step toward ensuring that the power of changing society lies in the hands of groups of people as opposed to corporations. The internet can play a vital role in this, yet we should still approach it with caution. The detachment of online interactions can actually limit people's abilities to develop skills of interaction with others and skills of relationship building. Face-to-face interactions are one sure way of developing these skills: the most essential skills in conflict resolution and peacemaking—and arguably in the building of any community or group. (While Boulding's work mainly preceded the internet age, I argue she'd likely agree with me on this.)

Peace cultures often place strong emphasis on all people being involved in the raising of children. Shared parenting offers parents—and most especially men—the opportunity to engage in the kinds of experiences that emphasize "gentling" and "sensitizing," characteristics that increase openness and vulnerability—two key elements in the practice of creativity that help people to have a fuller development of their skills. This is because they're open to seeing the reality they actually face and feel capable of being creative in their response. In this way, art is an essential element of any peace culture, as the practice of making and engaging with art expands our horizons of the possible and demands that we develop our creativity. Eventually, all of these characteristics embed themselves in people, with this process of change and growth opening space for a more complete personhood to take root within and flourish without. This process is feminist and queer as well, in that it can often decouple violence and conflict from the expression of gender.

Men have their own special role to play in the patriarchal culture of violence. Men can struggle with the role of manhood, and men's roles in modern Western society can be completely restrictive and soul crushing for those men who don't fit in these very tiny boxes. The development of caring and nurturing relationships across the gender spectrum, with adults and children, is a key component of this aforementioned gentling of men. Boulding places all of this in the realm of feminist critiques of power that have been essential in the field of peace studies, particularly in the emphasis on power *with*, or empowerment—as opposed to power *over*. This provides the key to the transformational modeling of the postpatriarchal system in which, according to Boulding, violence has no place.

Most important—almost foundational—to a peace culture is the role of play as well as fun. Play must be fun, and play must be an integral part of a peace culture's life. When play becomes competitive, tense, or violent, it stops being life giving or life affirming. It isn't even play in any recognizable sense anymore. It's important to note that any activity, including scientific research, can involve play. It's really more about the intent to be playful in all one's actions. When celebrations aren't playful, when art constricts relationship with others, when gift giving is exchange, and when performance is competitive, then they all lose the character of replenishing the human spirit and are a poor source of peaceableness.

Children have a unique capacity to contribute to these peace cultures, especially in their relationships with adults, caregivers, and parents. The best parenting is therefore based on shared responsibility—and shared respect—between adults and children. Children can contribute different perspectives and an ability to critique the status quo, while adults can contribute wisdom and a deep knowledge of how the world works. In such a way, the entire family can act as a model for how wider society can include all people with a range of skills toward the common goal of peacemaking.

How is all of this experienced, particularly in family life? I offer these two stories about my experience celebrating the Christmas holiday with two different families: my family of birth and my family of choice. One offers a vision of a family shaped by violence culture, while the other is a family shaped by peace culture. I offer these stories as brief illustrations of the profound impact that our families have on shaping the people we eventually become, both in our beliefs and the lives we choose to lead—thus, our *bodies*.

Brazos River Watershed (Texas), December 25, 1996: Violence Culture

One year, as my birth family was about to begin opening presents, my mother leapt up, declared that my brother and I didn't deserve any gifts that year, due to our distinct lack of duty fulfilled—and deference provided—over the last year, and with the words "Never mind, we're done," canceled Christmas. My brother and I were sent upstairs to consider the gravity of our errors, while my father was tasked with gathering the receipts and cleaning up from breakfast . . . which we had *just* eaten. I closed the door to my room with extreme care so as to not attract my mother's attention (and likely subsequent wrath) during this precarious moment of calm violence—with any expression of emotion through the sound a door makes when it touches the jamb and latches closed.

Emotion was a weapon in my house growing up—both in its expression and its withdrawal. Knowledge was also a weapon, particularly the knowledge of emotional vulnerabilities: If my mother experienced you expressing an emotion, she would catalogue what caused that emotion and would ensure that she knew everything about your experience of it. As a result, when she needed you to experience an emotion, she would simply . . . make it happen, somehow. Reality was whatever my mother said it was. In my family of birth, my mother's word was God's law, my father supported my mother in absolutely everything, my brother was lost in his own world, and I was simply trying to survive—both in the house and out of it.

I sat down on my bed, my heart and mind aswirl. I felt my body turn cold, and everything began to feel distant—until a lightning flash of rage exploded behind my eyes, as a powerfully dull thudding sensation grabbed my attention, and I caught myself pummeling my thigh with an unfortunate level of force. Mind you—I wasn't at all aware that I was doing this. I lay—gently, now: remember, make no noise—on the ground, wrapped my head in my headphone cocoon, turned the dial to ear-piercing, and began to furiously crank out the first of a thousand abdominal crunches. The blood flowed in my mouth as I spent the next hour chewing on my anger and pain (and my cheek) as I tried to come to terms with what had just happened. As my parents never apologized anymore (for *anything*, whatsoever), I was certain that I would be asked, in a few hours, to stand in front of my parents and explain not only my own recent behavior but my mother's response to it. It goes without saying that "recent" meant whatever my parents thought it meant, so it could be last week, last year, or the last decade: You never knew from day to day.

My parents had always been strict, with an extraordinarily clear hierarchy established within the family. I was the youngest, and thus was expected to abide by whatever my parents declared and to heed my brother as the older brother. Voices were raised sometimes, but I can still feel the cold encircle my heart when someone begins to get really, truly *quiet*. We were never given orders, as obedience was simply expected; how rigid the obedience required shifted as quicksilver within the murky depths of my mother's emotional state.

We were expected to regularly perform these rituals of public repentance in which we would explain my parents back to themselves and produce the proper expressions of gratitude if the boon of absolution was granted. Forgiveness was not guaranteed and could not be relied on. My parents were both quite intelligent, and my mother was an especially skilled debater with a gifted sensitivity to human emotion. Anything in your life that they decided was in their purview simply became so: The concept of a secret, or privacy, meant whatever they wanted it to mean. Over time, I was forced to develop keen powers of misdirection simply to have control over my own private thoughts and protection of my own inner feelings. In other words, I became an exceptionally skilled manipulator of the truth as a survival technique, not because I had any desire to lie and pull the wool over my mother's eyes.

I actually deeply admired and agreed with my parents' beliefs—still do, generally. My parents voted for the Democratic Party for their entire lives and were avid supporters of a wide sweep of progressive causes. My mother was a strict pacifist in a 1970s liberal, second-wave feminist, patriotic kind of way: Guns were evil, God is peace, but we saluted the flag and the American experiment in equal measure. My dad spent his twenties in a nuclear submarine beneath the Pacific Ocean in the service of the US Navy and respected the military but understood that I was never going to join. Yet, he only respected my pacifism because it stemmed from religious reasons—I still owed duty to my country, somehow. Duty shaped every decision they ever made as a couple, and they absolutely expected us to uphold our duties to God and to society.

While they were effectively socialists in their dreams for their ideal society, they'd instead insist that they were dreaming of the peaceable kingdom—and so they were. That's the answer I still give when I explain my political beliefs. My parents were quiet supporters of queer rights and most likely would not have rejected me had I ever come out to them; I never had the opportunity to test that theory. My father was the most dependable and reliable person I have ever met. He'd show up, ready to work, for whoever needed his help, for as long as they needed it. My mother was a storyteller gifted with a charming wit and an eloquent tongue: She could captivate an audience, holding it rapt in the palm of her hand. The full warmth of my mother's personality could hit with the power of a thousand suns.

However . . .

Breach a family rule, fail to completely obey, fail to conform: and in a flash! Order must be restored, duty acknowledged, and repentance delivered. My mother would spend *hours* talking *at* me, delineating my failures of filial piety in detail, and I would escape into the world behind my eyes, emerging whenever it was my time to perform the obedience rituals. I still needed my parents to be proud of me . . . and to love me—actually, truly. I embraced their vision of faith and duty and wanted to live a life of purpose and service. It was never good enough, though, because their true desire was my willing obedience—absolute acquiescence, more like—over anything else. By the time I had reached the later years of high school, I just marked time until I could leave the house and finally gain a measure of liberty.

Eight hours after this Christmas ordeal began, my brother and I were summoned downstairs, and we performed the requisite repentance rituals to my mother's satisfaction. (To this day, I haven't a clue what could possibly have set my mother off that morning.) She then permitted us to open presents—with the warning that should we not be suitably appreciative, she might "really cancel Christmas this time." I distinctly remember thinking, "I can't do this anymore, there has to be another way to live," as I pasted a smile on my face and tried to just return to being a kid at Christmas.

This is a family violence culture.

Herring Run, Chesapeake Bay Watershed, December 25, 2014: Peace Culture

My family of choice was awash in that blissful liminality of a late Christmas morning, after presents have all been unwrapped—toys and clothing and food all scattered across the room—and before any other holiday tasks demand attention. My daughter was playing dress-up, wearing a flamenco dancer costume and holding a pair of castanets in her hands. Her smile reached deep into her eyes, emitting a thousand watts of pure joy and fun and childhood wonder as she threw her head back, showering the entire room with *duende*, that inexplicable charisma prized in flamenco. She had learned about flamenco just a few weeks prior and was in thrall to its entrancing rhythms and riotous colors. Her castanets clicked, her mother and I began clapping, and—with a mighty *¡olé!*—she tossed her hands up in a dancer's pose. I simply couldn't resist capturing this moment of sheer, expansive, inexhaustible joy with a click of my camera.

"Daddy! You didn't ask for my permission to take my photo."

She was absolutely correct.

It wasn't anger, frustration, or even mild annoyance she was expressing: Instead, she was matter-of-factly reminding me of my own rules. I immediately acknowledged my fault, apologized, and deleted the photo. She thanked me, plopped down, looked straight at me, tossed her hair back with a flourish, and a smile simply exploded through her being as she declared, "Take my photo now!" I duly obliged and captured what I still consider the best photo I have ever taken of her. It hangs on my office wall, between a window and the computer screen, directly in my line of sight. This photo is now and will forever be the most beautiful thing in my office.

Its beauty emerges not from the absolute magnificence of that moment, captured in pixels and printed on paper, however. What I see in that photo, every time I look at it—like I did, just now—is a child absolutely secure in the knowledge that she is loved exactly as she is, that she will be treated with respect and dignity, that she has a say in the rules that define her existence, that these rules will be applied fairly and justly, and finally that her parents recognize that her body is hers *and hers alone*. This moment was far from unique, though. Her reciprocal respect of my wishes for a photo wasn't forced, demanded, or manipulated: It was immediate and instinctual, in the way that can only emerge from the constant and consistent immersion in a comprehensive way of life. In fact, this moment was truly a moment: Her smile flashed, and the next second she was right back in her state of play, dancing around the room, twirling the rambunctious folds of her dress around her legs as she snapped her plastic castanets with aplomb.

What I see in this photo is a child unbroken, protected from the poison of violence culture, who has no need or desire to escape, who has always known freedom *and* the responsibility that comes with it. I see in her face the child who has grown up to become a fierce advocate of mutuality, solidarity, respect, and justice. I see a child whose childhood was the antithesis of my own. I see a child raised in an environment shaped as much by a rejection of violence culture as an embrace of peace culture. I see a child flourishing, in which she embraces the interdependent, interwoven flow of love in a community, where energy and nourishment is given and received by all in the root networks and vine communities her body resides within, with a trunk shaped by the daily experience of the peace culture of our family.

I see a child who has created a peace culture of her own in the large community of friends she has gathered around her, of multiple genders, who respect and love each other, who apologize to each other, who are willingly vulnerable to each other—in other words, who abide with each other. I see a community of people who all feel entirely at home in our home—most especially those who know violence, injustice, and absolute obedience in their own families. I see a child rooted deeply in her family, standing tall, fiercely committed to making the world a kinder, gentler, more loving place. I see a child who has mended relationships, has offered her ear and her shoulder to any who need them. I see her friends committing to a different way of being. (One of her friends, Morris, drew the map illustrations in this book: a gifted artist and a beautiful soul.)

The kids are all right.

This is a family peace culture.

CHAPTER FOUR

Leaves/Interpretation

How Do We Interpret Divine Revelation?

Friends, deal plainly with yourselves, and let the eternal light search you, and try you, for the good of your souls; for this will deal plainly with you; it will rip you up, lay you open, and make all manifest that lodgeth in you; the secret subtilty of the enemy of your souls, this eternal searcher and tryer will make manifest. . . . Consider one another, and provoke one another to love and to good works.

—Margaret Fell, "An Epistle to Convinced Friends," 1656

Interpreting Light Through the Ecosystem

One of the hallmarks of the early years of the Friends movement in England—especially before the profound societal changes that accompanied the restoration of the Stuart monarchy in 1660—was the sheer exuberance of written material, published by Friends, that described the experience of being moved by the Light of the Divine Presence. In parts terrifying and awesome (in that sense of inspiring awe to a profound degree), this experience was also described as disorienting, discombobulating, disrupting, and disarming—particularly of the interior landscape of the Friend who allowed the "eternal light" to search, try, and deal plainly with their soul, ripping them open and showing the truth of who they really were inside.

This experience is still central to Quaker theology and practice, especially for those who—like the audience for Fell's letter and like me—have been "convinced," one of a profusion of unique terms, as noted in chapter 3, that have emerged from within the Friends community to explain the Quaker experience. (Albeit mainly to Quakers, alas.) While *convincement* could broadly be translated "conversion," *convincement* is more accurate, as it implies that one was persuaded of the truth of the Quaker understanding of the nature of God, of the meaning of the term *worship*, of Quaker ethical principles and practices, and on. The same applies to the experience of opening one's soul to the eternal Light: Convinced Friends (which in 1656 was inherently all Quakers, as the movement was only a few years old by this point) could attest to the truth of Fell's description of this experience, as they themselves had experienced their own powerful "laying open."

This description of the experience of engaging with the Light Within still deeply resonates with Friends, to the extent that the words in the epigraph opening this chapter are a part of Quaker shorthand, another in the list of phrases and concepts foundational to Quaker consciousness that are seen to encapsulate the central truths of Quaker experience and the worldview that results from orienting one's life around them. Fell's words can be an exhortation, an explanation, and a goal to pursue—and even all three at once.

They speak to the disconcerting way that the experience of the Light Within occupies two time frames simultaneously: the specific, individual moment of the discrete experience of encountering the Divine (often in worship, but also potentially at any time during one's daily life) and the effects of that experience that continue to reverberate through the Friend's soul, body, and life for ages afterwards—akin to the moment of the tolling of a bell and the resonating sound waves that continue to ripple out afterward. The eternal Light will search you, rip you up, and lay your soul bare, the experience being powerful enough to transform your inner makeup, so that you eventually become the kind of person whose testimony is so powerful that it can provoke others to act with a love reflective of the Divine love.

Of all of the elements of the Quaker theological ecosystem, *photosynthesis* is the most internal. *Climate* involves the entire landscape of the ecosystem. *Bodies* involves the shape and structures that frame our existence. *Flowers, fruit*, and *seeds* are all designed and intended to engage outward, with the rest of the ecosystem. As the biological process of photosynthesis transforms light within the individual plant into energy that the plant then depends on for life, however, *leaves* relates to the process of the individual interpreting their experience of the Divine Light for the purpose of transforming that experience into the energy needed for a life now defined by the presence of the Light Within.

In this way, while climate and bodies shape the ways we experience the Light—including whether we are even capable of opening ourselves to the potential for such an experience—leaves instead involves the process of transforming the experience. This happens through a process of *interpreting* the meaning of the *experience* for the individual person using theological tools that translate into the language of the Friends tradition. Using the energy that emerges from that process, the bodies of Quakers not only live but also power the processes of creating the flowers, fruit, and seeds that ensure the continued life of both the individual and the creation as a whole. As in any ecosystem, none of these elements is more or less essential than any other, and each depends on the others: As one cannot have photosynthesis without both leaves and an entire body structure, one cannot have flowers if one's body is incapable of transforming the experience of the encounter with the Divine Light Within into the energy necessary to grow them.

The process of interpretation that occurs in the leaves of Quakers—the process of theological photosynthesis—is like every aspect of the Quaker theological ecosystem in that it reflects the nonbinary (yet paradoxically dual) reality of Quaker theology as it speaks to the existence of universals within individuals, and of individuals embodying universals: Every person is capable of experiencing an encounter with the Divine Presence, yet not all people have them; every person must interpret—and make meaning—of their experiences in their own mind, heart, and soul, yet the tools needed for such interpretation are universally available; each person must find the energy needed to live their own life, yet the Divine Light shines everywhere, through everything, constantly and consistently and comprehensively. As I've mentioned previously, the distinct peculiarities of Quaker theology, in particular its dynamic nature and emphasis on personal experience, have led to a perception that it is untranslatable to the rules and structure of Christian systematic theology as broadly understood. This perception, again, is partly driven by Quakers themselves and their sense that their theology is inherently incapable of being comprehended systematically. This is not to claim that Quaker theology is developed in a structural vacuum; rather, Quakers place religious experience as the primary locus for theological reflection and development.

One useful rubric for charting the different elements of theology is the Wesleyan quadrilateral,[1] the idea that theological authority is developed in four

1. This is first referred to by Albert C. Outler in his edited collection of Wesley's written works. Outler notes the existence of the other sources yet stresses that they must all be read through the primary lens of Scripture. By treating the sources as equal partners and by allowing experience to take priority over the other sources, I am adapting the concept of the quadrilateral to my own theological purposes. Albert C. Outler, ed., *John Wesley* (Oxford University Press, 1964).

main ways: Scripture (the Christian Bible), tradition (the doctrinal statements of ecclesial structures, the creeds of the ecumenical councils, and theological schools built on the thought of certain theologians), reason (the application of logic and human reasoning), and experience (the religious experience of both individual humans and the gathered community of individuals sharing a common religious experience). Protestant Christian tradition has placed the greatest emphasis on Scripture, while the Roman Catholic and Orthodox traditions have emphasized Scripture and tradition as dialogue partners. While one can argue that every Christian tradition uses all four elements in some fashion in the development of its theology, it is not common to place the greatest priority on experience, with the argument that the inherently fragmentary and dynamic nature of experience makes it an unreliable foundation on which to say anything certain and universal about God. By thus viewing the other theological sources through the lens of religious experience, however, Quakerism dismisses the assumption that theology can ever be certain and universal and instead insists that it must be contextual, dynamic, nonuniversal, and developed through the dialogic interplay between the diverse interpretations of the religious experience of both individuals and the community.

Quaker theology is thus inherently interdisciplinary, as Quakers draw from multiple sources in an effort to develop language to comprehend their experience of the Divine. These multiple sources are placed alongside each other, with varying levels of authority granted to each source, depending on both the importance and the value each individual Quaker places on the available sources, all interpreted through the communal discernment of experience within each Quaker community. Thus, the construction of theology will bring all potential aspects of analysis to bear on an experience: the history of how such experiences have been interpreted within Quakerism generally, correspondence with scriptural passages (generally Judeo-Christian Scriptures, yet with increasing regularity Scriptures from other faith traditions), alignment with the written narratives and stories of respected Quakers throughout Quaker history, sociological analysis of how other Quakers interpret and apply similar experiences, and even examination of the experience in light of sociopolitical realities.

As Quaker theology is itself interdisciplinary, the act of interpreting the experience of the Divine Light is also an inherently interdisciplinary exercise and can present a case study for demonstrating this woven fabric of Quaker interpretation. I root my exploration in the writings of one specific community of Liberal Quakers: those who have given the Swarthmore Lecture to the annual meeting of Britain Yearly Meeting of the Religious Society of Friends, an annual lecture addressing an issue or subject relating to the testimony and work of Quakers, both British Quakers specifically and the global community of Liberal Quakers.

I've written about this community before, in my doctoral dissertation.[2] I chose this community of writers because it presented such a rich variety of reflections on the theological and ethical implications of living Quakerly, which were all also—in the astonishingly vast forest that covers the Christian theological watershed—rooted in the same tiny grove of trees. In other words, I was curious to see what bountiful theological variety would exist within this group of (mainly) British Quakers in the twentieth century (mainly, again), then determine whether this variety could be interpreted such that a framework for constructing Liberal Quaker theology could be envisioned. The journey I began with this group of thinkers fifteen years ago has led me here, with the book you are currently reading. Let's return to the first *leafing* of this idea, a chapter from my dissertation—adapted and updated, of course.

Leaves in the Wesleyan Quadrilateral

Experience: Continuing Revelation

Quakerism has a construct known as "continuing revelation," which refers to the belief that God is continuing to reveal aspects of God and God's truth to humanity through human interactions with God. Continuing revelation is intimately connected with the Liberal Quaker construct of progressive revelation, which argues that with each successive revelation, God is revealing more about God, lending (potentially) greater weight to the wisdom gained from latter revelations than from previous ones. Progressive revelation also demands that Quakers be open to the wisdom and perspective of other religious and secular traditions, as God might be revealed in a significant fashion through any pathway. This dynamic relationship to revelation ensures that Quaker theology is in a constant state of flux, with an openness to adaptation. This

2. Daniel (Christy) Randazzo, "The Interdependent Light: A Quaker Theology of Reconciliation" (PhD diss., University of Birmingham, 2018).

adaptability involves three main elements of continuing revelation: God's revelation to humanity, the processes of theological change, and an openness to "sources of truth" outside the Christian tradition. I conclude the section with Quaker critiques of how continuing revelation has been applied in Quaker thought and critique of the concept itself.

God's Revelation

Openness to God's continual revelation to humanity marks all of Quaker theological inquiry. Of course, this concept isn't exclusive to Quakers but is instead rooted in the flush of innovative theological reflection created by the opportunity to read and interpret the Bible for oneself that came about due to the Reformation. Quakers are thus engaging in what they view as a valid theological enterprise with deep roots in the Christian tradition. As such, Quakers argue that this theological approach is as valid as other theological perspectives that prioritize the Bible as the primary measure for assessing the validity of a new theological idea (*Scripture*) and that find primary value in the carefully crafted theological doctrines of previous generations in that specific ecclesial community (*tradition*). Quakers value this openness to newness, seeing it as a courageous and creative enterprise that doesn't fear the possibility of radical change and growth, especially as they view this perspective as rooted in God's good will for humanity.

Quakers acknowledge that this is a minority perspective. Yet, they value the possibilities for radical, even rebellious change in accepted theological paradigms that this open perspective provides. They feel that this is a prophetic act, something sorely needed in theology. They also acknowledge that this perspective has a flaw that, if left unchecked, could ultimately hamper the entire enterprise. The Quaker emphasis on always seeking the new, rooted in the interplay between individual experience and corporate discernment of that experience, could lead to a failure to come to any unity on essential elements of the new teaching that all Quakers will actually accept as binding. This is a particular concern when dealing with the Quaker openness to other sources of truth. While this openness might allow for deep and meaningful engagement with the ways in which God is interacting with other religious communities, it might also challenge the ability for Quakers to find any meaningfully—and distinctly—*Quaker* engagement with the Divine that would serve to draw the community of Quakers together. The new sources of truth could in fact prove to be as meaningful as the old sources, yet could wind up severing the connections between Quakers.

Quakers hold that God is continuously revealing Godself to humanity. This is a progressive revelation, in that the revelations of today have resonance for the contemporary moment and might dispute or advance previous revelations; thus, these revelations are said to be progressive in that they demonstrate a progressive movement toward a continuously more intimate and complete revelation of God. Russell Brain suggests that this concept has its roots in the Reformation, specifically in the excitement that was spawned by the acceptance of a right to private judgment on the interpretation of the Bible as opposed to the communal authority of the Roman Catholic curia—the administrative institutions of the Vatican and the central authoritative body of the Roman church. This movement would allow humans the freedom to hear God more completely without the potentially restrictive mediation of the curia. Brain argues that the intense power of this realization sobered the leaders of the Reformation in Geneva, especially as it related to the rapid development of religious movements that sought to view the Bible through the lens of metaphor. This frightened Protestants away from any recognition of progressive revelation that was not read as a further interpretation of the Bible, limiting, Brain suggests, the ability for Protestant theology to adapt to any situation or theory that did not have a biblical parallel.[3]

This willingness to be open to new revelations, especially those that relate to modern circumstances that might not have obvious parallels in the biblical text, is presented as a strength of the Quaker approach. Maurice Creasey suggests that the Quaker emphasis on the direct experience of God ensures that Quakers do not fear any new theological idea. If an idea is tested through Quaker worship and discipleship, alongside past experience—in the form of reason, tradition, and Scripture—and is found to be true, Quakers can then incorporate that idea into their theological structures of belief. However, if the idea is found wanting, Creasey argues, it is either tested further in order to glean some form of wisdom from it or it is discarded. Creasey affirms that this entire process is performed by Quakers as they explore the boundaries of the Quaker understanding of revelation as the experience of God within both the individual and the community.[4]

---

3. W. Russell Brain, *Man, Society, and Religion* (Swarthmore, 1944), 67.

4. Maurice A. Creasey, *Bearing, or Friends and the New Reformation* (Friends Home Service, 1969), 28.

Quakers acknowledge that they tend to emphasize the potentially wild influence that new revelation might have on their willingness to adhere to doctrine. In this vein, Gerald Priestland notes an epistle from Yorkshire in 1919 that stated that the Holy Spirit had not ceased to inspire, despite the settling of the New Testament canon.[5] He argues, however, that even an examination of the presentation of God in the Bible demonstrates that God is continually revealing new truths and offering new perspectives. As Priestland states, the picture of God presented in Genesis is significantly different from that offered by Jeremiah, for example, and both are very different from the perspective that the Christian Gospels offer on God.[6] However, this is not to claim that this process opens Quakers to simply following theological trends. Priestland suggests that the Quaker emphasis on silence and expectant waiting in worship might actually be an unintended barrier against what he terms "radical religious ideas" that could stem from an emphasis on progressive revelation.[7]

Processes of Change

Quakers are a minority religious group, in that they are both demographically small and have few parallels with other religious traditions. Yet, they are ambivalent about that status as well as the role that such status plays in their approach to theological change. Some Friends willingly claim minority status and in turn accept what such a status often entails: a dynamic openness to theological change, with an attendant willingness to abandon (or at least adapt) theological beliefs and the structures that are built on them.

Barratt Brown is representative of the perspective embracing minority status. He provides a framework for understanding Quakerism as a minority, especially in relation to processes of theological change. Brown suggests that minorities—including religious minorities (such as Quakers, of course)—develop a rebellious temperament stemming from religious convictions that are prophetic, pushing against the established truth of the majority tradition. Brown argues that this rebellious approach to religious belief and practice

5. Gerald Priestland, *Reasonable Uncertainty: A Quaker Approach to Doctrine* (Quaker Books, 1982), 15.

6. Priestland, *Reasonable Uncertainty*, 38.

7. Priestland, *Reasonable Uncertainty*, 14.

is prophetic, due to the minority's willingness to see alternatives to current orthodoxy as well as its willingness to find value in the "fresh upspringings of life" that emerge from unexpected areas and people.[8] Brown acknowledges that oftentimes these new revelations are difficult to understand and incorporate into current worldviews, even for many in the minority group. Brown insists that these new revelations are often from God, demanding our engagement. They can provide liberation from obsolete perspectives and methods and shed new illumination on perspectives that still have value.

John Hughes makes a similar argument about the necessity of revising theological structures in the face of new revelation. Hughes states that it would be tantamount to intellectual dishonesty to hold tight to old and obsolete doctrine in the face of new information and perspective. Doing so would cause Quakerism to lose out on vital opportunities to engage in a complete and prophetic way to new circumstances. Admittedly, however, such an openness to the new can present potential challenges. One example is the need to be cautious about turning a respect for the potential present in the flush of vitality that can accompany new revelation into a dependence on this enthusiastic energy: Groups must instead steer a course between enthusiasm and a "contented and timid" insistence on adhering to tested and potentially obsolete methods.[9] Quakers might be in greater danger of not being able to come to any unity on essentials, thus risking losing out on the benefits that minority status offers for a group with such a significant emphasis on prophetic action.

Openness to Truth

A common thread among Quakers, even of decidedly Christian leanings, is the acknowledgment that while unity would be of great benefit, much can still be gained through dialogue with other traditions, along with an openness to their potential for truth. Representative of an explicitly Christian Quaker perspective, Harry Silcock suggests that Quakers can find much of value in non-Christian religions, especially in light of (and in repentance for) the spread of Christianity under the banner of converting "the heathen in

8. A. Barratt Brown, *Democratic Leadership* (Allen & Unwin, 1938), 18.

9. John A. Hughes, *The Light of Christ in a Pagan World* (Allen & Unwin, 1940), 52.

his blindness."[10] Edgar Dunstan takes this one step further by invoking the language of duty, arguing that Quakers have a responsibility to be open to "new light from whatever source it comes." He claims that only this openness will fully equip Quakers to aid those who are searching for God and who have given up hope of finding answers within the Christian community.[11] This focus on seeking is rooted within the Quaker heritage, Dunstan argues, for this is the ministry that George Fox and the early Friends devoted their lives to.

A common critique of this approach acknowledges the value of openness while also insisting on openness being channeled toward the ultimate goal of greater connection with God. Having a ministry to seekers does not grant Quakers leave to be on a continuous search simply for the sake of the hunt, however. Every spiritual seeker must have the goal of eventually finding God, or else they are seekers in search of the wrong thing. "New light" is therefore a tool for aiding in the search of God and not the point of the search itself. The search must therefore stem from a deep respect for the other tradition from which may come new light.[12] Being open to other sources of truth requires a recognition that as God is present in every person; other traditions may also be speaking a truth about the revelation and truth of God. It also requires that Quakers respect that other faith traditions have unique ways of speaking about the experience of God, which may only be fully understood in the context of that tradition.

Continuing Revelation and Tradition

Continuing revelation as an overarching concept is not without critics, however, especially from more explicitly Christocentric expressions of Quakerism. Paul Anderson, a biblical scholar from the Evangelical Quaker tradition,

10. Harry T. Silcock, *Christ and the World's Unrest* (Swarthmore, 1927), 19. Similarly, Margaret Harvey suggests that this openness to the truth from other traditions is the logical outgrowth of the idea of continuing revelation: Once a group is open to new revelation coming from any of its members, even revelation with the potential to dramatically change the theological perspective of the group, it is a logical next step to find new revelation within the wisdom of other traditions. Harvey, *The Law of Liberty* (Allen & Unwin, 1942), 41.

11. Edgar G. Dunstan, *Quakers and the Religious Quest* (Allen & Unwin, 1956), 11. This phrase was placed into the Book of Discipline in 1931 and has been maintained in subsequent editions as well as the current edition of Faith and Practice. Yearly Meeting of the Religious Society of Friends (Quakers) in Britain, *Quaker Faith and Practice* (Britain Yearly Meeting, 1994).

12. Doncaster, *God in Every Man*, 52.

typifies the critiques from that tradition in his concerns that Quakers privilege immediate revelation over Scripture and the body of Quaker revelation (tradition) gathered over centuries.[13] In his view, Quakers run the risk of using the reality of divine guidance as an excuse for privileging immediate revelation, thus reflexively always assuming—mistakenly—that older revelation loses value as soon as newer revelation emerges.[14] He argues that Quakers must instead be more cautious in their approach to incorporating continuing revelation and its attendant theological openness, ensuring that they develop strong means of testing leadings and subjecting them to strict scrutiny within the communal structure of the meeting. Anderson is thus arguing for a more cautious approach toward accepting immediate revelations as stemming from the movement of the Spirit.[15] This approach insists on a greater level of testing newer revelation against older revelation that has been demonstrated to have significant value, including both the Bible and the theological tradition.

Richenda Scott makes a similar argument to Anderson, in terms of the necessity of using tradition to test the validity of leadings and of discerning whether they are continuing revelation. Scott insists that tradition is a vital tool for Quakers to discern ethical standards of conduct to formulate theology.[16] Scott likens tradition to a vessel in which the history of a people is carried forward to the present. This vessel carries all of the lessons learned from the mistakes and successes of the past and the stories and heritage of the community. As such, tradition cannot simply be dismissed as useless or as something new revelation has evolved beyond. Scott acknowledges that tradition often involves viewpoints from the past that truly are outdated and unhelpful, and that new revelation might be showing ways to advance beyond such tradition. However, Scott insists that tradition that is alive and engaged with current revelation can serve as an effective standard against which to measure new revelation, in a dynamic conversation.[17]

---

13. Paul Anderson, "Continuing Revelation—Gospel or Heresy?," in *Good and Evil: Quaker Perspectives*, ed. Jackie Leach Scully and Pink Dandelion (Ashgate, 2007), 26.

14. Anderson, "Continuing Revelation," 27.

15. Anderson, "Continuing Revelation," 28.

16. Richenda C. Scott, *Tradition and Experience* (Allen & Unwin, 1964), 5.

17. Scott, *Tradition and Experience*, 5.

Scripture: The Bible and Continuing Revelation

Quakers have a complicated relationship with the Bible. One significant complicating factor is the Quaker stance toward continuing revelation. The challenge of this concept, in terms of the Bible, is that it can open *all* previous revelation (including both the Bible and previous theological reflection) up to examination and possible reassessment in light of the most recent revelation. Admittedly, those who view the Bible as a static document argue that while, yes, it is not open for change in terms of the specific words of the text themselves, the document is alive in terms of how it is interpreted by new generations of people. This reinterpretation must wrestle with aspects of the text that succeeding generations may not in fact find applicable to their specific context. Christians have discovered a variety of ways of approaching this challenge without making the radical choice to dismiss the text in its entirety. Quakers do the same, viewing the Bible in any of five separate ways: as an authority, as a guide, as one Scripture among many others of equal status and importance, with ambivalence, and finally with hostility.[18] None of these readings grants the Bible the same level of authoritative status granted the text in most other Protestant Christian denominations, where the Bible is seen as the final arbiter in constructing modes of meaning, framing belief, and commanding behavioral changes—all based solely on the authority of the text itself.

By contrast, if the Bible is viewed as authoritative in any fashion for Quakers, it is as an area of contact with God, in which God can speak through the individual's experience of the document and thus gain authority from the experience itself. In general, Quakers seek to answer the following questions when deciding how to approach the text: How do we interpret the Bible? Will these interpretations make demands on Quaker behavior? Finally, to what extent will the Bible influence Quaker belief? Quakers approach these questions from two main perspectives: the role of continuing revelation in interpretation, and Quaker biblical hermeneutics. The roots of this approach to the Bible can be seen in the proceedings of the Manchester Conference, to which we now turn.

---

18. Pink Dandelion, *A Sociological Analysis of the Theology of the Quakers: The Silent Revolution* (Edwin Mellen, 1996), 136.

Historical Background: The Manchester Conference

In 1892, in response to growing tensions between the evangelical wing of British Quakerism and those inspired by the liberal religious movement of the late nineteenth century—and in good Quaker fashion—British Quakers formed a committee to assess the situation. In 1895, the committee held a conference in Manchester, England, to discuss the current state of Quakerism—in the Atlantic world alone, unfortunately.[19] Representatives from meetings across Britain were invited to participate along with several American Quaker scholars.[20] This was the first time that many of the new ideas of liberal theology that had been bubbling under the surface were given a public platform.[21]The conference also gave Quakers interested in these new ideas the opportunity to meet and begin to develop a common vision for a new Quakerism.[22] One of the main points of division at the conference fell along the question of the main sources of theological authority.

Early in the conference, Frederick Sessions outlined what he envisioned to be the Quaker sources of theology: the witness of the Scriptures, which he understood to be the Bible; the application of reason to the Scriptures; and finally, the experience of the "good fruits" that the Scriptures had brought forth in the ministries of Quakers.[23] Sessions presented what he understood to be a broadly accepted recognition of the significant role that the Bible played in British Quaker religious life. Joseph Bevan Braithwaite, a noted Evangelical Quaker, echoed Sessions's sense of the vital place of the Bible to Quakerism, stating that the Bible was at the root of all religious truth for Quakers.[24] This "Truth" could withstand any modern attempts to examine its historicity and

19. Martin Davie, *British Quaker Theology Since 1895* (Edwin Mellen, 1997), 67.

20. Paul Lacey, *The Unequal World We Inhabit: Quaker Response to Terrorism and Fundamentalism* (Quaker Books, 2010), 35.

21. Margaret Heathfield, *Being Together: Our Corporate Life in the Religious Society of Friends* (Quaker Home Service, 1994), 64.

22. John W. Graham, *The Quaker Ministry* (Swarthmore, 1925), 70.

23. London Yearly Meeting, *Report of the Proceedings of the Conference of Members of the Society of Friends, Held, by Direction of the Yearly Meeting, in Manchester from the Eleventh to the Fifteenth of Eleventh Month, 1895*, 3rd ed. (Headley Brothers, 1896), 36.

24. London Yearly Meeting, *Report*, 211.

accuracy, Braithwaite argued, in direct response to the arguments of younger Quakers. Braithwaite argued that the Old and New Testaments balanced each other in a harmonious tension and that the Bible could still be viewed in modern times as it had been viewed in ancient times: as the full and complete expression of Divine revelation to humanity.[25]

The prevalent view toward the historicity and truth of the Bible among the respondents, however, was deeply contextual, reflecting the influence of the new critical methods of biblical interpretation that had begun to develop earlier in the century, particularly within the new (at that time) liberal expressions emerging within Christianity around the turn of the twentieth century. Silvanus Thompson and Thomas Hodgkin delivered strong addresses expressing a deep skepticism toward using the Bible as the primary source of religious truth for Quakers. Reflecting the new thinking of liberal theology, Thompson questioned the reliability of the writings of the Christian Bible, wondering whether—between the complexity of their composition and the political maneuvering involved in choosing which books to include in the canon—they could accurately be said to offer the "pure Gospel" of Jesus Christ.[26] The early ecumenical councils piled on, dismissing the necessity for historical accuracy while insisting on the importance of certain beliefs—beliefs powerful church leaders held dear and thus promoted over other, potentially more "accurate" beliefs. Thus, Thompson argued, the councils fashioned a document that was inherently flawed.[27] When coupled with the traditional Quaker aversion to concrete and immutable theological statements/creeds/creedal formulae, Thompson argued that Quakers needed to not be bound by the theological concerns of people from centuries ago and should instead reject all the ecumenical creeds.[28]

Hodgkin continued this critique of the Bible by pointing to the limitations of the text as established by the scientific methods of interpretation.[29] These limitations led Hodgkin to claim that while the Bible might contain

25. London Yearly Meeting, *Report*, 214.

26. London Yearly Meeting, *Report*, 231.

27. London Yearly Meeting, *Report*, 233.

28. London Yearly Meeting, *Report*, 239.

29. London Yearly Meeting, *Report*, 208.

any number of spiritual truths, the contemporary methods of interpretation had demonstrated to "intelligent Christians" that the writers of the Bible were in a state of "childish ignorance" as to the scientific truths of the universe.[30]

The context of Hodgkin's words lies in an extended critique of applying biblical perspectives on the nature of creation and the historical accuracy of the texts; the subtext, as Martin Davie notes, was that Christian faith needed to develop beyond its childish phase toward a complete integration of the teachings of science and the ethical teachings of Jesus.[31] Frederick Thompson (no relation to Silvanus, but the Quaker world has never been large), meanwhile, expressed this in the more diplomatic language of progress.[32] Thompson viewed progress from the perspective of achieving the improvement of character, promoting equal opportunity for all, and the encouragement of free inquiry in all religious and moral directions through the removal of any obstacles in the "path of progress." Presumably, this would include any religious beliefs that clung to what Thompson might consider outmoded, nonscientific visions of truth.

This optimism in the possibility of human spiritual and ethical growth is reflective of the theological tradition as a whole and is still a strong thread of Quaker theology. Thompson's call for Quakers to "welcome any fresh light which comes to us," even if that new information should destroy previously strongly held convictions, is not only reminiscent of the scientific method but is also reflected in the Quaker emphasis on the continuing revelation of God. I should note, however, that this was not an entirely new thread in Quakerism, as the concept of continuing revelation was a core idea of Elias Hicks, an early nineteenth-century American Quaker, and the Hicksite movement of Quakerism that used his name. Thompson's application of continuing revelation to scientific discoveries is reflective of liberal theology, however, and was a new expression of this idea.

The seeds sown in the Manchester Conference regarding a uniquely Quaker approach to the Bible—recognizing the value of the Christian heritage of Quakerism while integrating the concept of progressive revelation—continue to bear fruit in Quaker perspectives on the Bible. Again, I must

30. London Yearly Meeting, *Report*, 208.

31. Davie, *British Quaker Theology Since 1895*, 80.

32. London Yearly Meeting, *Report*, 146.

note that, despite this skepticism, Quakers generally still make a point of recognizing the value the early Quakers placed in the Bible (tradition) and thus still acknowledge that the Bible is an essential aspect of the Quaker heritage.[33]

The Role of Continuing Revelation in Quaker Biblical Interpretation

From a Quaker perspective, it can be argued that the closing of the canon, and the difference between the context of the authors of the biblical text and the present context, makes the Bible a static revelation. This static nature challenges a religious expression that insists on dynamic revelation.[34] Herbert Wood argues that the complex history of the Bible's composition, including the significant differences between an oral-history view of historical accuracy and a scientific, modern view of historical accuracy, preclude the development of any vibrant and robust Christian theology based on biblical infallibility.[35] These issues make the case for biblical inerrancy an impossible one for Quakers, especially if inerrancy means without any error in any sense whatsoever. This also troubles any argument for granting the Bible a sense of authority based solely on the text itself.[36] Quaker writers have offered reasons as to why this might be the case, especially for members of a tradition with a strong aversion to any claims of authority, especially with issues of theology and interpretation. They include literary, experiential, and historical-critical readings.

Edward Grubb approaches the issue from the perspective of literature, suggesting that the construct of biblical infallibility rests on the argument that human words have the ability to express the complete experience of the biblical revelation, which itself rests on the ability of human words to express the fullness of divine infallibility. Grubb dismisses this idea as fit only for those who have failed to "properly consider what language is." For Grubb, the only way to approach the Bible is through the language of metaphor, poetry, and

---

33. For example, Doncaster argued that the Bible has always been an essential element in Quaker belief and as such is the one authoritative text for assessing the Quaker experience of God (*God in Every Man*, 5).

34. Charles F. Carter, *On Having a Sense of All Conditions* (Swarthmore, 1971), 22.

35. Herbert G. Wood, *Quakerism and the Future of the Church* (Swarthmore, 1920), 27.

36. Edward Grubb, *Authority and the Light Within* (James Clarke, 1909), 31.

lived experience, with an appreciation for the beauty and power of the words themselves and the truth of the experience behind them.

Charles Carter insists on assessing the authority that experiential and contextual readings grant the Bible. He first dismisses any interpretive construction that treats the biblical text as prescriptive, limiting behavior and structuring the shape of acceptable belief.[37] Carter argues that not only is this ultimately a complex act of eisegesis (reading our own perspectives and interpretations into the text), but it's risky and creates opportunities for people to gain innumerable damaging interpretations from the text, that—as this is the *Bible*, after all—will then carry the weight of divine authority. Instead, he argues that Quakers should view the Bible as a reflection of God and that we can understand what the text asks us to do and to believe only by experiencing God in the text, both individually and corporately. Thus, the text has authority for Quakers only as Quakers experience God in the text itself.

Finally, Gerald Priestland argues—again, in good liberal fashion—for a historical-critical approach to the text, in which Quakers view the Bible from the perspective of discerning its original context: As the original circumstances of the composition of a text govern the primary meaning of the text for the original audience, they also color the modern understanding of the original intent of a text.[38] When the original intent can be identified as closely as possible, Priestland suggests, the next step is to determine how to apply that meaning in the current context, remaining aware of differences in language and worldviews between the biblical context and today.[39]

Recognition of past value does not always translate into present value for Quakers.[40] This is represented in a variety of perspectives, from the text having inherent value to its having no more value than any other sacred text. Margaret Harvey, for example, represents the inherent-value end of the spectrum, viewing the Bible as a resource of highly relatable, universal lessons

---

37. Carter, *On Having a Sense of All Conditions*, 22.

38. Priestland, *Reasonable Uncertainty*, 51. This reflects John Ormerod Greenwood's earlier assertion that the context of the biblical documents is entirely alien from any contemporary, Western context, more than a reading of the words themselves might imply. Greenwood, *Signs of Life: Art and Religious Experience* (Friends Home Service Committee, 1978), 4.

39. Priestland, *Reasonable Uncertainty*, 51.

40. Dandelion, *Sociological Analysis*, 137.

and stories within which humans can always experience commonality and answers.[41] Harvey uses this literary perspective to call Quakers to continually view the text through two simultaneous and equally important lenses: the text of the Bible itself and the present context. Harvey thus places value on the text *as* text. George Gorman, however, suggests that the Bible maintains an authority only due to the gathered experience of thousands of years of human interaction with the text, and the experiential power of the biblical narratives.[42] This authority might be inherent within the text due to the demonstrated power of the experience of God, Gorman implies, yet this authority, for Quakers, is not implicit in the text *as text itself*.[43] Janet Scott represents the most insistently skeptical perspective on the value of the text, stating unequivocally that the Bible should not be taken as literally true or authoritatively binding in any fashion on Quakers.[44]

In this, as in many aspects of Quaker theology, diversity is paramount, and even potentially overwhelming! This is actually the state of biblical interpretation within Liberal Quakerism: either chaotic cacophony or beautiful harmony, depending on each Quaker's own tolerance for diversity and disagreement. Quakers have sought to bridge these divisions, however, offering potential avenues of dialogue and areas of commonality. Christopher Holdsworth represents a helpful approach to acknowledging the importance of progressive revelation while granting the text its own inherent value. Holdsworth stresses the importance of locating the original meaning of the text, while also suggesting that this is only a step toward the ultimate goal of having Quakers immerse themselves in the text *as text*, allowing themselves to locate places of meaning within the narrative itself.[45]

This is an imaginative endeavor that requires that the person engage with the text slowly and in a complete way, acknowledging any aspects that are

41. Harvey, *Law of Liberty*, 33.

42. George H. Gorman, *The Amazing Fact of Quaker Worship* (Friends Home Service Committee, 1973), 61.

43. Gorman, *Amazing Fact of Quaker Worship*, 61.

44. Scott, *What Canst Thou Say?*, 67.

45. Christopher Holdsworth, *Steps in a Large Room: A Quaker Explores the Monastic Tradition* (Quaker Home Service, 1985), 33.

confusing or challenging without dismissing them. Holdsworth emphasizes the necessity of viewing the text through the lens of metaphor and poetry, allowing the conventions of those literary forms to structure one's response to the text itself.[46] This form of biblical interpretation is, for Holdsworth, authoritative both due to its roots in the practice of *lectio divina* and due to its ability to have the text serve as a space to experience God in one's present and individual context.[47] As this model brings all of the concerns of the other approaches in conversation, I suggest that this model is the most holistically Quaker approach to the biblical text.

Apocalyptic Hermeneutics: The Bible as Comedy

OK, let's play with Holdsworth's idea. The Bible is the story, a narrative, of God's relationship with God's people and of the people's relationship with each other, as understood through the prism of their creaturehood as part of God's good created order. When the Bible is understood as a metanarrative of God's care and love for God's people, however, and when viewed through that classical ancient Greek binary of comedy/tragedy, it becomes glaringly obvious that the next logical step is to conclude that as narrative, the Bible must definitely be understood as a divine comedy. To be certain, tragic elements abound in the narrative, as do elements of romance and fairy/hero tale. The slavery in Egypt, the exile, the individual sufferings imposed on so many of the characters in Israel's story, even and especially up to the death of God in Christ—all are terrible, tragic events. Yet, the irony of Joseph welcoming his brothers into his home after they had exiled Joseph from theirs, the gift of the rainbow after the flood, the spectacular chaos of the languages at Pentecost, and again, the glorious victory of the resurrection are all significant events in the life of God's people and are most decidedly comic.

The Bible begins with God inaugurating the created order for seemingly no other reason than because God can. By the end of Revelation 20, time is ended: Satan and all of his forces have been defeated, while everyone (and everything) has already been judged. God could have stopped there and held another Sabbath, having completed an entire circle of creation and destruction. Following the trajectory of the story through to its conclusion, however, in the

46. Holdsworth, *Steps in a Large Room*, 43.

47. Holdsworth, *Steps in a Large Room*, 34.

Christian Bible God again raises the new Jerusalem for seemingly no other reason than to give God's creation a place to be joyous and to spend their time in worship. The end of the Hebrew Bible follows a similar pattern. It places 1–2 Chronicles as the final book, with the final passage relating that Cyrus, the pagan emperor who had just broken the haughtiness and arrogance of Babylon—the ruler of a massive empire—was somehow inspired by God to turn his attention to tiny Israel, and to thus specifically allow the people to return and to rebuild the temple. Yippee! After all that has happened, Israel is rescued by God in the face of the Persians, and their land and temple are returned to them—thus completing the comedic circle. The tragedy was not the dominant metanarrative; it was proven to be simply an element of the narrative.

The separation of narrative into such defined categories as comedy and tragedy is misleading if it leads us to see them as two separate aspects of human experience. The classic definition of comedy and tragedy appears to hinge on their conclusions: So as in tragedy all ends in tears and division, in comedy it ends in laughter and celebration. From that perspective, again, the Bible must be considered a comedy. The Bible, in its conclusion, is closer to *Twelfth Night* than to *Hamlet*. Even in the flow of its narrative, the Bible is no closer to tragedy.

The distinction lies in the fact that, as mentioned above, while tragedy is a significant element in the biblical narrative, it does not define the narrative entirely. Comedy and tragedy are absolutely related to each other and are each present in the other: Comedy has elements of tragedy, and vice versa. Rosencrantz and Guildenstern are fools and add a wonderful element of hilarity in the midst of Hamlet's gloom. The obverse can be seen in *Twelfth Night*. The story begins with a shipwreck and continues with Viola being forced to suffer the pain of deception. All comedy must possess elements of tragedy or else the irony and puncturing of pride so integral to comedy would lose its power and pathos.

One prime example in modern cinema is the movie *You've Got Mail*. Meg Ryan plays a woman who owns a small children's bookshop that is under threat from a mega-chain bookstore conglomerate that has just opened down the street. Tom Hanks plays the son of the conglomerate's CEO and owner—who is hilariously beleaguered due to his father's tendency to collect new wives, thus bestowing new stepmothers. Hanks is managing the construction of the bookstore branch threatening to put Ryan out of business. Near the beginning of the movie, the inevitable confrontation between Ryan and Hanks ensues. Ryan scores emotional points on Hanks yet cannot defeat Hanks and his bookstore: Her store closes and ends Ryan's dreams, breaking her heart. However, due to the standard romantic plot devices, Hanks winds up falling in love with Ryan. After much confusion, awkwardness, repentance, and eventual acceptance, the pair fall in love and end up together by the end of the movie. Yet, even though they are both lucky in love, the bookshop is still closed, Ryan's dreams are still dashed, and Hanks is still left with the pain of having been the person responsible for it all.

The same can be seen in Job. Job becomes the sport of Satan, and he loses everything, with the sole exception of his long-suffering wife. He even realizes that he has lost his supposed friends. After much suffering (and a terror-inspiring theophany), Job's fortunes are restored, even double what they were previously. Yet, the critical point to remember is that those children are not the same as before, and neither are the cattle and all of the other people tied to Job's land and house. His time of suffering is not taken away or forgotten. The comedy of Job does not deny suffering—in fact, it makes the suffering an integral aspect of the story. God never actually answers why he elected to provoke Job to such an extraordinary degree. Yet, in the end, Job gains a new perspective on his suffering and permits himself to peer through the fog of his suffering to a horizon where he is still alive and still able to appreciate joy. The Bible is a narrative of God's people, in which God is asking us to take a different perspective on life—the long view, if you will. While suffering and intense tragedy are an aspect of our lives, in the end, God has us in God's hands, and we will be restored, joyfully, to a new Jerusalem.

Tradition: Creeds and Quaker Belief

Quakers have a well-developed aversion to creeds, or the fixing of belief in any doctrinal statement. This stems from a positive sense of the overwhelming, indescribable experience of God that many Quakers attest to in their lives and in worship, and a sense of the inability of any theoretical formulation to encapsulate the variety, truth, and meaning of Quaker experiences of God.[48] Quakers state that affirming a doctrinal faith statement would affix

48. Dandelion, *Sociological Analysis*, 94.

as unchangeable an aspect of God's revelation, which runs completely counter to the Quaker experience of a God who is constantly adapting to new circumstances.[49] For Quakers, affirming any specific faith statement would establish a boundary around what is an acceptable expression of Quaker belief, even if the boundaries were written in the most vague and ambiguous way possible.

Quakers' opposition to creeds stems in part from continuing revelation: any defined formulation of belief that appears to limit the potential for continuing revelation must therefore be at least interrogated, if not rejected. Creeds not only crystallize belief, leading to an ossification of faith, but are also not true to Quakers' dynamic experiences of the Divine. Rejecting creeds therefore means that Quakers can remain open to what they see as a more complete expression of God's desire for humanity, which includes an appreciation for the vicissitudes and variety of a life of faith. This does not allow for rigid dogmatism, or at least what Quakers would view as such. While this is a main tenet of Quaker theology, there is a spectrum of ways in which Quakers approach this. These include exploring the role of creeds in the development of faith and belief, examining the role of creeds in the experience of faith, and being ever vigilant of the danger that anticreedalism presents for Quaker theological unity.

The Development of Faith and Belief

A common thread for many Quakers is the insistence that a strong focus on developing and then ascribing to a specific creedal formulation places undue emphasis on correct belief. Hugh Doncaster is representative of this perspective. He emphasizes the value of developing an awareness of the promptings of the Spirit, especially those that lead us to act in a loving and truthful manner toward others.[50] Any examination of our experiences should seek to develop a greater understanding of how experience works, what lessons can be learned from it, and how people can use such lessons to understand and interpret the experience of God in their own lives.[51] That effort fails, however, when the experience is examined through the lens of dogmatism, for such a lens crystallizes the experience into permanent and thus authoritative interpretations

49. Dandelion, *Sociological Analysis*, 99.

50. Doncaster, *God in Every Man*, 36.

51. Doncaster, *God in Every Man*, 33.

of the "truth" of the experience. For Doncaster, therefore, creeds exclude the experience of any and all whose experience of God—and any subsequent interpretation of that event—differs from what Quakers view as the univocal nature of creeds.

Dunstan presents a similar argument to Doncaster, yet with an insistence on being open to new sources of truth—due to the influence of continuing revelation. This openness ensures a corollary openness to the possibility that the experience of God will fundamentally alter a person's awareness and understanding of God.[52] This radical openness is essential because God might be calling each person to a radically new way of life that could run counter to what a strict adherence to a creed would demand. Dunstan asserts that creeds are dangerous, therefore, because they claim to be exhaustive and universally applicable to all people, everywhere. This claim to universal truth is antithetical to a God who continually calls on people to seek God's truth in the dynamic flow of human life.[53] Belief cannot be universal, especially when universals are based on the highly contextual experience of God. Doing so would immediately exclude other experiences, Dunstan argues, and would make the experience of God seem untrue to those who could not subscribe to such supposedly universal beliefs.[54]

The Experience of Belief

Quakers place great value on the role of truth in the development of belief yet differ in their definitions of truth and of its applicability to questions of faith and belief. The main division lies with the value Quakers place on rationality and whether the Divine can be said to be rational: Can the "truth" of faith in God be understood as rational, as God is rational; or is faith (and thus any corresponding "truth" that stems from such a faith) never rational, as God is inherently irrational?

Arthur Eddington approaches this question from the perspective of science, because as one of the preeminent British astronomers of the twentieth century, of *course* he would incorporate science in his faith life. Eddington claims that one can reject creeds without rejecting belief, for belief is a living

52. Dunstan, *Quakers and the Religious Quest*, 4.

53. Dunstan, *Quakers and the Religious Quest*, 43.

54. Dunstan, *Quakers and the Religious Quest*, 13.

and dynamic response to an experience.[55] Creeds are the attempt to settle the questions of faith and the experience of God for all future generations. Science, however, eschews establishing any fact or belief as creedal (i.e., authoritative and determinative) and instead allows facts to be dynamic in the light of new evidence. In science, Eddington argues, belief occurs as a willingness to accept the intellectual responsibility to continue to search for answers, while we must have faith that such answers will eventually emerge as we question.[56]

Michael Rutter quotes Eddington in order to make the argument that the Quaker rejection of creeds is actually an effort to locate order within their lives.[57] This occurs, Rutter argues, due to the dynamic nature of the pursuit of truth that Eddington describes: As Quakers strive to interact with a dynamic world, they hold close to values they have developed as a result of their faith experience of interacting with God.[58] The values are flexible in their application and can allow for any necessary response to a change in circumstances with a change in *belief* about that circumstance. However, this flexibility can only occur as a result of being firmly rooted in a strong system of values that are in turn rooted in the experience of God. The world is guaranteed to be in constant flux, Rutter suggests, and will constantly challenge beliefs. Holding too tight to beliefs will only hamper one's ability to fully engage with the world, which would in turn distance Quakers from the experience of a God fully engaged with the world. Values, not creeds, are thus the proper Quaker response.

In a similar vein, Richard Ullman emphasizes the dialectical nature of truth, claiming that a person who is fully certain of the truth of their faith experience might still be able to be open to new and potentially differing senses of truth.[59] This occurs as a conversation, in which the seeker engages with others about their beliefs and faith experience with the intent of finding areas of commonality. In the process of such dialogue, if the seeker is truly in pursuit of the truth of the other's experience, the seeker will inevitably be

---

55. Arthur Stanley Eddington, *Science and the Unseen World* (Allen & Unwin, 1929), 56.

56. Eddington, *Science and the Unseen World*, 55.

57. Michael Rutter, *A Measure of Our Values: Goals and Dilemmas in the Upbringing of Children* (Friends Home Service Committee, 1983), 16.

58. Rutter, *Measure of Our Values*, 105.

59. Richard Ullmann, *Tolerance and the Intolerable* (Allen & Unwin, 1961), 44.

open to accepting that their own experience of truth might not be complete. Ullman argues that this experience of engaging with the faith of another empathetically opens the seeker to locating a potentially greater truth beyond the truth they currently understand, which in turn opens them to changing their beliefs.[60] As God is both dynamic and present within the community of all seekers, then the experience of God and any subsequent belief structures are inherently fluid. This conception of truth dismisses any essentialized definition of truth as simply the opposite of error. While this binary formulation is the basis of many creedal formulations—and the belief structures that are dependent on them—the pursuit of truth is necessarily more dynamic and thus requires freedom from any restrictions in order to be true to the dynamic nature of faith experience.[61]

In contrast to Eddington and others, Creasey emphasizes the irrationality and disorder of God. He suggests that God's existence can never be proven in any satisfactory way, nor can any belief structure be created that could completely and in a rational fashion explain the nature of God.[62] The Divine cannot be defined by human terms if God is the ground of all human existence, as any method for investigating any claim about God's nature or existence will thus be hampered by the finite awareness of the human intellect. The Divine nature of God is infinite, however, and while it may connect with humanity in a very close and real way through the Divine Presence in creation, God is still the mysterious cause of all existence. Creasey suggests that the only proper response to this is to accept it and to live in response to a God "in whom we live and have our being." This is a response *to* God and not an effort to define what can be understood *about* God, which is the flaw inherent in all efforts to create creedal statements.[63] Instead, Creasey insists that Quakers strive to

---

60. Ullmann, *Tolerance and the Intolerable*, 45.

61. This is similar to Grubb's argument that faith necessitates the struggle to come to terms with the irrationality of the human experience of God, in light of the role that intellect plays in the development of faith. Grubb insists that as belief involves the entirety of the person, a complete faith must include the application of the intellect and a reevaluation of beliefs based on such application. Edward Grubb, *The Historic and Inward Christ: A Study in Quaker Thought* (Headley Brothers, 1914), 31.

62. Creasey, *Bearing*, 40.

63. Creasey, *Bearing*, 35.

develop words that respond to their faith experience and then test those words against this experience, creating a dynamic interaction between a lived faith and an intellectual response to it.[64]

Internal Critique

The main critiques of the Quaker rejection of creeds revolve around the acknowledgment that creeds have inherent value for many believers and as such shouldn't be dismissed entirely. John MacMurray is representative of this perspective. MacMurray focuses on the universality of creeds with the intent of demonstrating what he sees as the danger of developing two levels of belief: the universal and the other. He argues that those who could not ascribe to the universal belief would be thus grouped as other and would suffer harm due to their status as outsiders. He examines this dynamic in light of the development of creeds during the time of the ecumenical councils.

The creeds were developed in the context of an effort to specify a universal understanding of the truth of God, which in turn created an atmosphere of competition between several doctrinal systems, all of which claimed to be universal.[65] The schools that fell outside orthodoxy were inevitably termed heresy and were thus dismissed.[66] The universal church saw these competing systems as threats to its dominant status within Christianity, as they attested to different interpretations of God and thus threatened the church's exclusivist claims to power within the Roman Empire.

In response, MacMurray argues for the creation of modern ecumenical councils, which would strive to correct the universalizing tendencies of the ecumenical councils of the patristic period. These councils would build unity through finding common ground among Christian groups, while avoiding the imposition of unity. MacMurray notes that Quakers—both individual

64. Creasey, *Bearing*, 36.

65. Grubb made a similar argument, focusing on the challenge presented by the council's insistence on the belief in the two natures of Jesus. As these creeds have become standards of belief for all Christians, future generations have been barred from wrestling with that question and possibly coming to a different conclusion based on their experience of God and their intellect. Grubb argued that the impossibility of resolving such a paradox would be untenable for many Christians whose faith would be challenged by the incompatibility of the doctrine and their experience. (*Historic and Inward Christ*, 21).

66. John MacMurray, *Search for Reality in Religion* (Allen & Unwin, 1965), 57.

Quakers and the wider community of Friends—might never find a doctrinal statement to which they could assent, due to the Quaker testimony against making such a statement. He wonders whether this aversion might eventually distance Quakers from the rest of Christianity to an irrevocable extent, reflecting concerns about the divisive possibilities of new interpretations. MacMurray argues that a possible corrective to this, without accepting a creed, would be for Quakers to strive to be in dialogue with other Christians and to continually seek to develop Quaker theological thought in concert with the broader theological conversation.[67] As this is the intent of this book, I agree with MacMurray. Obviously!

Priestland agrees with MacMurray that the ecumenical councils that developed the Nicene and Athanasian creeds were seeking to make universal statements about the experience of God, which could then be used to bring the entire empire under one common understanding of God.[68] He argues, however, that the creeds were beneficial in the sense that they preserved truths that had been confirmed by many Christians in a variety of contexts, and ensured that they could be available as a heritage for posterity.[69] They also gave a communal sense of the often-individual experience of God. Continuing revelation, he argues, presents a challenge not faced by creeds: That new light might actually be harmful to the group. Instead, creeds create a standard against which to measure the validity, and potential danger, of experiences.[70]

Richenda Scott approaches the question somewhat differently, focusing on the challenge presented by the lack of any firm foundation in a specific belief structure: It renders Quakers vulnerable to being swept up in the fervor of an overwhelming new theological trend. Scott argues that the rise of evangelicalism in British Quakerism during the early part of the nineteenth century demonstrated this, in that evangelicalism rapidly changed the culture and belief of British Quakers.[71] Evangelicalism found root in Quakerism due to the simple fact that it spoke directly to the needs of many Quakers for a

---

67. MacMurray, *Search for Reality in Religion*, 72.

68. Priestland, *Reasonable Uncertainty*, 25.

69. Priestland, *Reasonable Uncertainty*, 25.

70. Priestland, *Reasonable Uncertainty*, 26.

71. Scott, *Tradition and Experience*, 28.

biblically based theology that sought to engage with the world. British Quakers, Scott suggests, found this combination irresistible due to their intense desire to reengage with both the Bible—and the world!—after two centuries of the hedge of the Quietist period cutting them off from the rest of the world.

I will lay aside the question of whether Quakers should or should not have engaged with evangelicalism—I try to avoid engaging in alternative history exercises, as it's impossible to make any *intentionally* accurate prediction (as opposed to *accidentally* accurate ones) about the direction of history. I also will not argue for Quakers to embrace creeds now—I am convinced by the arguments above about the potential for ossifying belief. And yet: The rapid and profound impact of evangelicalism on British Quakerism *absolutely* demonstrates the vulnerability of a creedless faith to being consumed by new light. However, another implication is blindingly clear to me as well: If Quakers keep insisting on the freedom to adapt belief to changing circumstances, then they/we must actually engage in the work of theology *more*, not less.

Reason: Doctrine and Quaker Belief

The differences between the meaning of the words *creed* and *doctrinal formulation* on one side, and *doctrine* on the other—as they relate to constructing Quaker theology—are a matter of permanence and codification versus theoretical experimentation, with *reason* being the act of using one's intelligence and reason to develop belief that is flexible and adaptable yet also applicable to specific contexts and practices. For Quakers, creed and doctrinal formulation refer to the same pursuit: the effort by an ecclesial body to permanently codify into an authoritative and determinative belief structure the experiences that a community has with God, the faith in God that develops as a result of that experience, and finally the beliefs that emerge from that faith. A Quaker approach to doctrine, however, stresses the development of theories about that experience that are tested and adjusted through their continuous experimentation in the presence of God, and which are fundamentally temporary guideposts with the flexibility to bend and adapt to changing climates: theological and otherwise.

One significant critique of Quaker theology lies with its inability to effectively translate its core beliefs and tenets due to its focus on the individual experience. The Quaker aversion to acknowledging any person, corporate body, piece of the theological tradition, or teaching as authoritative—other than the individual experience—has stripped Quakers of the ability to influence the behavior and private life of individual Quakers.[72] The powerful witness of an entire life structured by Quaker values has been individuated, as Quaker values are interpreted individually and often without reference to the rest of the meeting community. Instead, Quakers can be Quakers in some settings and can take off their Quaker identity in other settings. This has led to the separation of an individual Quaker's life and witness into a secularized private life and "Quaker life" when they are engaging in specific activities with other Quakers.[73] In this sense, time itself becomes bifurcated between "Quaker time" and the rest of their lives—the vast majority of which, again, is not spent explicitly within the Quaker community.

Some Quakers claim that while it might be necessary to bring the individual experience of God into conversation with the communal experience of God (including the Bible and theological tradition), Quakers must be cautious to avoid granting any inherent authority to the communal experience per se, as well as any doctrine that might emerge from it. William Charles Braithwaite cautions that the key to developing effective educational tools for translating the Quaker experience to others—witness of a life of Christian service and theological doctrine—lies in focusing on developing the intellect, skills, and spiritual lives of all members of the Quaker community.[74] Quakers must keep the tools and aspects of Quaker heritage, including the Bible, from becoming authoritative and thus serving as the central means of maintaining the cohesion of a church community. According to Braithwaite, authority structures will only destroy the true source of authority in the spiritual life: the individual conscience developed through the individual experience of God amid the training of the community. Quaker doctrine, therefore, must serve the main purpose of developing the conscience of Quakers.[75]

Others dismiss these concerns, however, arguing that Quakers have much to gain from the creation of doctrine. Reflective of this, Charles Carter

---

72. Dandelion, *Sociological Analysis*, xviii.

73. Dandelion, *Sociological Analysis*, xxvi.

74. William Charles Braithwaite, *Spiritual Guidance in the Experience of the Society of Friends* (Headley Brothers, 1909), 107.

75. Braithwaite, *Spiritual Guidance*, 107.

dismisses arguments against creating Quaker doctrine as reductive and simplistic, stating that the Quaker aversion to theology is simply a desire to allow their thoughts to remain vague and their experience of God unexamined and untested.[76] I suggest that Carter is touching on the Quaker focus on the individual experience. This focus shifts attention away from the inherent "rightness" of the experience by claiming the experience as authoritative, but only to the individual.[77] Allowing the community to test the experience opens up the possibility that the individual leading might be found insufficient or incomplete. Theology, however, must be tested by the community, must stem from the experience of the community, and must be seen as having some claim over the lives of the community. Avoiding theology allows the individual to avoid granting the community any substantive influence over the individual, and thus it places the individual on a throne of their own individual authority. Therefore, I argue that a greater focus on the work of translating Quaker experience into the language of Quaker doctrine might strengthen Quakerism by addressing the challenge of an excessive focus on the individual experience. However, another correlative response would be focusing on the role that the meeting community has always played in Quaker life.

Quakers, as noted above, struggle with the challenge of explaining their experience of God in somewhat universally translatable terms while recognizing that their words might fail to encapsulate the entirety of their experience in a manner applicable to all Quakers. This aversion to pursuing universality has discouraged Quakers from engaging in the development of doctrine, to the admitted poverty of the tradition. A way forward lies with Quakers viewing doctrine as I have defined it above. In this section, I develop a model

---

76. Carter, *On Having a Sense of All Conditions*, 50.

77. Along this line, Grubb suggested that one of the greatest challenges the early Quakers faced in expressing the full extent of their experience to others was in their inability to translate their inward experience to other Christians using the orthodox frames of Christian theology. They were quite able to gain converts to their cause when they engaged in personal interactions with individual people who witnessed the "sober consistency" of the Quakers commitment to their values. Yet, the weakness of the Early Quaker approach was demonstrated through their inability to translate the experience of those personal interactions into anything that could guard them from the theological attacks of others, even those whose beliefs might not have been too far removed from those of the Early Quakers. Grubb, *Authority and the Light Within*, 79.

for constructing Quaker doctrine that can be expanded in the service of creating a Quaker systematic theology. Quaker doctrine must incorporate these elements: an emphasis on the role of the community, an insistence on honesty about the effectiveness of doctrine, strong humility about the inherent value of continuing revelation, a willingness to continually test the doctrine in the light of experience, a rooting in Quakerism's Christian heritage, and finally an insistence that doctrine reflect Quaker testimony.

Community

John Punshon notes that the process of removing the communal aspect from the development of Quaker doctrine and ethics has eroded both the meaning of Quaker doctrines and their place in the belief structure of Quakerism. Punshon argues that Quakerism has seen an influx of people who were drawn by its ethical structure but not the theological underpinning of that structure.[78] Punshon sees the process of individual adjustment of corporate doctrine (described above) at work through the gradual shift in the meaning of Quaker doctrines such as the Inward Light; this change is so profound, he argues, that individual Quakers seek to see themselves in a humanistic, ethical vision of the testimonies, as opposed to the theological vision of the testimonies as outgrowths of the experience of God. I agree with Punshon that Quaker ethical life and doctrinal development must reflect the traditional Quaker emphasis on the corporate experience of God, including the experience of the Quaker Christian heritage, or else it fails to remain religious in any meaningful sense of the word.

Testimony

Harvey insists that Quaker doctrine reflect Quaker testimony, especially simplicity and practicality.[79] Doctrine must be useful, understandable, precise, and clear. It must express its point completely, without logical games. In short, doctrine must fulfill its purpose without insisting on its own importance. Hughes agrees, stating that theology—the development of the conscience, values, and faith of individual Quakers—is an essential element of the Quaker

78. John Punshon, *Testimony and Tradition: Some Aspects of Quaker Spirituality* (Quaker Home Service, 1990), 41.

79. John W. Harvey, *The Salt and the Leaven* (Allen & Unwin, 1947), 78.

life precisely because it has a practical purpose.[80] Theology is an inherently practical pursuit, as the ideas that are discussed under the banner of theology are the ideas with true power to guide human behavior as they are rooted in the awareness of the experience of God.[81] Reflecting that emphasis on practice, Richard Peters argues that reason—which he defines as taking account of both facts and the "connectedness of human activities"—is essential to developing what he calls the middle way: a life that is neither bound to a strict code of conduct nor entirely self-determined.[82] Peters argues that reason must stem from a passion for justice and fairness, an openness to both accepted facts and new realities, and a willingness to integrate both the old and new into a way of living that reflects both.[83] This sounds similar to the multifaceted definition of doctrine I have advanced.

Honesty

Michael Rutter adds that doctrine must be respected as an essential aspect of the Quaker heritage and be able to be simplified enough to be taught to children.[84] An essential aspect in the fulfillment of the educational purpose of doctrine must be the honesty of all Quakers toward their individual experience of doctrine. While Rutter argues that Quakers must have theological doctrines that can inform Quaker faith and practice and that reflect the entirety of the Quaker doctrine, Rutter also insists that the community must always be open to internal critique by Friends who experience a doctrine negatively, or are incapable of accepting it as authoritative.[85]

Humility

Gerard Priestland insists on maintaining a sense of humility toward all aspects of doctrine. He first insists that Quakers not view doctrine as a tool for making people good by acting as a pathway through which people who believe in the

---

80. Hughes, *Light of Christ in a Pagan World*, 49.

81. Hughes, *Light of Christ in a Pagan World*, 49.

82. Richard S. Peters, *Reason, Morality, and Religion* (Swarthmore, 1972), 75.

83. Peters, *Reason, Morality, and Religion*, 50.

84. Rutter, *Measure of Our Values*, 80.

85. Rutter, *Measure of Our Values*, 80.

doctrine can be transformed.[86] Instead, Priestland argues that doctrine must be viewed through the lens of a people desperate to discover some aspect of the truth of God—and thus to teach others about that truth. Doctrine exists to serve its purpose with humility and must be able to be adapted in the face of new information or even be dismissed entirely. Priestland insists that doctrine is thus only a tool for humans to learn how to change their lives and open their hearts in order to receive the grace and love of God.

Priestland critiques the certainty that can bleed through the Quaker prioritizing of continuing revelation, instead insisting that humility demands that Quakers accept the value of previous revelation. He states that Quaker faith in progressive revelation has created in Quakers an arrogance in which they assume that "no generation till ours had a valid religious experience."[87] The insights of the past can offer present Quakers a window into the experiences of the past. These experiences can be inhabited, giving Quakers the opportunity to learn valuable lessons about different experiences of God that might be difficult to encounter in modern life. Therefore, absolute certainty about the fullness of the contemporary experience will actually limit the breadth and depth of Quakers' exposure to the experience of God, which would run directly counter to the Quaker insistence on extrapolating doctrine from direct experience.[88] Thus, humility can ensure that Quakers have the best opportunity to develop the most complete doctrine.

Experience

Harvey Gillman places a high value on the respect and patience he experienced when he first joined the Quakers and was striving to make sense of his place in the community. Gillman speaks fondly of the respect he encountered from the community for theological and philosophical differences, and the patience that was offered for those who were still struggling to find themselves in the community and in its values.[89] Gillman notes that this created a space for him to not only find his place in the community and to feel comfortable being his

---

86. Priestland, *Reasonable Uncertainty*, 48.

87. Priestland, *Reasonable Uncertainty*, 48.

88. Priestland, *Reasonable Uncertainty*, 48–49.

89. Harvey Gillman, *A Minority of One: A Journey with Friends* (Quaker Home Service, 1988), 80.

honest (and flawed!) self, but also to discern how he could contribute to the life of the community. This reflects my argument that the creation of doctrine requires a flexible interplay between the experience of God in the community and in the individual, and a respectful willingness to engage in a continuous process of theoretical development and testing.

Christianity

I suggest that if Quaker doctrine does not reflect its Christian heritage, it will fail to fully represent a Quaker identity. Christianity and Christian doctrine are essential elements of both the Quaker heritage and its contemporary worldview. The planting of a Quaker doctrine requires a respect for the common doctrines that Quakerism shares with other Christian communities. This creation also requires an insistence on viewing those doctrines through the same testing process that Quakerism requires all other doctrines to undergo. This has the potential to open spaces for engagement between Quaker and other Christian theologies. As John Harvey argues, modern theology shares with Quakers the struggle to engage with doctrine. This creates an opportunity for Quakers, Harvey suggests: Quakers can guide this engagement and can thus guide the development of Christian doctrine.[90]

This is not to call for the inclusion of Christian doctrine that has been untested or fails to reflect Quaker distinctives in the creation of Quaker doctrine. T. R. Glover argues that Christian doctrine has historically not undergone as rigorous a testing process as was necessary, for much of the doctrine about God that was later proven to be incomplete was initially installed as an authoritative creed, enshrining what Glover terms heresy—along with truth.[91] He acknowledges, however, that even incomplete truth about God may be useful in order to open dialogue about doctrine and thus to discover where the truth lies. This process of correction will be hampered by the establishment of creeds, yet it will eventually be corrected. This occurs due to the inexorable power of the "Spirit of Jesus" to continuously move the Christian community—or church—toward adaptation and improvement.[92] Glover suggests, however, that certain doctrines have remained central to the experience of the church

90. Harvey, *Salt and the Leaven*, 78.

91. T. R. Glover, *The Nature and Purpose of a Christian Society* (Headley Brothers, 1912), 21.

92. Glover, *Nature and Purpose*, 21.

through many centuries of testing their truth through the experience of individuals and the life of the community.[93] The doctrines have proven themselves to be both flexible and strongly rooted in the truth of the church's experience of God.[94] This long history does not excuse Quakers from fully engaging in the process of continuous testing, however. Instead, he argues that they are of central importance due to the fact that the process of testing them has consistently revealed new aspects of God.

In a similar vein, Herbert Wood suggests that this heritage of testing Christian doctrine is strikingly similar to the Quaker method of testing doctrine, demonstrating a strong kinship between doctrine in the wider church and Quaker doctrine.[95] This kinship provides an opportunity for Quakers to respond to what Wood views as the weaknesses of much modern theology: an inability to respond in a manner, both simple and profound, to the challenges of scientific materialism without resorting to fundamentalist answers. Wood terms this a theology that could interpret life's meaning and purpose while maintaining balance between the heritage of the historic revelation of God and the new revelations of truth present in science.[96]

Lackawanna River Watershed (Pennsylvania), Christmastide 1990–1991

It's funny to consider the experiences that become the ones that stick in our memories, the ones not only that we return to time after time but also wind up becoming the foundational memories on which we build our sense of self, including our beliefs and concepts about the world. One of the most surprising, to me, is the time my aunt told me that God doesn't make mutants.

When I was ten years old, I visited my grandfather's house to celebrate Christmas with my family—just like every year. An entire branch of my family lived within an hour's drive of my grandparents' house, meaning that the house was absolutely packed to the rafters with people. In other words, if anyone made a fuss, *everyone* would hear it.

93. Glover, *Nature and Purpose*, 31.

94. Glover, *Nature and Purpose*, 33.

95. Wood, *Quakerism and the Future of the Church*, 50.

96. Wood, *Quakerism and the Future of the Church*, 29.

I also should note that my family was blended before that descriptor had become commonplace. Just on my mother's side of the family (the ones that lived in Pennsylvania), I had aunts, uncles, and cousins from both my grandfather's first and second marriages. I had aunts, uncles, and cousins who weren't related by blood but were considered close family just the same. Some people were born in northeastern Pennsylvania and had lived their entire lives there, whereas others had been born—and lived their entire lives—elsewhere. The entire spectrum of Protestant Christianity was represented, from Pentecostals to evangelical fundamentalists to mainline Methodists to leftist Christian socialists, not to mention the presence of a surprising number of agnostics and freethinkers . . . as well as the Roman Catholics in my own household. Some people were absolute rationalists, whereas others were fans of whatever conspiracy theory happened to be popular on television at that moment. In other words, each person in that house approached the *interpretation* of theological truth through an entirely unique-to-them set of *leaves*, such that the process of *photosynthesis* manifested itself in a panoply of ways.

Yet, the family culture emphasized inclusive tolerance and open-minded curiosity, and this especially extended to the topics traditionally avoided in polite company; instead, religion, politics, economics, and human nature were all fair game. In other words, this was a group well-versed in the complexities of navigating complicated conversations and sought out opportunities to practice these skills.

It must be noted here that the culture of my extended family did not always align with that of my birth family, obviously. Would it surprise you to learn that my parents were different people when they were outside our home than the parents they were behind closed doors?

It was in this context that I brought out my Teenage Mutant Ninja Turtles dolls, so as to have toys in order to play with my younger cousins. The Teenage Mutant Ninja Turtles were cartoon characters who became overwhelmingly popular during the 1980s. The key to understanding these characters lies in their hyperaccurate name: These were turtles who had encountered toxic sludge in the New York City subways, mutating their bodies until they could not only stand on two legs but actually developed the skills necessary to become trained ninjas. Oh, and they were teenagers, who were impetuous, bratty, angry, goofy, and addicted to pizza: Basically, they were just like every kid who had ever imagined themselves as a Ninja Turtle—which was a shocking number of us. Their story was an obvious fantasy to me, and that's why I loved it: These characters would never exist in real life . . . but imagine if they did! I loved the Teenage Mutant Ninja Turtles as if they were my brothers—and I think I still do.

My aunt Linda, however, did not share my feelings. She did not see beauty in the fantasy of mutant turtles and instead saw the work of something evil and dark that disrupted the necessary order of God's good creation. While I was beginning to flirt with a nascent Christian universalism, with hints of socialism (how else are we to understand Acts 2, for example?), my aunt was firmly rooted in the Assembly of God church. This meant that while we both worshipped Jesus and considered ourselves Christians, these words (*Jesus* and *Christian*) held *vastly* different meanings for the two of us. I wasn't exactly sure whether I agreed with my Roman Catholic priest that church tradition was the best place to begin one's exploration of theology, but I was certain that I disagreed with my aunt's overwhelming insistence on hewing to the literal meaning of the biblical text. I was even more certain that—following my extended family's culture—I had every right to speak and defend my own opinions and beliefs, regardless of who I was speaking with—so long as I was respectful, of course.

I was several years older than the cousins who happened to be my aunt's sons, and I loved being able to spend time with my cousins by playing with toys that I might be embarrassed to play with in any other setting than during the holidays at my grandparents' house. So, when I broke out my Teenage Mutant Ninja Turtles paraphernalia and started introducing my cousins to these characters I loved so much, I was having an absolute blast, as were they. Imagine my utter shock when I heard my aunt whisper, "Oh no," and saw her storm into the room. I whipped my head around, and when I had made eye contact with her she said, with a shout of utter horror, "Put those toys away this instant—God does *not* make *mutants*!"

Do you remember when I mentioned that the house was absolutely stuffed with people? Well, suffice it to say that everyone heard my aunt's words, and in short order the room we were occupying went from relatively calm and empty to uncomfortably awkward and stuffed with every member of my family who could be considered an authority figure. Once I'd overcome my shock at having somehow done something so apparently heinous, I began to defend myself insistently. I emphasized that Teenage Mutant Ninja Turtles was simply fantasy; yet even if it weren't, and mutants were somehow possible in the physical plane we occupy, then God would still love mutants, as there is nothing present in the creation that was not created, lovingly, by the Divine who creates all things. I had been trained to express myself, and I was becoming quickly incensed: How dare my aunt embarrass me in such a public manner and shame me for sharing something I loved! Also, I was simply unwilling to allow my aunt to proclaim something so antithetical to my own experience of a loving God.

After clearer heads had prevailed, and I had put my toys away—in the end, these were my aunt's sons, and she had the right to say what she would and would not allow my cousins to play with—my family came up to me in ones and twos for the rest of the evening in order to check on me but also to share their own perspectives on what had rapidly become a focus of the evening: the ethics and theology of mutants. Each person approached this question differently, reflecting the diversity of their own foundational assumptions, whether theological, ethical, philosophical, anthropological, political, cultural, or even biological. Several people tried to explain what the building blocks of my aunt's worldview were, forcing me to engage in the intellectual empathy necessary in order to understand the depths of my aunt's horror. I was not required to agree with my aunt, nor even to accept her perspective as truth—no one else really wanted to tell me, a kid, that my beloved toys were actually works of the devil—but I was expected to understand where she was coming from.

For years later, I kept gnawing at this question: Why would God not have a hand in making mutants, and why should their status as mutants put them outside God's love? I followed each of my family members' perspectives from their roots all the way to their conclusions and began to see patterns emerge. For example, if people began their theological reflection from the Bible, their arguments would follow certain pathways. They might come to vastly different conclusions, but their processes for getting there would be similar. The same goes for those who began their reflection from what Christian tradition has said about mutants (as can be expected, precious little). I realized then that I didn't begin from either of these traditional places but instead from my experience of feeling the overwhelming love of God within both the human zoo that is the city and in the vast forests and rolling hills that surrounded Forest City. I *knew* I experienced the Divine everywhere I went, because I felt that love wherever and whenever I sought it: I could feel the love as if it followed me. I experienced that love in the surprising diversity of my family and as I began to discern that I was rather different, in uncomfortable and unsettling ways, from other kids I knew. I didn't know that I was queer then, but I knew that something was different, and it both frightened me and excited me in equal measure.

Basically, as I experienced God's love amid the dizzying diversity of the creation, I was certain that God loved everything that God created, and nothing existed that God didn't create, so therefore God must have a hand in making mutants, ensuring that they were just as loved as I was: a weirdo outcast for whom the courage and overbrimming self-esteem of the Ninja Turtles was inspirational. As I experienced God in this way, I inevitably wound up shifting my theological frameworks to reflect this experience, reading the Bible and church tradition through the lens of experience. Once I realized how this pattern worked, I've continued to see it everywhere: Your foundational assumptions about the sources of theology frame your perspective to a profound degree and will irrevocably shape the interpretation and theology that emerges as a result.

As this chapter demonstrates, when you begin with experience, the theology that results will appear profoundly different from those theologies that begin from the Bible or tradition, regardless of whether the result from each theology is similar. For example, Quakers are pacifists because we believe that as we experience that of God in each and every person, to harm another is to harm those with whom God is in the closest possible relationship. Mennonites, however, are pacifists because of the biblical witness: Jesus specifically said (most particularly in Matt 5), and God specifically said (most particularly in Exod 20), that we are not to ever kill another person. We arrive at the same belief and perform the same action—serving as peacemakers and living as pacifists—but for very different reasons. Yet again, individual universals and universal individuality reigns supreme, as humans express a near-limitless diversity of ways of interpreting the world around them, while the fact that we interpret the world uniquely is actually a universal truth for all humans, shared by every single one of us.

CHAPTER FIVE

Flowers/Testimony

How Do We Live Truthfully and Beautifully?

So let your lives preach, let your light shine, that your works may be seen, that your Father may be glorified; that your fruits may be unto holiness, and that your end may be everlasting life.

—George Fox, "Epistle 200"

We need in every community a group of angelic troublemakers who really will disrupt. Our power is in our ability to make things unworkable. Not with any weapons because that is not our weapon. The only weapon we have is our bodies, and we need to tuck them in places so things, wheels don't turn.

—Bayard Rustin, 1963

Alabama River Watershed, Mid-February 1956

In 1956, Martin Luther King Jr. applied for a gun permit.[1]

When Rosa Parks took her fateful bus ride in Montgomery, Alabama, on December 1, 1955, the building blocks of what became the Montgomery bus boycott had already been laid through decades of work by Parks herself, alongside an entire ecosystem of activists both in Montgomery and across the South. This community was committed to nonviolence as a useful tactical approach, yet many in the movement argued that nonviolence should be seen as the foundation for the work, informing everything they did. When Parks was arrested, the activist community in Montgomery immediately recognized that her case

1. David Garrow, *Bearing the Cross: Martin Luther King, Jr., and the Southern Christian Leadership Conference* (W. Morrow, 1986), 49.

presented an opportunity to begin a campaign to boycott the Montgomery public transit system—Black people comprised the vast majority of riders, after all. Their numbers could be leveraged to test whether the Interstate Commerce Commission's recent decision in *Keys v. Carolina Coach Company*—only a month earlier—to disallow segregation in interstate travel would also apply to travel within states themselves.

We often assume—incorrectly and unfairly—that our heroes emerge fully formed somehow, that they don't need to grow into the circumstances thrust on them. While King had studied peace theory in college and seminary—mainly reading some Henry David Thoreau and a few Christian peace theologians—he was far from the image we celebrate today of the fierce prophet of peace and justice. He actually had to be convinced to lead the boycott and was mainly chosen because he was new to town and the white leadership of Montgomery didn't know him yet. In other words, when a campaign to bomb the houses of Black leaders in town commenced the next month and a bomb was found under King's porch—with his wife and young children inside—King was easily convinced to post armed guards at his home as well as to apply for a personal permit to carry a firearm.

While he is best known as *the* person who made the famous March on Washington happen in 1963 (you might have heard of a somewhat notable speech, delivered by King, commonly known as the "I Have a Dream" speech, which occurred during the event), in 1956 Bayard Rustin had already been a leader in the peace movement for decades. He not only served a prison term during World War II because of his conscientious objector status, but he also traveled to India in 1948 to study Gandhian nonviolence tactics and theories. Admittedly, Rustin had a head start on King when it came to pacifism, having been raised by grandparents who were active in civil rights work. His grandmother had been raised a Quaker and instilled Quaker theology and ethics in the way she raised her grandson. When he was old enough to make his own choices about his faith, he committed to Friends (this is actually an important edit, as it is an important distinction) and joined Fifteenth Street Monthly Meeting in Manhattan.

Rustin—who was both Black and gay—viscerally understood the stakes he risked with his fervent commitment to and incandescent passion for both peacemaking and civil rights. Besides his previous arrest, he faced significant difficulties due to the rampant homophobia of the time, including an arrest in 1953 for having an intimate encounter with another man in a car.

Despite the revulsion many people in the civil rights movement had for his homosexuality, it was generally accepted that he was exceptionally talented at organizing, and his presence was thus grudgingly welcomed by leaders in the civil rights movement. He demonstrated his deep understanding of the principles of peacemaking—and of the Quaker peace testimony—by serving on the committee that wrote the massively influential pacifist treatise *Speak Truth to Power: A Quaker Search for an Alternative to Violence* in 1955, published by the American Friends Service Committee.

When Rustin said that the world needed angelic troublemakers who would be so committed to peacemaking that they'd jam their bodies in places to disrupt the wheels of oppressive systems to ensure that these systems ceased to function, he meant it quite literally. I'd argue that Rustin ate, slept, and breathed the peace testimony, becoming a walking representation of it in all that he did, so that his life would itself preach to the world about the truth of the presence of God everywhere—including and especially within a gay Black activist who represented everything that white supremacists hated . . . and feared.

When the boycott began, Rustin traveled to Montgomery to teach King about Gandhian nonviolence tactics. Rustin immediately recognized that King had a lot to learn about the tactics of nonviolent direct action, but also saw in King a potential kindred spirit when it came to nonviolence as a spiritual, political, theological, and cultural framework. King, in turn, recognized Rustin's immense value—particularly because he was drowning at that point in his life.

In less than three short months, King had gone from being a young preacher still new to his first position serving as head pastor, trying to get his bearings and not yet making many waves—to being in immediate and immense danger as the face of a mass movement. Other clergy leaders had already escaped a fiery death by inches and miracles. King's phone daily clanged with the rings of death threats to him and his family. Before we judge King here, let's try and imagine ourselves thrust into such a central role at such a crucial and overwhelming moment and missing the mental infrastructure of beliefs, spirituality, and experience in peacemaking that Rustin was blessed with. In that situation, in that context, applying for a gun permit makes a great deal of logical sense—to this pacifist, at least. We're all only human! King's life had been completely upended, and they were threatening his family (his babies!) and his home: I absolutely empathize with his fear and confusion.

When Rustin entered King's home amid all of this action and chaos, he noted the guards, saw King's state of mind, and recognized that he needed what in the South is called a come-to-Jesus meeting: a confrontation where someone is shown the truth in the hope that they will realize what needs to change and actually do it. Rustin began to ask King why he had guards outside his home and a gun inside—sitting on a chair at the kitchen table, no less. Rustin and King then spent the rest of the evening and parts of several subsequent days talking about peace as more than just a useful tactic, as a natural embodiment and expression of one's Christian commitments.

Rustin was caring and compassionate—while painful at times, telling Truth can be done gently—but also insistent about the inherent alignment of nonviolence with a life devoted to embodying the life of Christ in one's own life. There's no record of what was actually said in the conversation, so we can only speculate about what arguments Rustin would have used. From what is known about Rustin, however, gathered from both his words and his actions, it's highly likely that he emphasized that an effective practice of nonviolence requires a rooting in a holistic framework of nonviolence, around which one builds one's life in its entirety: Peacemaking is lived into, therefore, and not simply assented to.

King was eventually convinced that the weapon did actually represent all of the fantasies of power and security that are so deeply embodied in American gun culture. Let's be honest, if someone wanted to harm King, they could have easily done so, likely with impunity—in that time and place—regardless of whether King carried a revolver. Why is that? He was a Black man, living in what was the first capital of the Confederacy (1861), who was the public face of a desegregation battle in the same city that would later witness Governor George Wallace's 1963 inauguration speech, famous for Wallace's declaration that he would "toss the gauntlet down at the feet of tyranny, say[ing] segregation now, segregation tomorrow, segregation forever!"

No—all of King's guards, with all of their firearms, would have been powerless to protect King from any number of potential scenarios that were extremely familiar to the Black community of Montgomery. For example, all the authorities needed to do was arrest King, and once he was safely behind bars and far from the public eye, he could have easily encountered the same kind of "accidents" (i.e., vicious beatings) that regularly befell incarcerated Black people in that time and place. Instead, King decided to commit wholesale to nonviolence, and the fundamental vulnerability that accompanies it, as a defining principle of his existence for the rest of his life.

Admittedly, Rustin wasn't the only person trying to convince King to commit more completely to nonviolence and get rid of the weapon: Several other leaders in both the peace movement and the civil rights movement had similar conversations with King. I'll readily admit, I'm biased and want to focus on Rustin's contribution. I am a queer Quaker who has a picture of Rustin in my office, after all, who cherishes this Friend as an embodiment of Quaker testimony: It's no surprise that I'd focus on Rustin's conversation. What is notable about Rustin's engagement with King on this issue, though—and which speaks to a Quaker understanding of testimony—is that Rustin stayed in King's life, serving as a friend, yes, but also as a mentor and elder, seeking to always speak truth to King, truthfully.

This makes logical sense: You cannot simply drop truth on people and walk away, expecting that you've made any actual impact on their lives or on their way of thinking about the most fundamental issues—such as the safety of one's family or whether violence is acceptable in any form whatsoever in one's life. Instead, you demonstrate that you actually care about the person themselves, for their own sake, by remaining in relationship with them: Again, show your love through your actions, not simply your words.

In this moment, Rustin effectively demonstrates the intersections of testimony—the *form* of a way of being expressed through the *function* of a way of life. What made the specific instance of Rustin's testimony so effective is that it was consistent: King could sense that Rustin was speaking truth in that one specific moment in time because King could trust that Rustin's life was itself *true*—King could have had the same conversation with Rustin a week earlier or a year later, and Rustin would still seek to help King embody the truth of peacemaking through living truthfully, responding to the Truth of God's love for all people.

To claim that testimony is a balance of form and function is, admittedly, a novel approach, yet is also arguably consistent with traditional Quaker understanding. Testimony is understood to be the marriage of *testimony* as a way of being shaped by the human response to "that of God" in all people with *testimonies* as the ways that this response has presented itself in the actions of

Quakers. For example, Quakers have long held that the act of peacemaking is a necessary outgrowth of a life shaped by the fundamental belief in the presence of God in all people: You cannot harm and kill what the Divine has made sacred and instead must act peacefully toward all. Testimony is thus double-sided, containing aspects both negative (what we cannot do) and positive (what we must do).

In this way, *peace* means many things simultaneously. It makes claims about God's fundamental being (God is peace), God's desire for creation (the peace of God), and God's actions (God creates peace). It also makes similar claims about the fundamental nature of humanity (humans are most human when at peace), morality (peace is central to human character), and ethics (humans must act peacefully). These meanings overlap and interact with each other to such an extent that each definition nests within each other, yet they are also noticeably different and unique: While peace as ethical action is inherently different from peace as state of being, each depends on the other to make sense. The process of the human act of peacemaking cannot be understood without one already possessing a definition of *peace* as state of being, as one cannot make something without a definition of the thing being made; concomitantly, the state of peace cannot make sense if one has not experienced acts—and moments—of peace in one's life. Peace is therefore both form and function, for both testimony and testimonies.

Flowers

When seen through the lens of the ecosystem, testimony can be expressed in the metaphor of *flowers*, for flowers are complex structures that are themselves a balance between form and function: The highly complex and structured outward form provides a framework for the function of fertility (within flowers that fruit, of course—no metaphor is perfect) and the hope of new life. I will return to this metaphor throughout the chapter, exploring in much greater detail the ways that the metaphor of flowers expresses truth about testimony. Let's first explain the metaphor, though.

Fundamentally, a flower is the structure/form on a plant that performs the function of reproduction. Flowers are composed of a combination of vegetative organs that work together to protect itself, attract pollinators, create pollen, distribute the pollen grains, and finally provide a safe harbor for the development of seeds within the outward form of a fruit. Flowers are highly structured, in that within each flower is a complex array of different component parts whose forms have evolved to serve particular functions.

Flowers, as a category, are quite ordered in form. They are generally composed of the same types of structures (perianths, stamens, and pistils), with combinations of structures and forms unique to each species of plant. Similarly, while each individual flower on a plant is composed of the same structures—serving the same function—as every other flower on the plant, no two flowers will be exactly the same. In this way, both the form and function of flowers is ordered, structured, and intentional: Flower structure is a result of the specific needs of each plant, reflected in the form unique to each plant species.

Flowers are also inherently chaotic in the sense that pollen is intended to be spread chaotically—as anyone with allergies can attest! Whether through clinging to the feet of bees or expelled out into the wind, each individual pollen grain makes its own capricious journey out into the world, a journey the flower cannot control. In this way both the form and function of flowers is chaotic: Flowers can dictate neither which pollen grains will fall into the reproductive structures nor whether any individual flower will be fertilized at all. Flowers, therefore, are a balance between form and function, a marriage of structure and chaos.

I make a distinction between *flower* and *blossom* in this chapter, despite the fact that these two words have historically meant the same thing: the entire structure of the reproductive organs of a plant. In current English usage, however, *flower* has taken on the general definition of the reproductive structure for any plant, while *blossom* is reserved for the reproductive structures of fruiting plants. As my metaphorical schema here involves fruit and seeds, I'll refer to the structure of the flower as a blossom.

Blossom: How Does Our Experience with the Divine Meet the World?

Truth and Beauty

Truth

I've always appreciated what happens when you place two Quakers—from vastly different contexts—together, addressing the same topic, having a conversation, as it were. Their significant differences can actually act as harmony for each other, revealing the significant similarities: a framework for a life lived in beautiful tension between the *form* of becoming a person whose life is patterned to the love of God for all and the *function* of actually doing the work of dismantling the systems of oppression that work so very hard to destroy what is beautiful about a life fully lived. The quote at the beginning of the chapter, from George Fox, represents the first, while the one from Bayard Rustin represents the second.

The phrase "Let your lives preach" has become a helpful Quaker shorthand for testimony, as it encapsulates both the form and function of testimony: a form of life shaped by one's response to "that of God within all" is expected to preach (or *speak*, in more recent framings of this concept) to the world through the function of the actions performed. This is not unique to Quakers, as the well-known Christian phrase "Preach the gospel at all times; if necessary, use words" refers to a similar framework. While the phrase is overwhelmingly misattributed to St. Francis, it rings true to Francis's mission and vision of ministry, so I'd argue that it doesn't really matter whether he actually said it. Effectively, both phrases capture a truth about the Christian—and Quaker—life: Your actions must reflect the love of God, demonstrating an alignment between belief and action such that it preaches truths about God's love that people can see and learn from.

Put in the form/function framework of this chapter, one can learn about the form of a Quaker's life through the function of their actions. This phrase has become so ubiquitous in some Quaker communities that it's become axiomatic. Align your beliefs and actions such that your life speaks, and for Liberal Quakers especially, one should limit one's speech to such an extent that the only thing speaking—or preaching, for that matter—is one's life. If you wondered whether this emphasis is fed by and in turn feeds into Quaker reluctance to engage in the work of theology ("words about God"), you'd be on to something true about the Quaker condition.

What is often lost in the constant repetition of this phrase is that when read in the midst of its original context—Fox's context, in which the work of theology was seen as the work of a hierarchical clergy elite, which actively sought to silence and censor unapproved voices—it actually becomes a theological statement about the inherent truth of the Quaker way of embodied theology and the need to insist on this truth at all times in every aspect of life. The rest of the passage demonstrates this through its insistence that all Friends who dwell in—and feel—the power of God (which Fox assumes should be all of them) must live into this truth both internally and externally, such that it transforms the person so completely that their life can serve as a beacon for others to follow, "a city set upon a hill" that all can see for miles around. People don't become Quaker when they declare themselves convinced but are actually molded into Quakers through a continuous dedication to the Quaker way of life.

This way of life is both true and Truth for Fox. It's true because it contains no falsehoods, and because it is the most complete and true way of life for humanity. It's Truth because it speaks to the fundamental nature of God and presents the most complete way of following God's desire for humanity. Fox embraced the idea that Quakers answer that of God in others as a confrontation of truth with falsehood, in which the true testimony of Quakers is exemplary for the rest of the world to such an extent that the false lives of others will crumble under the one-two punch of the truth of Quaker testimony speaking directly to the Divine Presence within. Thus, the human living a "false" life encounters the truth of Quaker testimony from without (through the evangelism of the Quaker example and the passionate fervor of Quaker speaking) and from within (through the work of the Divine Presence continually working to shift the hearts, minds, and souls of humans).

Another famous phrase from Fox makes this framing more explicit. In 1656, Fox wrote in his journal that Quakers are to "spare no place, spare not tongue nor pen, but be obedient to the Lord God and go through the world and be valiant for the Truth upon earth; tread and trample all that is contrary under."[2] Fox does not mince words here: Obedience to the will of God requires that Quakers "walk cheerfully over the world," trampling anything within other people that is false. Testimony is truth and Truth for Fox, and a Quaker living truthfully must—out of love for both God and the person themselves—never shirk the command to confront what is untruth with every fiber of their being. Just as flowers are highly visible to the world—intentionally, as the form of flowers has evolved to attract attention from pollinators—Quakers must live in the open, preaching the truth of testimony through every aspect of their lives, attracting attention from others who could spread that

2. George Fox, *The Journal of George Fox*, ed. John L. Nickalls (Religious Society of Friends, 1997), 263.

message through the form of their own lives. Read in this context, Rustin's instinct to confront King, however lovingly, is rooted directly in the very foundations of the Quaker movement.

I need to note, though, that this framing of truth/Truth requires that Quakers accept that answering that of God within demands a fundamental, foundational epistemological certainty that one can actually make the same binary choice of truth/deceit that Fox outlines. The irony for modern Friends is that Fox would very likely challenge the foundational, epistemological uncertainty (and subsequent tolerance for diversity of thought) that marks much of modern Quaker theology.

When read in light of Fox's emphasis on truth being the form of testimony, and Rustin's own act of loving confrontation with King, Rustin's framing of the function of testimony as "angelic troublemaking" and holy disturbance resonates with a deeper power. For one, Rustin does not accept half measures in the functioning of testimony: When confronting oppression and injustice—systems mired in deceit—we must be willing to sacrifice everything we have, even and especially our own bodies and lives. This is the function of the thoroughgoing nonviolence Rustin explained to King. Rustin insists that we look at nonviolence through a true lens: These systems of deceit will not go down without a fight, and if we fail to have a clear-eyed awareness of the depth of commitment the fight will require of us, we will fail.

This is where Rustin's organizing genius emerges. He recognizes that, in the face of a system with access to a wide array of weaponry—and a willingness to use as many of them and as often as is necessary to defend the status quo—nonviolence will appear ineffectual and weak. King himself wondered, so early in his life, whether the only choice left in the face of extreme violence was the deployment of violence in return. Rustin argues that if you accept this framing—that the only effective response to violence is violence—you are actually limiting the scope of your thinking and hampering your capacity for creativity.

Rustin recognized that these systems are actually often quite vulnerable, as they themselves depend on the consent of humans and their willingness to dedicate their efforts to ensuring the seamless continuity of the system's inner workings. Place enough people at enough of these vulnerable points, people absolutely committed to gumming up the works and slowing down the system, and you can disrupt them. Use your creativity effectively and your resources wisely, placing people at the points most likely to cause the most damage possible, and there's a good chance you can make the system unworkable to the point of collapse.

The crux of Rustin's argument here rests on a comprehensive understanding of testimony: The effectiveness of the functions of peacemaking depends entirely on a complete commitment to an entire way of life. Consider any discipline one can master, and you quickly see the truth of this. What separates a master carpenter from an apprentice? The apprentice is versed in the function of carpentry: They can measure, cut, follow blueprints, and with these skills can build things competently. Yet, it takes a master to not only respond effectively to the challenges that inevitably emerge when making something but also see into the future and respond both effectively and creatively to challenges that the apprentice cannot even imagine yet. The apprentice is following rules, while the master transcends them. The apprentice is able to build a bookshelf. The master, however, has been so deeply formed by the discipline of carpentry that they can envision and build an entire library.

When faced with the overwhelming power of the system of Jim Crow segregation, Rustin argues, you need to be a master peacemaker, one who has been so shaped by peace as form that they can envision not only innumerable different functions of peacemaking but a form of the system that is itself shaped by peace. Rustin understood that nonviolence is form first, or it is nothing. Jim Crow can respond effectively to the functions of peacemaking: Use enough force, employ enough violence, and you can stop a march, break up an encampment, or even wait out a boycott. Jim Crow cannot—and did not, as we know—respond effectively to the power of peace as form to transform the conscience of a country.

Beauty

In his famous poem "Ode on a Grecian Urn," John Keats declares—in the voice of the urn itself, actually—that "beauty is truth, truth beauty—that is all Ye know on earth, and all ye need to know." Admittedly, this poem is the face that has launched thousands of terrible high school English essays—including my own painfully awful attempt at eloquence that quivered with all of the powerful emotional immaturity I possessed at fifteen years old. Yet, regardless of how I feel about the rest of the poem—did I mention that my experience of it involved a significant amount of pain?—I have always been struck by how true this correlation feels: how it seems to capture something essential about the nature of beauty, the beauty of nature, and beauty's relationship with truth. This relationship between truth and beauty has a feeling that is experienced first and foremost, that cannot be known conceptually until it has been experienced emotionally and physically.

We first experience beauty at the opening moments of our life, independent of our mother's womb, before we have the mental capacity to frame any thoughts about beauty as concept. I mean this literally: We are born into beauty, and it shapes us fundamentally, before our thinking minds have been able to conceptualize anything beyond the most basic and true human experiences of touch, hunger, surprise, and love. When I say that beauty is truth, and truth beauty, this is what I mean: the particular kind of beauty that exists when something is so true, so well aligned to the fundamental rhythms of life and so beautifully crafted, that we can experience it as a window into the foundational truths of existence. These are the moments when words seem to fail us, when these experiences become a language unto themselves, a shorthand that speaks truth to such an extent that we might even become impatient with words as they continue to fail to capture the essence, the power, the beauty of what we have experienced.

There is a rich theological tradition that has addressed moral beauty, the beauty of the created order (natural beauty), spiritual beauty, beauty as philosophical concept, beauty as an expression of the Divine Reality, and of course, the beauty of art. Theologians have also spilled plenty of ink examining the marriage of beauty and truth. Quaker theology, in contrast, has historically expended little effort on beauty as a distinct category worthy of exploration or analysis—perhaps unsurprisingly.

That's not to say that Quaker theology ignores beauty completely. It's simply that beauty is far more likely to be explored on the way toward exploring something else. Beauty has historically been understood among Friends as something that emerges as a consequence but rarely as something to be pursued for its own sake. The main reason for this has been the primary Quaker concern for stripping away anything that separates the human from the experience of the Divine and that creates divisions between humans based on their access to beauty and beautiful things.

For example, the spare, sparse beauty of Quaker meeting houses emerges as a consequence of the aesthetics of "plain." Quaker plain is multifaceted, a foundational concept that is expressed in the design of meetinghouses in ways that are practical, moral, and spiritual. This can be seen through the shocking lack of any kind of ornamentation in meetinghouses, whether the historic (mainly eighteenth- and nineteenth-century) meetinghouses that proliferate in the Delaware River watershed or the meetinghouses of more modern construction that can be found in the American West.

Meetinghouses have always had one, central function: gather the community in one space, where they can engage in the practice of waiting on the Divine together. Anything that doesn't directly serve this purpose alone, and instead distracts people from their focus on listening to the still, small voice of the Divine Presence, is not only practically unnecessary but also morally wrong—because it wastes resources unnecessarily and because it could cause one to focus on the beauty of the ornament and not on the beauty of the Divine. Thus, Quaker meetinghouses will have walls, ceilings, floors, benches, windows . . . and essentially nothing else. There's even controversy that surrounds the tradition of placing flowers in the center of the main room of the meetinghouse: While some find such displays acceptable because they represent the beauty of creation and help people focus their attention toward the beauty of the Divine, others are adamant that they are just another distraction—and a worldly one at that, as flowers in a vase are by definition dead and thus serve only to waste money (if they were bought at a store) or to waste life by killing living flowers.

Yet, all of this lack allows you to experience abundance in surprising ways. When you're left without ornament to delight, entertain, or instruct you, you can actually experience light unfiltered, pure, and dizzyingly abundant. Light splashes in from everywhere, it seems, bouncing off floors, walls, and even the ceiling, heightening the impact of what color does exist. Yes, the link here between the natural light of the sun and the Light of the Divine Presence is entirely intentional. Similarly, when you strip away visual ornament, you are able to finally notice sounds that might have been missed in other settings that are louder sonically and louder visually. Again, this is intentional, for one of those sounds you are now free to hear is the voice of God—the entire point of being in this space in the first place. This is a beauty that is true in that its form is a direct response to its function, while its function is made most complete by its form.

The beauty of flowers follows the exact same framework, in that they are also a harmony of form and function, in which each is dependent on the other and only makes sense in light of the other. The overwhelming diversity of the forms of flowers—the blossoms—is a direct consequence of the overwhelming diversity of plants themselves and the ways that each individual species of plant has responded to the universal imperative function to reproduce that they all share. Flowers are beautiful forms, no doubt—that's simply true in a way that sunsets are beautiful. Yet, just as sunsets are also the inevitable functions of a planet spinning on its axis, in which the beauty is the result of light waves interacting with the atmosphere, the beauty of flowers is functional. Plants depend on the reproductive function of flowers, and what we experience as a beautiful form is function to a pollinator seeking nectar and a plant seeking pollination in order to reproduce. Yes, the form of bright colors and pleasant scents attracts pollinators, but mainly in service of the function of reproduction. Also, yes, the function of flowers entirely depends on the ability of the form to be visible to the world and attract attention.

Now we finally return to testimony. Once we understand the ways that form and function are inextricably linked in truth and beauty, we can see how testimony is the point where beauty (moral and spiritual) in form meets the function of acting in the world as we are intended to do, by which someone is true to both their nature and to their intended purpose. Testimony is plumb and balanced where it is formed exactly as it should be so that it has the exact, particular form to perform the function it was designed for. It thus functions truly in that one can experience truth enacted through actions that speak to truth. Beauty expressed in function, perfected.

Virtue Theory and Flourishing

To this point, I have sketched out a vision of testimony that is a harmony between theology and ethics. This reflects the Quaker theology of Divine-human interdependence. Quaker interdependence theology is expressed metaphorically, in which the metaphor of Light expresses the Quaker experience of a Divine Presence that is individually connected to every part of creation (including, of course, every individual human) and therefore also connected to all of creation, serving as the ground within which all of reality is rooted and from which all of creation grows. Every single speck of creation is therefore interdependent with every other speck, as all are connected through the ground of Divine being.

Yet, this also means that the Divine is drawn into an interdependent relationship with all of creation as well. *Testimony* is the *form* of life that emerges when humanity—shaped by this Divine interdependence—responds to it. As Quakers view this as a truth of the human condition, they term this response testimony: something that is spoken, a faithful witness to something that is true. Testimony is therefore understood to be a holistic reflection of the Quaker community's core theological beliefs and ethical convictions, in which Quaker interpretation of these beliefs and convictions is embodied and expressed in the actions of Quakers.

Quaker thought has taken the concept of the testimony of a Quaker's life, rooted in this faithful response to and expression of the worship of God, and developed from that collection of testimony a typology of specific ethical norms, also termed *testimonies*, within which the overall Quaker ethical framework can be placed. This has led to the development of a variety of Quaker collective testimonies over the years, often reflecting the theological and ethical concerns of the specific Quaker community developing the list, in each specific time and context.

These testimony lists transform the ambiguity of testimony as a way of life into something concrete and specific, and thus often serve as effective—and handy!—pedagogical and evangelical tools, allowing Quakers to teach others about some of the core doctrinal elements of a tradition known for its insistent rejection of anything smacking of dogmatism and creed. One of the challenges of testimony lists, however, is that their handy portability can easily slip into the very same kind of creedalism that an emphasis on testimony as a way of life seeks to avoid. For example, Liberal Quakerism in the United States has developed the mnemonic SPICES, which includes testimonies to simplicity, peace, integrity, community, equality, and stewardship/sustainability. While each of these particular testimonies certainly speaks to something essential about Quaker testimony, in practice they are often used as a shorthand for explaining the essentials of Quaker theology and ethics—a task for which they are actually poorly suited. I've already focused a great deal of attention on two ideas—peace and truth—that not only have been seen as central to the idea of testimony as a broad vision of a way of life but have also been understood throughout Quaker history as essential to any testimony lists that emerge from reflection on testimony.

These particular testimonies are not simply known, as if they were thought processes one could rationally follow, step by step. They are also not rules in the sense that one can apply the particular testimony to peace as a universal rule for handling all situations that involve the potential for violence. Instead, particular testimonies are experienced in relationship: with each other as overlapping approaches to and perspectives on testimony as a way of life embodied by people who enact testimony in their entire being. In this way, particular testimonies are communal, experienced in the intimate places of personal relationships and in the physical places where people live their lives. These particular testimonies must be nourished and taught in all places of a person's life, such that a person becomes themselves an expression of testimony: They embody Quaker testimony completely, to the extent that they express testimony with every breath they take and every action they perform.

Neither the theology nor the ethics that responds to it is unique to Quakers. In many ways, this is a form of virtue ethics, an ethical framework that emphasizes the development of moral character over moral behavior, such that one shapes oneself around the form of the character of a virtuous life expressed in the function of particular virtues that emerge from that foundational, virtuous character. Aristotle is perhaps the most well-known secular theorist of virtue ethics, while Thomas Aquinas is the most well-known Christian theorist.

While Quaker ethics has long acknowledged this significant connection between testimony and virtue ethics, Jackie Leach Scully has made the most complete argument for seeing testimony as a form of virtue ethics—albeit with some notable caveats.[3] Scully also sees challenges with the development of testimony lists as mnemonic shortcuts, suggesting that they limit the concept of testimony to that of a list of moral and ethical guides divorced from an underlying theological framework for the Quaker life.[4]

Instead, she argues that Liberal Quakers should envision particular testimonies as constituent virtues rooted in an overarching testimony of love for that of God within each person, in which testimony is the ground out of which each of the particular testimonies would grow. She also notes that each of the particular testimonies is itself a complex weave of values—what

3. Jackie Leach Scully, "Quakers and Ethics," in *The Oxford Handbook of Quaker Studies*, ed. Stephen W. Angell and Pink Dandelion (Oxford University Press, 2013), 535–48.

4. Jackie Leach Scully, "Virtuous Friends: Morality and Quaker Identity," in *The Quaker Condition: The Sociology of a Liberal Religion*, ed. Pink Dandelion and Peter Collins (Cambridge Scholars, 2008), 107–22.

she terms an "ethical collage"—in which each value makes sense only in relationship to the others, and each of the particular testimonies also only makes sense in relationship to the others, as aspects of an overarching Quaker ethical structure rooted in a dynamic, lived testimony. Thus, the testimony to peace is incomplete without an awareness that conflict is rooted in inequality, corruption, and materialism, all of which intersect with particular testimonies to equality, integrity, and simplicity—which themselves overlap as interdependent and interconnected elements of testimony, elements with ambiguous and fluid borders.

While testimony is centered on the faithful life, virtue ethics is often centered on the "good life," one Aristotle argues is demonstrated by the presence of what he terms eudaimonia: often translated as "happiness" but which can more helpfully be defined as "flourishing." One of the reasons for adopting this definition is that the concept of a good life is inherently dependent on one's definition of good, which by necessity includes a framework for understanding not only whence good emerges but also what type of life would be most likely to manifest such good.

Should one follow Epicurus's lead, for example, pleasure—and its pursuit—is seen as the fundamental purpose of human existence, in which a good life is one that is defined by the pleasure that one is capable of enjoying. Of course, we are now faced with the challenge of defining pleasure. If we're seeking to become Epicureans, we would be required to frame a definition that includes virtue, as Epicurus insists that a life defined by pleasure would inherently be a virtuous one. We would then need to adopt a definition of pleasure that actually insists on disciplining the appetites. This might sound surprising to modern audiences living in a world where the maximization of pleasure most often consists of an indulgent hedonism instead of a more tempered recognition of pleasure. Thus, pleasure is more akin to Goldilocks and the porridge: a life defined by achieving that balance between too little and too much, in which pleasure is more about contentment than Dionysian abandon.

Pick at this question from the perspective of testimony, I'd argue, and a picture emerges of a journey between two points, in which one's definition of good sits at one end and a demonstrative, exemplary life exists at the other, a life formed by living most completely into the virtues that emerge from the good. In a sense, the exemplary life can serve as a pedagogical function, teaching us what the good is by demonstrating how that good manifests in one's life. We are engaging in teleology here, in which the telos, or end purpose, of life is demonstrated in lives defined by testimony, and in which learning is experiential: We experience the good of peace and truth, for example, as we encounter people attempting to embody these virtues in every aspect of their lives.

This can become a virtuous feedback loop, in which we encounter examples of lives testifying to peace through embodying peace, in which action reflects the direction of an inner compass, which is then calibrated through a continuous listening to the Divine Presence (the root of the good) and which itself is then tested through the actions one performs as one seeks to follow the example of the lives of those around us that testify, or speak. This process of embodiment and reflection is continuous throughout one's life, for life is inherently dynamic: As the world around us constantly changes, we must constantly return to the source of good and then attempt to live into that good through embodying that good in our lives, with exemplary lives serving as markers to help guide our way.

This form of ethics is not allergic to rules, per se; it's more that rules are inherently temporary and contextual and cannot be universal or timeless in any way that would be acceptable to natural law theorists, for example. An example of this is the testimony of hat-honor. In the context in which the Quaker movement was birthed—seventeenth-century England—class distinctions were not only seen as essential for social order but as essential to human nature: Some humans were simply better than others due to the circumstances of their birth, particularly the class into which they were born. Class was a theological, ontological, and anthropological reality as much as it was a political, cultural, and economic one: It was the way God created the world, and to reject the assumptions on which class was based was to question the very nature of the Divine.

One of the rules that emerged from this ontology was that those of lower class were expected to recognize the gulf between themselves and those of higher rank in every aspect of their daily lives, even and including baring one's head—doffing one's hat—in a form of salute. People of lower rank could experience dire consequences if they didn't perform this action, up to and including legal consequences: Either recognize the fundamental reality of your lower rank (and thus affirm the inherent inequality of people) by taking off your hat, or you might permanently lose the ability to ever wear a hat again.

I'll let you ponder what I mean by that.

When seen within its context, hat-honor shifts from a silly thing that ancient people cared way too much about into an act of significant importance for an entire society. Quaker theology insisted on the absolute equality of all people before God, however, in that every person had equal access to the Light of Christ within, king and peasant alike. Class was a human construct based on human needs and desires, therefore, and needed to be rejected wholesale. Thus, early Friends declared a testimony to hat-honor, in that Quaker testimony demanded that Friends keep their hats firmly on their heads, regardless of who was in front of them—again, king and peasant alike.

This was a rule in that Friends understood this to be an inevitable consequence of their theology. To act differently than testimony required was to reject the truth of that testimony and thus to reject the fundamental truth of absolute equality before the Divine. Once the rules of society moved on and the laws about hat-honor were abolished, the testimony to hat-honor itself faded away. The testimony to hat-honor wasn't about the act of doffing your hat, therefore, but about a rejection of the inequality of class, a testimony that has remained evergreen across the centuries and now presents itself as the particular testimony to equality. This applies to any number of different testimonies that Quakers have expressed over the years, where rules about dress, marriage, money, furniture styles, intoxicants, and so on and so forth have all emerged and faded as Friends have responded to their own changing contexts and circumstances.

Let's return to our discussion of the good life. When viewed through an ecotheological lens, the telos of Quaker testimony is best defined as *flourishing*, as "the good" from an ecotheological lens is that which sustains life and helps it become abundant—or flourish. Central to any understanding of flourishing, then, is fertility and reproduction, which involves pollen (the substance in flowers that actually does the fertilizing), to which we now turn.

Pollen: How Do We Fertilize Our Lives with Our Testimony?

Fertility and Reproduction

Pollen is messy—intentionally so. Tree pollen generally comes in two forms: anemophilous (wind-loving) and entomophilous (insect-loving).

Anemophilous pollen is the stuff that is released by pine trees (usually) in those massive yellow clouds that settle everywhere and cause so many of us such agony during late spring. It is designed to be carried wherever the wind—and gravity—takes it, in a chaotic explosion of hope for the future. Entomophilous pollen is the kind that gets stuck in the hairs that cover pollinating insects as they dig deep in the structures of the blossom for the nectar they need to survive. As they travel from flower to flower on a plant, some of that pollen—all jumbled in a sticky, chaotic mess, matting in globs on the insect—will fall off into the pistil of each flower. In both forms, the chaos and mess are intended to mix up pollen grains from a variety of trees, allowing for genetic diversity and increasing the likelihood of pollination.

The chaotic, blurry mess of pollen is the response of a being that is literally rooted in place and faced with the challenge of pollinating itself: Flood the zone with as many sperm cells (what pollen is, effectively) as possible. This process depends almost entirely on the fertility of other beings and nature itself to ensure that enough pollen lands in enough pistils to pollinate enough flowers, to create enough seeds, that will then land in soil that is fertile enough, with favorable enough climatic conditions, to root and have enough trees grow, so as to ensure the continuance of the species. In other words, the reproduction cycles of trees depend on the fertility—that is, the ability to produce offspring and sustain life—of an entire ecosystem (a community of beings and natural forces). The tree can control only one aspect of the fertility of this entire cycle: the quality and volume of the pollen released. Everything else is out of its control.

When the practice of testimony is viewed through the metaphor of pollen, some obvious overlaps emerge, most especially the messiness, chaos, and uncontrollable nature of embodiment inherent in the pollen metaphor: The only thing we really ever have control over is how we respond to the chaotic, uncontrollable messiness of life. We cannot ensure that our enacting of testimony, in the form of particular testimonies, will be fertile and reproduce testimony in anyone else's life, because that is dependent on factors far beyond our control. The climate and soil of the narratives in which we are rooted dictate the structure of the world, and the flow of history, at a level far beyond any individual's ability to change or manipulate them. The *roots* and *trunks* that frame our realities similarly act on our *bodies* far more than we are able to act on them.

Finally, if each individual flower is akin to an individual human, metaphorically, then we also cannot control how photosynthesis feeds any other flower other than our own: I can only adapt and change the ways I interpret the experience of the Divine and cannot control whether another will share my interpretation or even experience the Divine in any meaningful way. All we can do is send the pollen of our embodied testimony out into the world through our own actions, remaining faithful to the Divine vision of a testimony well lived, and hope that it is all enough.

Embodied testimony is messy. It requires that we get up close and personal with those around us in a deeply intimate way, an embrace close enough for the pollen of our lives to get sticky and chaotic and globby with the pollen of others, in which I share all that makes me *me* with others, and the community we create in the relationship we've formed is fertile and rich. At that point we are alive and are becoming the fruit that will form the seeds of the next generation. This is beauty, and this is truth. This is also *flourishing.*

Embodied testimony is when all of the larger aspects of the ecosystem finally come together in one point, where the energy of the Divine Light—which has been coursing throughout the entire ecosystem, giving it the energy of life—settles in and adds its spark to the action of pollination in a particular life, shaped by the *blossom* of a particular way of life, connected to a particular community, rippling out in waves across every blossom, within every community, within the entire ecosystem. Once you have created new life within the blossom, it begins to grow into *fruit*—with the *seed* of the future and new *hope* growing inside. This fruit is *doctrine* because the intimate, closely lived experience of testimony is what matures into teachings that speak so true—and truly—to the community that they are accepted as true: They reflect what is True about the Divine, the creation, and the relationships between everything. They sustain the community, and protect as the community plants the seeds of hope for the future wherever the seed eventually falls, on ground close to home or in places far away, surprising and unexpected and frightening and daring. This is a theology of life, chaotic, beautiful, messy life, ever dynamic and meant to be lived completely and with joy and abandon.

I truly believe that this is what emerges when you root your theology in soil, fertile and alive, as the spiritual mothers of early Friends taught us to do at the very first planting of that grove of trees known as the Religious Society of Friends. This is also what happened when Bayard Rustin welcomed Martin

Luther King Jr. into his life and invited King to do the same. Rustin drew King intimately close, so close that the pollen of Rustin's blossom could pollinate King's life and thus make manifest on the physical plane an interdependence that was already present on the spiritual plane as the energy of the Divine Presence danced through the community of their relationship.

Sure, the power of Rustin's argument for nonviolence as the most complete shape of the flower of King's testimony of justice was no doubt powerfully persuasive—Rustin most certainly had a talent for turning a phrase. What actually made King's soul fertile ground, however, was the essence of who Rustin was, the absolute commitment he showed to his Quaker nonviolent faith, and the ways this faith presented itself in his life. Rustin the man—the truth of his character and the beautiful way it presented itself to the world—caused King's blossom to open, and the beauty of his soul poured forth from the blossom of his earth-shaking prophetic power. Even today, the pollen of King's testimony fertilizes the world with the life-affirming truth of his life.

Pollen Testimonies

Particular testimonies are pollen because they fertilize our lives but also because they bounce against each other, blurring boundaries between them and remaking them in novel and fascinating ways. These *pollen testimonies* are peace, integrity, sustainability, justice, interdependence, and humility. I've already outlined some of the aspects of the particular testimonies to peace and truth above, in my analysis of Rustin's actions in response to Martin Luther King Jr.'s desire to own a weapon. As noted above, these two particular testimonies are multifaceted and complex, foundational aspects of Quaker testimony as a *form* of life shaped by the embodying of Quaker interdependence theology as well as particular expressions of that form in the *function* of specific actions that emerge in response to this embodiment. I must state at the outset that I am not looking to examine every potential aspect of these six particular testimonies. Instead, I want to first sketch out some core elements of each particular testimony as it is currently understood by Friends and then view those elements through the lens of pollen and ecotheology.

As has been my approach throughout this book, I am describing a mindset, or a worldview, that emerges when one engages in the work of theology from a certain perspective, using a specific set of tools, in a particular way: that of Quaker theology responding to the climate crisis. My account of each of these particular testimonies will therefore be answering the question, "What particular testimonies would emerge if one viewed Quaker testimony through the lens of life in its abundance: its beauty, its flourishing, and its fertility?" This is an admittedly novel approach to Quaker testimony, but not unprecedented. I've already engaged in the same exercise from the perspective of reconciliation theology and an ecotheology of Light.

My arguments here will be brief for two reasons, one practical and the other fundamental. The practical reason is simply that this is a book of sketches, a snapshot of what emerges when theology is viewed through a particular approach. I really only have space and time to sketch out a skeleton and will have to provide flesh and muscle to this approach in future volumes. The fundamental reason is by far the more intriguing, however, in that it makes claims about what particular testimony is: fundamentally, a set of tools that only fully come alive as they are embodied and enacted.

In this way, particular testimony must be reimagined each time it is applied in one's life, as the meaning of peace can morph and transform over time, even from one circumstance to the next. Similar to a carpenter using the same plane on two different pieces of wood but in vastly different ways, particular testimony has a universality to it that is nevertheless expressed only in specific ways, in specific contexts. One can write an entire book on the peace testimony, for example (or edit one![5]) and still discover that one has only scratched the surface of this testimony. Thus, take these sketches as guidelines, which only come alive when the color of life is applied.

Peace

As noted above, the particular testimony to peace is fundamental to any understanding of Quaker testimony, meaning that it is the necessary testimony within which any Quaker ecotheological testimony is rooted. This particular testimony is itself rooted in the concept of Divine/human interdependence underlying testimony as a whole, with the inevitable result that we must treat each individual molecule of life with the same respect and empathy we would treat the Divine, for the Divine is actually present throughout the entirety of the creation. Also, as God loves the entirety of creation, we must

5. Paul Anderson, Christy Randazzo, and Lonnie Valentine, eds., *Quakers and the Future of Peacemaking*, Quakers and the Disciplines 8 (Full Media Services, 2024).

as well, meaning that any violence against creation is itself inherently violence against God.

Peacebuilding is therefore the necessary beginning point for Quaker ethics and practice. Peacebuilding is also a natural outgrowth of the truthful beauty of worshipping a God whose love energizes the entire creation. In this incarnational vision of peace, the interdependent God demonstrates this love to its fullness, providing an example that Quakers are called to actively embody. For Christian Quakers, the most complete example of this incarnational life of loving interdependence is the life of Jesus. Yet, what still joins Quakers across all of our many divides is the insistence that we can encounter this incarnational love in our own lives and use the resource of the stories of exemplary Friends—who are understood to have exemplified this embodied peacemaking—as guides on the journey of living this form of life.

The peace testimony therefore depends on a holistic vision of peace. Peace must be understood to be the most complete expression of the human condition, embodied in everyday human interactions, in order to become so rooted in a person's character that it can shine through in their pursuits of peacebuilding on a broader scale—the state of peaceableness I examine in chapter 3, as described by Elise Boulding. This is a vision of peace as flourishing, in which peace is the state at which life flourishes in all of its abundance, marked by the presence of peace far more than simply the absence of immediate, direct conflict—the anemic definition of peace crafted by the binary world of peace/war so common in the language of empire.

Integrity

We have already experienced the dynamism of truth, in which truth expands in ever-widening ripples of impact, from the specifically individual (truth as being honest in one's individual dealings with others), through an alignment of one's life to a communal way of life that is true (such as peacemaking), finally lapping at the solid shoreline of the Divine as Truth itself. Truth must be true at every point of impact: The ethical frameworks of honesty that Quakers have long emphasized as integral to the particular testimony to truth must be rooted in an understanding of the Divine as True, in which the truth spoken by the individual Friend is a direct response to the truthful nature of the Divine. Truth is therefore dependable and can be relied on to reveal what is true, in which truth is understood as that which is both foundational to the world and necessary for maintaining the harmony and balance of the good order of creation. To live truthfully is both to always be honest in one's dealings with others and to align oneself with the essence of Divine Truth.

The practice of a testimony of truth as integrity is embodied by Quakers consistently speaking truth through their words and actions at all times, in all places, such that a life shaped by truth becomes an integrated whole. This embodied testimony reflects the presence of the integrated, interdependent Divine within, with the consequence that integrity is both universal and particular: universal because the Divine Truth is present in the entire creation, particular because individual human beings experience the Truth of the Divine presence in the dazzling diversity of human particularity. This dynamic interplay of the particular and the universal appears paradoxical but is actually reflecting the truth of an interdependent ecosystem that integrates multiple experiences of truth at once, each one coexisting alongside its fellows. The particular testimony to integrity is thus as much an approach to living truthfully in the messiness of our daily lives as it is an alignment of creation toward the Divine Truth.

Sustainability

A particular testimony to sustainability has emerged as many other things do: first very slowly, and then suddenly all at once. Sustainability is a testimony that coalesced into an explicit testimony—for some Quaker communities—only quite recently, yet it has roots that go deep in Quaker history. For example, John Woolman's concern for creation was itself rooted in the theology of life of early Quaker women. Admittedly, Quakers—as a body—have only recently begun to recognize that Woolman's vision of Quaker plain extends to an explicit care for creation, dependent on a fundamental sense of humility toward the place of humanity in God's creation.[6]

As I noted above regarding the impact of Quaker plain on the design of meetinghouses, plain reflects an entire framework of simplicity underlying every aspect of a person's interaction with the world, in which Quakers are called to focus their entire attention toward hearing the voice of the Light Within and removing anything that becomes an obstacle to embodying that focus completely in one's life.

---

6. Rachel Muers, *Testimony: Quakerism and Theological Ethics* (SCM, 2015), 175.

The most well-known expression of plain emerged during the time known as Quietism, which ran roughly between the end of the seventeenth century and the first few decades of the nineteenth century. Quaker plain in this period meant a specific set of consumption patterns and practices and economic concerns, and a stylized framework of aesthetic expression—known as "Quaker grey" . . . for potentially obvious reasons. Look up "Quaker grey clothing" on the internet, and you'll immediately see what I'm talking about here. Over time, however, this framing of plain as a uniform fell away, and plain began to morph into what we now term as a testimony to simplicity.

Quakers do not now have anything even remotely resembling a uniform—although a consistent thread from the plain of the past to the simplicity of the present has been a recognition of the call to focus all of our resources of attention toward placing the Divine at the absolute center of our selves, such that our every thought and action aligns with the Divine will.[7] One can easily see how a complex, interconnected web of specific practices and frameworks would emerge from this, and it has. Quakers might not have a uniform, but we will apply the principles expressed in plain as a framework for resource stewardship: a preference for thrift-store clothing over department-store clothing, as one potential example. In this way, it can be argued that simplicity is already aligned with an ecotheological framework, meaning that developing an explicit testimony to sustainability would not be necessary.

In the twentieth century, some Quakers developed a testimony of stewardship as an acknowledgment of the systemic injustice and waste that had consistently emerged from the selfish anthropocentrism (centered on the concerns and perspective of humanity alone) of much of human history, perfectly distilled in modern industrial practices.[8] A testimony of stewardship, therefore, ensures we expand the personal emphasis on simplicity into a systemic emphasis on correcting anthropocentrism and the dominion theology on which it depends, instead moving toward placing humanity as one element of an entire interdependent creation.

Yet, a testimony of stewardship is only a step along the path toward the more complete testimony: to the sustainability of life on this planet.

---

7. Lloyd Lee Wilson, *Essays on the Quaker Vision of Gospel Order* (Celo Valley Books, 1993), 173.

8. Muers, *Testimony*, 173.

Stewardship is itself not enough of a corrective, as it still centers humanity as the primary stewards of creation, with the primary role of caring for the creation as one within the creation but also somehow beyond it as well. This continues to feed into a hierarchical understanding of humanity as the center of creation rather than as simply one creature in a web of relationships with the rest of creation. Instead, a particular testimony to sustainability moves humanity out from the center toward a more humble—and scientifically accurate—place as simply one element of the chaotic abundance of life in an entirely interdependent creation. The particular testimony to sustainability is thus in a close relationship with particular testimonies to justice and humility: Only when we have the necessary humility to make the radical changes to our oppressive, unjust, and destructive structures of industry and domination will we be able to arrest the rapid ecological destruction we have unleashed on our planet.

Justice

Quakers have not delineated a specific testimony to justice, yet many of the same elements that constitute justice (redressing imbalances, the protection of rights, social restructuring, and restitution from harms done) also reside within the traditional framework of the particular testimony to equality. Justice stems from the fundamental Quaker theological tenet that the Divine is present within all. Equality emerges from a logical extension of this: As the Divine is universally present throughout creation, that necessarily implies that the Divine is universally present within particular persons, while these persons are brought into unity through the Divine present in each and every one of them. The action of Divine love both flattens and makes sacred the particularities of each person. The love of God is complete, whole, and unified, and as such individual persons are all equally loved by the Divine presence in creation. However, as God shows love through the act of creation, this inevitably includes each individual person, meaning that God is not just present within the particular but that God's love is also intended for particular persons as unique individuals.

Reflecting Quaker testimony, therefore, Quakers are called to show the love of God for others by ensuring not only that all people are equally free from oppression, injustice, war, violence, and poverty but that they are given space and the actual, physical resources they need to grow into the unique gifts given them by God—for bringing into being the Divine will but also for human enjoyment. Justice therefore seeks to offer redress for any imbalances between people, including ensuring the rights of marginalized groups and offering actual restitution for injustice. The pursuit of both justice and equality will inevitably lead to reenvisioning the structures that undergird society as well as the relationships that bind and give form to human communities.

Quakers have devoted significant attention to developing the outlines of the testimony to equality, such that Quaker discussions of equality are always issues of justice, whether racism, gender equality, economic injustice, and countless other examples. Quakers have also examined innumerable issues of violence from the perspective of equality. Quakers view equality as the lens through which to frame questions of justice and explain their particular approach to achieving justice through the methods they have developed to achieve equality across humanity.

Interdependence

A Quaker particular testimony to interdependence replaces and more clearly expresses the concerns currently expressed by the Quaker particular testimony of community. What distinguishes a particular testimony of interdependence are the ways Quaker theologies of interdependence radically expand the concept of community far beyond its current focus on human community. A testimony of interdependence rests on the foundation of the fundamental unity of all creation through the presence of the Divine within all people, which renders sacred all human life. This reflects the emphasis on existential humility expressed throughout this section, which insists that Quakers consistently recognize their actual place as only one element among many others within a fragile, interdependent ecological system, whether the global ecological community of earth or the specific contexts of the actual lived communities of watersheds. This is not a new approach, something imposed on Quaker testimony, but—as demonstrated by its presence throughout this section and actually throughout this entire book—is instead rooted deep within the history of Quaker theology and testimony.

Expressing this testimony in our lives requires that we recognize the truth expressed in the terms of Quaker interdependence theology: that we live fully into our humanity only when we see human beings as interdependent with the rest of creation, experiencing the pain and suffering of the rest of creation, and opening ourselves to align our entire way of life to relieve that suffering—which is itself often the result of human hubris and narratives of radical independence and freedom.

This is intensely personal and intimate work. It demands a willingness to be uncomfortably—and even dangerously—vulnerable to others in creation to a far greater extent than we are often comfortable with. The beauty of this work, however, lies in that it also opens us to experiencing the profound beauty and intimacy that develops as a result of close, vulnerable relationships—not only with other people but with all entities in creation. We are not simply experiencing the overwhelming love of God for creation, but we are experiencing the messy love of particular people, the joy of connecting with individual creatures, the awe inherent in engaging in the difficult and rewarding work of caring for the plants, trees, and fungi on which our survival depends.

Humility

I began this section by arguing that Quaker testimony from the perspective of the ecosystem is fundamentally shaped by the lens of life in its abundance: its beauty, its flourishing, and its fertility. This necessarily realigns testimony from a central focus on human needs and concerns toward an existential humility, in which the will of the Divine for the entire creation instead becomes the center of our theology and testimony. Arguably, therefore, every other particular testimony in this hexagonal vision of pollen testimonies contains aspects of the particular testimony to humility.

It is only through a fundamental humility toward our place in creation that we can (1) work toward ending our violence against creation and other human beings through dismantling structures of violence and injustice that depend on centering human desires for power and control; (2) free ourselves from the prison of lies that undergird dominion theology, accepting the truth of our interdependence; (3) develop the deeply intimate relationships with other human beings and creation that are inherent in the design of this interdependent creation; (4) dismantle the unjust systems of supremacy and oppression that perpetuate the division, poverty, and ecological exploitation marring the beauty of God's creation; and finally, (5) cultivate the perspective of interdependence necessary for us to reject not only dominion theology but also any role that in any way distances humanity from its true, intense intimacy with all creation as only one piece of its complex, interdependent beauty.

CHAPTER SIX

Fruits/Doctrine

What Are the Implications of "That of God Within"?

These things are worthy of note. I do not want to dwell too much upon Scripture authority. *We too often bind ourselves by authorities rather than by the truth.* We are infidel to truth in seeking examples to overthrow it.

—Lucretia Mott, "Not Christianity, but Priestcraft"

The Tree Is Always Known by Its Fruit: The Letter of James

My brothers and sisters, do not claim the faith of our Lord Jesus Christ of glory while showing partiality. For if a person with gold rings and in fine clothes comes into your assembly, and if a poor person in dirty clothes also comes in, and if you take notice of the one wearing the fine clothes and say, "Have a seat here in a good place, please," while to the one who is poor you say, "Stand there," or, "Sit by my footstool," have you not made distinctions among yourselves and become judges with evil thoughts? Listen, my beloved brothers and sisters. Has not God chosen the poor in the world to be rich in faith and to be heirs of the kingdom that he has promised to those who love him? But you have dishonored the poor person. Is it not the rich who oppress you? Is it not they who drag you into the courts? Is it not they who blaspheme the excellent name that was invoked over you? If you really fulfill the royal law according to the scripture, "You shall love your neighbor as yourself," you do well. But if you show partiality, you commit sin and are convicted by the law as transgressors. For whoever keeps the whole law but fails in one point has

> become accountable for all of it. For the one who said, "You shall not commit adultery," also said, "You shall not murder." Now if you do not commit adultery but you murder, you have become a transgressor of the law. So speak and so act as those who are to be judged by the law of liberty. For judgment will be without mercy to anyone who has shown no mercy; mercy triumphs over judgment. What good is it, my brothers and sisters, if someone claims to have faith but does not have works? Surely that faith cannot save, can it? If a brother or sister is naked and lacks daily food and one of you says to them, "Go in peace; keep warm and eat your fill," and yet you do not supply their bodily needs, what is the good of that? So faith by itself, if it has no works, is dead. (James 2:1–17 NRSVue)

I've always imagined the writer of the Letter of James to be a deeply practical person, the kind of person you could imagine as a highly effective community organizer, who sees the world clear-eyed and free from illusion, the kind of person who will instinctively hit at the core truth of a thing and be capable of explaining that truth plainly and effectively—the person who follows Lucretia Mott's call to be bound not by authorities but only by truth.[1] The central themes of this passage are obvious on their face, and James's argument is similarly clear and to the point. If you live a life rooted in faith in the love of Jesus, that life will inevitably leave traces around it through the actions you perform in the world. The markers of such a life involve fairness, mercy, love, compassion, and practical action (literally feeding people); one cannot be said to truly live in the faith of Jesus without these markers inevitably showing up.

James begins the passage (2:1) by stating plainly that the gospel of Jesus Christ does not permit anyone to play favorites and show partiality to any one over any other. This is a call for redress, however, for the community James addresses needs to be reminded that the equality of the gospel life is nonnegotiable. Yes, the systems of the world around you might demand that you accept different levels of worth and in turn demand that you police these levels yourself (2:2–4). When you do that, however, you are not only forgetting

---

1. This section is adapted from Christy Randazzo, "The Tree Is Always Known by Its Fruit," Political Theology Network, September 2, 2024, https://politicaltheology.com/the-tree-is-always-known-by-its-fruit/.

the core truth of the gospel—God chooses to focus their attention on the needs of the poor and the powerless (2:5)—but you have somehow become the same as those who oppress you, who ignore justice and use the courts as their playthings (2:6) and who use your adherence to the gospel as a central justification for their oppression of you (2:7, 9). Instead, you are called to show love toward your neighbor—not an affable willingness to do what is necessary to just get by but a true love that centers their needs—as the gospel demands of people when they show love the way Jesus showed it (2:8, 10).

This calls for an understanding of our lives as a collection of threads, radiating out from our souls within, that are woven together with the threads of everyone else (2:11). We are so shaped by these threads, and the way of life that emerges as a result of centering the law of love (2:12), that our faith will inevitably emerge through our actions (2:14). For example, you would be merciful more than judgmental (2:13), and you would ensure that all people had their basic needs met (2:15–16). A life truly shaped by the faith of Jesus will result in actions/works that speak of the life of Jesus all on their own. In other words, if you are capable of not acting when you see a need to show mercy, or to feed someone who is hungry, or any of a number of different ways that a life shaped by the gospel can manifest in someone's life—a life without works, in other words—then you cannot say that you actually have faith. Again: Faith by itself, if it has no works, is dead (2:17).

Now that we've laid out the general framework of this passage, let's return to the specific circumstances to which James was referring: People were showing partiality to people who not only didn't need it (due to the massive amount of power they held) but also didn't deserve it (due to their deceit, manipulation, oppression, and abuses of power). This is a situation that is easily understandable, for it needs no translation: a fundamentally unfair and unjust power imbalance in which those without power are forced to accommodate the desires and egos of those with power. This is the very definition of unfair, and we can all understand why.

We seem to know, almost instinctively, what feels fair to us and what doesn't. Almost from birth, we have a firm grasp on what emotions we feel—and how those emotions make our bodies feel—when we are convinced that we are being treated unfairly. Give one child two of something, give another child one, and regardless of how carefully you explain why you did so, I can almost *guarantee* that the child with one thing will cry foul. They will invoke the sacred chant, known to literally everyone, everywhere: "That's not fair!" Cue the inevitable explosion of anger, mingled with a gut punch of frustration, shock, and disappointment, and you have all of the essential elements of the experience of unfairness that every human has felt at least once in their life. Some among us, lest we forget, have this experience with far more regularity than others.

Of course, the challenge inherent in judging by the metric of fairness lies with the lack of any standard, universally accepted, objective measurement of "fair" that would apply equally to all at all times. Fair is irretrievably bound to circumstance and context, as fairness is nearly devoid of meaning outside people interpreting its meaning. For example, I am an adjunct in the humanities, whose main ministry vocation is in writing the kind of stuff you're reading right this minute. I am deeply enmeshed in the life of my faith community, work that demands countless hours of work a week, work that I will never get paid for. I am certain that very few people see the balance between my paid labor and unpaid labor as fair. Yet, that wouldn't tell the entire story of fair, at least not as I view it.

Here's the argument made by so many idealists and dreamers to justify their often paltry income: Life isn't just about making money. While some of you might be wearing a knowing smirk right now, please do not mistake me: I am a true believer. I know that I am not earning anywhere close to what I could in some other fields. And I've come to accept that each dollar less in my paycheck equals one minute more I get to spend alone and doing work I love. In this specific circumstance, in this specific context, I have come to see a pathway for me through life in which I can accept a measurement of fairness that serves my own needs and answers to my own terms.

Yet, on another level, this situation will never, ever be fair—vast income/power equity imbalances exist within academia as much as any other industry, especially as state funding started drying up a few decades ago and then private equity firms swooped in to start having their fill. For my *entire* life—as I was born just a hair before the beginning of the Reagan revolution—the financiers and capitalists and money men have looted and pillaged their way across every single aspect of human existence in the United States, such that a scant few hundred people own over 90 percent of the accumulated global wealth and at least as high a percentage of property: both real and financial assets. The very foundations on which society is built, and the fabric that weaves it together, are fundamentally, radically unfair. You will never be able to convince me of the fairness of this Salvador Dali surrealist fever dream of reality. Interesting times, indeed.

Any attempt on my part to find some measure of fairness in a system that is unfair at its roots is a way to reclaim my autonomy from the system's rapacious clutches. For the market, exchange is everything, and so finding a level of exchange one is willing to accept in order to engage in the life of the market is unavoidably bound up in power and the vastly unequal distribution of power across society that is a core feature of late-stage capitalism. In a world in which money is the primary means of exchange, in which money's interests are seen as primary above the interests of anything else, it is nearly impossible to avoid engaging with the market on its own terms. Refusing to allow the inherently unjust, unfair, and sinful market to dictate your own sense of personhood, of value and worth, of identity and belonging: This is what James is talking about here in James 2:1 with his argument about partiality.

James states clearly that his readers are to never mistake an attitude of deference toward the wealthy and powerful as being the same as the Divine message. It's rather straightforward: You might be forced to acknowledge that the world you live in is fundamentally unjust—and adjust your actions and choices to account for that reality—but you should never take the next step to allow the values of that world to become the values that shape and give meaning and purpose to your life. You will know the tree by its fruit, and the faith by the life that accompanies it. Imagine what a world we could have if we judged someone solely by their fruits and not by their power, status, and possessions. In the meantime, in this world, our best resistance to injustice and unfairness is to never accept the narrative that they are somehow acceptable or even inevitable: The story of the market is not now, and *never has been*, the story of God's will for the creation.

The *fruit* that grows from the *flowers* of *testimony* is the one central theological doctrine (or foundational teaching) in Quaker theology: that there is "that of God" within all and that Quakers must act as if they are encountering the Divine whenever they meet another—because they *are* encountering the Divine Presence within another. Akin to the peace testimony, which has weight due to its consistency throughout Quaker history, the doctrine of "that of God" has weight due to the consistency with which Quakers have confirmed their experience of this doctrine since the beginning of the movement.

The theological import of this term has expanded and evolved over the years, meaning that this doctrine has been expressed in various ways across the entire Quaker theological watershed—as should be expected from any doctrine that must be open to continuing revelation. When read through the ecosystem, however, a few central elements emerge.

For one, as that of God is understood to be present within us, it involves an intensely intimate interdependence between creation and Divine, demanding a vision of the Divine that transcends boundaries while also being immanently present and alive. Take the implication to its logical conclusion, and you have the Divine fully present in every atom and every subatomic particle, down to the electrons that carry the energy of life and the particles that are the foundation of matter. I use the natural metaphor of *cloud* to connote this experience of being completely surrounded and immersed in the Divine Presence, akin to that all-encompassing way that being in a cloud, or in fog, can encapsulate you completely and become reality. Cloud also works on a practical level as a metaphor for interdependence, because it's impossible to deny human interconnectivity when everyone in a cloud is literally breathing the exact same fog. This is the Spirit of God, a Divine Cloud that interpenetrates creation—universally, everywhere—and makes life alive.

The other implication of "that of God" is the incarnation of the Divine in actual people and the ways those people respond to that presence. This includes the Christian doctrine of Jesus as incarnation, and the implications of the historical witness of Jesus the human on our understanding of the Divine as *particular* and present in specific individuals.

Quakers do not focus significant attention on developing an atonement theology. That being said, any theological statements Quakers make about atonement reflect the theological variety present not only within Quaker theology but also within Christian atonement theology. Generally, Quakers view the passion, crucifixion, death, and resurrection of Jesus—and any potential salvific consequences of these acts—through two main lenses: an assertion of the drawing of humanity into full participation in the divine life affected by the crucifixion, and a rejection of the salvific uniqueness of Jesus. This represents the twin strands of Christianity and universalism within Liberal Quakerism especially. Again, the diversity of theological belief among Friends means that not every Friend accepts the truth of both statements, let alone even one of them.

Any statement on the role of the crucifixion in the atonement, even a rejection of its importance, remains a theological statement, so Liberal Quakers therefore have both a positive and negative theology of the atonement. The fluid nature of Liberal Quaker theology is demonstrated in that Liberal Quaker theology avoids making specific claims about the meaning of the incarnation, the crucifixion, or the resurrection—and its historicity. Quakers who acknowledge that the cross had a role to play in the drama of Jesus seem willing to simply accept that there is in fact a connection. They are more interested in the implications of the connection, especially in terms of ethics. This approach would likely fall within the nonviolent atonement branch of theologies of atonement and reconciliation.

An important distinction, however, is that for Quakers, every theology of the atonement is read through an underlying rejection of violence having any positive role to play in the life of God. In other words, Quakers are deeply skeptical (an understatement) of any atonement theology that requires Jesus's violent death to effect God's will—*especially* substitutionary atonement. Yet again, this is a point of intersection between Quaker theology and ecotheology: Both reject violence as having any core role to play in the life of God. Quakers emphasize the peaceful rejection of violence, while ecotheologians reject the implication that the God of life would require a violent death in order to heal the relationship between creation and Divine. This is coupled with an assertion that humanity is drawn by God into full participation in the Divine life, affected by the responsibility to live "as incarnation" in a life of service, such as the affirmation mysticism framework developed by Rufus Jones.

Finally, this affects time and human perception of it, leading to an understanding of eschatology that exists in two time scales: realized and realizing. *Realized*, in that the Divine Presence everywhere means that the atoning work of the Divine has already occurred, and time simply continues to run without any future "end" of the world; and *realizing*, in that the work of bringing about the kindom of God is ongoing, and requires human effort.

This focus on healing creation's relationship with itself and with the Divine constitutes a form of "living atonement," in which atonement occurs through a relationship of profound intimacy between the Divine and the creation, in which both seek only that the creation *flourish*. This means *all* of creation, in which every single atom is capable of flourishing while it is their time to exist, in balance with its ecosystems while existing, and releasing their energy back to the biosphere once they cease to exist. Atonement thus necessarily involves both Divine and human action, in which both the Divine Cloud and the creation—in their own unique and particular ways—seek to heal the injuries suffered by the creation due to cruelty, selfishness, greed, or any of the numerous other forms of harm humanity (especially) is so good at inflicting on itself.

The Divine Cloud

Electron Clouds and the Cosmic Microwave Background: *Long Island Sound Watershed, Late 1980s*

Weekend nights when I was a kid involved watching a great deal of whatever was playing on the local public television station. Certain shows were nationally televised, beautifully interwoven with whatever locally focused culture and history documentaries happen to get a regular slot during the prime-time "weekend family activity for the nerdiest, most introverted people alive" schedule. Depending on where you were in the country, your evenings consisted of a Britcom (British sitcom, for those in the know), possibly a *NOVA* (*the* science documentary series of the 1980s and 1990s), *Doctor Who* (the original series, while it was running new shows), a British crime show (why only British ones? because the PBS audience can sometimes be *ever* so slightly snobby), and then it was past my bedtime.

When you're a kid, your world is most often defined for you by those holding care of you. I am *indelibly* marked by having grown up idolizing Tom Baker's scarf (*my* Doctor Who: Oh, those gloriously long, cozy, exuberantly eccentric scarves!) and having science explained to me in a way that was *just* entertaining enough that I was willing to accept that my parents were spending my life away, hour by *slightly* entertaining hour, as I learned about science—my dad's favorite subject and my least favorite.

Occasionally, though, *NOVA* would just drop the *hammer* on you, delivering a banger of an episode that asked all the juicy philosophical questions I cared about. Oh, you thought that people just *become* theologians? Oh no, you are *grown*, and the roots of your weird obsession with complicated questions go deep. Show me a nature documentary with breaching whales or hyenas being creepy, and I'll show you the entirety of my eyelids. Start theorizing about the ultimate nature of reality? Oh, you are *on*, science documentary show!

I adored those episodes when some physicist sitting next to astonishingly massive and complex technical equipment—wires as veins everywhere—was forced to enter the world of story and poetry and metaphor in order to find a way to close the yawning chasm between the ignorance of the vast majority of the world and the deep knowledge of these experts in fields whose Wikipedia pages I cannot fathom. One night in the late 1980s I was watching an episode on the Big Bang when I was introduced to two ideas that embedded themselves so deeply in my soul that they were eventually two of the building blocks for my understanding of the Divine: cosmic microwave background radiation and the electron cloud.

The beauty of the Big Bang theory is that while it is difficult to master, it is fairly easy to learn, at least in bare outline. The universe as we know it began as an unfathomably dense and hot singularity of space-time, which expanded outward at an unimaginable rate, effectively making existence exist. Effectively, the universe began as a tiny dot with a density of metaphysical proportions. As this "big bang" (hence the name and its absolute perfection: It's truly a thing of beauty) sent literally everything hurtling out throughout the current boundaries of our observable universe, there is a universal presence of microwave energy (or radiation) across the background of the cosmos as well: the cosmic microwave background. The cosmic microwave background holds an intriguing distinction: It contains the vast majority of all photons (elementary particles that comprise all electromagnetic fields, including Light) in the universe. In other words, the background foundation of the universe is a universally present light energy. (Yes, I am going exactly where you think I am going here.)

Later in the show, I learned that electrons aren't actually specific particles in space captured in orbits around the nucleus, such as the traditional planet-and-orbiting-moons image we associate with atoms due to the universal use of that symbol to represent radiation. This caught my attention because my father worked at a nuclear power plant, and I was quite familiar with this image. Instead, the physicist explained that the best way to visualize an electron in this new, quantum mechanical atomic model was *cloud* itself. As more scientists spoke, attempting the delicate work of trying to explain quantum physics to the general public using metaphor and poetic imagery, I could tell how uncomfortable it made some of these folks to enter that imprecision; many would apologize for having to resort to imprecise imagery in order to explain some impossibly complex mathematical equation. Why?! They were finally speaking in a language I could understand!

The electron cloud is uncertainly certain in that the probability field of the electron (where you could probably expect to locate the electron at any point in time) is *cloud*, entirely encircling and enveloping the nucleus. The uncertainty of the electron cloud remains even at absolute zero Kelvin, vibrating away in this is/isn't existence while the rest of existence appears still. This was mind-blowing for me, because it opened all doors at once: If the atom—the literal foundation of life—was fundamentally uncertain and instead was the embodiment of change, what ripples would this cast out into the bedrock certainty of existence and existing?

That's the thing, though: Electrons *do* exist and are certain. I typed this on a computer, with a monitor, that entirely depends on the existence of electrons (and their inherent uncertain certainness) to come alive. Never mind the electrical storms firing in my brain at this moment, either, using the energy of the sun (filtered for me through the plants I eat, the air I breathe, the water I drink) to cause these words to exist before you. No electrons, no atoms, no existence.

Eventually, this *seed* took root within a watershed *climate* whose rivers included interdependence reconciliation theologies, Christian mysticism, the metaphorical theology of Light, the individual/community tension in Quaker waiting worship, ecotheology, Western individualism, and panentheism. My *body* experienced the Divine over the years, in innumerable ways each and every day. These encounters led me to seek out a way of life—a *testimony*—in which my life would *blossom* as I was shaped by the Love at the foundation of all existence. My *leaves* interpreted this Energy as being the reconciling Spirit—interpenetrating within me and interdependent with me, material and immaterial, uncertain certainty. Finally, the *fruit* of the images of the Divine as Light energy, and Spirit as Divine Cloud, flourished within my soul.

Now, this wasn't a seed that took root immediately. As you can see, all I know about the context is a time frame of a few years: I don't remember anything other than what else was in the image of that one specific moment when the thought flashed through my brain, and "child watching *NOVA*" is a rich store of memory snippets to rummage through. Admittedly, there's very often randomness in which seeds embed in our sou(i)l. Yet, the idea that reality is at core a cloud of uncertainty, where everything is possible *and* impossible—simultaneously—obviously stuck around, as I wrote a book laying out a comprehensive vision of the nature of reality that you decided to read. The seed took *root*, grew, and produced *fruit*, did it not? The right seed, at the right moment, in the right location, nurtured and protected, can slowly consume a person such that they are defined by the seed, now one of their pillars. It's the power of a plant body to assert its autonomy over concrete and to flourish in sheer cliffs. Life finds a way, and ideas are alive: They want to be cast to the winds, to spread far and wide, to land on *fertile* soil and take root.

The measure of a metaphor lies in its capacity to capture, in a simple and effective image or concept, an entire cosmos of complex shades of meaning: Similar to electron clouds, metaphors are clouds of uncertain certainty, in which language is transformed from practical tool to poetry. In an act of continuing revelation, engaging with the language of quantum mechanics results in a new metaphorical theology. These two metaphors combine with the metaphor of incarnation to explain the relationship between the persons of the Trinity as a relationship of matter and energy: *the Divine Cloud*.

The Creator provides both the structure of existence and the Light energy that animates life as it pulses in the background, universally present throughout the cosmos, even in the darkest places: the Divine Presence as the Light Within. The incarnation is the Divine Presence experiencing existence from the perspective of creation, in the most intimate, vulnerable embrace possible, across the entire cycle of life from birth to death. The Electron Cloud is the Divine Presence as the paradoxical, uncertain certainty of this embrace: Spirit as both the animator of creation from within and the foundational structure of reality from without. Or, in more traditional Christian theological terms: the Trinity of the Divine Cloud is Light (Creator), Incarnation (Jesus Christ), and Electron Cloud (Holy Spirit).

Biblical Imagery of the Divine Cloud

However novel this metaphorical framework might appear, it is actually rooted deeply within the Christian tradition, present in both the Jewish and Christian Bibles, most prominently in six locations: the wind over the formless void in Genesis 1:2, the animating breath of God in Genesis 2:7, the silence Elijah seeks in 1 Kings 19:11–13, the promise of the Advocate (the Spirit) in John 14:15–17, the experience of the Spirit at Pentecost in Acts 2:1–13, and the long discourse on the spiritual gifts of 1 Corinthians 12–14. Each location speaks to a core aspect of the Cloud.

The NRSV of Genesis 1:2 states, "The earth was a formless void and darkness covered the face of the deep, while a wind from God swept over the face of the waters." *Wind*, however, has also been translated as "Spirit." As divine, Spirit existed before and outside time. As wind, the Spirit is immanent at all places at once, moving at will in and through creation. The Cloud is not mentioned in the remainder of the first creation story, Genesis 1:3–2:1, yet the absence of comment does not imply an absence of the Cloud during the remainder of the story, nor a retraction of the Spirit of God from the creation. It can be surmised, therefore, that the Cloud existed before time—and as God's presence over creation has existed throughout time.

In Genesis 2:7, the Cloud of Spirit is the animating breath of God breathing life into the first humans. The Spirit exists outside creation, yet is also breathed into all of creation, animating creation and making life possible. This is a common biblical understanding of the Spirit: A person's spirit or *pneuma* is the Divine within that person. Wherever life exists, the Cloud of Spirit hangs over it, interpenetrating it and soaking it through.

First Kings 19:1-18 tells the story of Elijah fleeing for his life, heading toward God's mountain (Mount Horeb) to give God an earful for requiring him to prophesy to monarchs who actively sought his death. While I've never felt the hounds of Jezebel nip at my heels, I've done my fair share of complaining to and ranting at God—in churches, on mountains, in my living room, and on—and I can appreciate the head of steam Elijah has built within him. He's so flummoxed that angels tell him to eat some food and take a nap—the universal cure. He finally arrives at Mount Horeb and explains to God that while he has been "very zealous" for the Lord, the government God put in place (kings were still understood to have gained their legitimacy due to God's approval) was destroying everything he was trying to build, including killing all of God's prophets. In other words, Elijah is pleading and complaining, simultaneously, asking God to step in: "Please help me, I'm backed against a wall here, and I'm doing what you *told* me to do!" God responds:

> [The word of the Lord] said, "Go out and stand on the mountain before the Lord, for the Lord is about to pass by." Now there was a great wind, so strong that it was splitting mountains and breaking rocks in pieces before the Lord, but the Lord was not in the wind; and after the wind an earthquake; and after the earthquake a fire, but the Lord was not in the fire; and after the fire a sound of sheer

> silence. When Elijah heard it, he wrapped his face in his mantle and went out and stood at the entrance of the cave. Then there came a voice to him that said, "What are you doing here, Elijah?"

This passage mentions a powerful wind, yet it is not the Spirit of God, nor is Spirit in the earthquake and fire. These three images were traditional symbols of God's presence and power. Elijah, however, recognizes that by presenting themself only in the powerful silence, Spirit is teaching him to experience God's presence through its seeming *absence* as much as its presence—perhaps even more so. God is stressing to Elijah that God exists on both the immanent and transcendent plane—both in the cacophony of creation and in the mysterious silence we experience deep within our souls.

In John 14:15–17, Jesus promises to send the Advocate, which will abide with the disciples. The Advocate is the Spirit of Truth, which, as verse 17 states, is known by the disciples, "because he abides with you, and he will be in you." The entire passage, 14:15–31, continues the theme of the divine interpenetration, in which Jesus makes explicitly clear that God exists in him as well as in all of creation. This interpenetration is dependent on God's love regardless of humanity's recognition of that love. The use of the present tense in verse 17 implies that Spirit already exists within the disciples. They are aware of Spirit within themselves due to the awareness that they have gained by rejecting the world's values and living by the commandments of Jesus, which involve loving God and neighbor.

This passage can be interpreted to imply that Spirit resided in the world before the specific historical time period of Pentecost, existing within all people. It stresses that we can come to a full knowledge of this fact only by living a life of complete love of God and the creation: thus imitating the life of Christ. We can attain a more complete union with Spirit through love. In Spirit, the will of God is no longer external to ourselves, for Spirit manifests itself within us, working alongside us to aid us in remaining in accord with the divine will.

The inbreaking of Spirit in Pentecost, as related in Acts 2:1–13, demonstrates that Spirit is dynamic, moves without restriction and according to its own will, and is universally present in all of humanity. The timing of Spirit's movement is sudden and without warning, taking every person present by surprise. Spirit has little care for the negative social impact on those in whom it moves—it disregards sarcastic comments about folks being day-drunk just as much as it disregards any other "worldly" perspective. Spirit does not discriminate by the differences of human culture, instead inhabiting people from what the writer of Acts understood to be the entirety of the known world.

The "gifts of the Spirit" passages in 1 Corinthians 12–14 are central to Paul's theology of Spirit. The key themes vital to the Cloud of Spirit are that the diversity of gifts given to the Corinthians are all equal in value and measure, and are all given by the one, unified Spirit (12:4); the diversity in and among the body of Christians is equivalent to the diversity of God, and as God does not show favor within the Godhead, all the members of the Christian body are of equal measure and status with each other (12:12–13); any manifestation of Spirit pales in greatness to Spirit itself, and Spirit is complete love poured out by God on the creation (13:1–3). Remember: The manifestations of the Spirit in 12:1 are actually charismata, gifts from God to the community, and not anything the Corinthians could gain themselves.

At-one-ment with the Divine Cloud

The reconciliation *pneumatology* of Divine Cloud makes the bold claim that God desires union with humanity and that human meaning and purpose stem from this union. God interpenetrates all of creation as Spirit, breathing over creation and animating all of existence. God exists as the grounding of creation, on whom the creation owes ontological dependence, for nothing/no-*thing* would exist were it not for the energy continuously poured from the Divine into the Cloud. This grounding comes with a necessary corollary: As Cloud, Spirit is embodied in the entirety of creation to such a full extent that the divine is omnipresent within every individual body of creation. The community is thus embedded in Spirit, and any rift in the community serves to divide the union of persons and Spirit in the Divine Cloud. The work of the Spirit is thus integral to any effort at reconciliation.

This relates to the fact that a spirituality of reconciliation is *panentheistic*. Panentheism deals with the fundamental paradox presented above: that God's complete transcendence exists in relationship with God's complete immanence. The immanence and transcendence are neither aspects nor attributes of God: They are the very essence of God. While this coexistence of two divergent constructs may appear a paradox, it is this very paradox whose tension gives meaning to God's panentheistic existence within creation. Spirit resides within humanity, therefore, and connects humanity to all of creation through the

Divine Cloud.[2] This is transcendence amid immanence—a paradox that can be experienced and even examined but never truly *known*.

This unknowability is not entirely due to God's transcendence, although that plays a role, reflecting the Christian mystical tradition's stress that Spirit can be comprehended only in outline. This is a paradox of material immateriality, in which the Divine can be a definable something, in the "something" of the soul—yet also be pure nothingness. This nothingness is often what we experience when we encounter God. As Friend Pink Dandelion states, in the context of Quaker worship, access to God may give an individual feelings of remoteness, otherness, and dependence before such power. In Quaker worship especially, there is a peculiar combination of experience in which what is beyond and absent is felt as present, while what is clearly present is experienced in terms of its absence or transcendence.[3]

This state of remoteness, otherness, and dependence forces us to deal with the utter transcendence of God. We stare into Kierkegaard's abyss only to discover that either we cannot recognize what stares back at us, or—even more daunting—we cannot tell whether anything stares back at all. Admittedly, language is often left without resources to explain the experience of Divine encounter. When faced with the task of explaining the interrelationality of the Trinity, the inestimable Augustine was left without any words to use to describe the paradox of three in one.[4] He was eventually forced to use imperfect words to avoid being reduced to complete silence on the issue.

The immanence of God is a presence with us, a sharing in our human nature. The immanence resides within us, sharing our joys and sorrows, as the Divine Cloud. The transcendence of God is a complete otherness, existing on a plane beyond human existence as the Divine Other. God and humans

2. McFague envisions the entire universe, in particular the earth, as God's body. As she explains, "There is one obvious advantage to this model [the body of God]: it allows us to think of God as immanent in our world while retaining, indeed, magnifying God's transcendence. The model of the universe as God's body unites immanence and transcendence. At once a powerful image of divine immanence, for everyone and everything becomes potentially a sacrament of God, it is also, though perhaps not as obviously, an image of divine transcendence." Sallie McFague, *The Body of God: An Ecological Theology* (Fortress, 1993), 20.

3. Pink Dandelion, *The Liturgies of Quakerism* (Ashgate, 2005), 14.

4. Ola Sigurdson, "Is the Trinity a Practical Doctrine?," in *The Concept of God in Global Dialogue*, ed. Werner G. Jeanrond and Aasulv Lande (Orbis Books, 2005), 120.

cannot be delineated by status or place, for status has meaning only on the same plane. God is therefore neither king nor monarch—or any other symbol of status in human culture. As humans can exist only on the plane of immanence, to compare our status with God is to place God firmly on the plane of immanence and to deny the plane of transcendence. This can be seen in the language of God's essence and God's "energies" in Eastern Orthodox theology:

> One interesting aspect of the power aspect of God is the fact that the Eastern Orthodox Church at an early stage made a distinction between God's transcendent essence (*ousia*) and his "energies" (*energeiai*). His essence could never be grasped by human beings, but his energies could be known through his activities in the world. . . . In a similar way, the relationship to God may be experienced in energetic terms. God is not only the powerful Other out there, but is the source of strength and vitality. The faithful person waits for power and strength from God.[5]

God's mystical reality is impossible, holding dual truths in tension: God's essence is transcendent and thus beyond comprehension, while God's energies are present in God's actions. God's essence is the energy of creation, therefore. Dietrich Bonhoeffer claimed that creation only existed because God's existence permeated it—and through the diverse unity of the Triune God changed creation into the very image of Divine incarnation.[6]

God's essence is the core of reality and energizes all of creation: Creation exists only because God already existed, exists, and will exist. We are permeated by God, we breathe in the life of God and are changed by the diverse unity of the multiplicity of God into the very image of the Divine. This mystical reality of permeation by the Divine Cloud is perhaps best defined as an "endless ocean of love," a community and society of lovers mutually indwelling and united to one another: a mutual indwelling in the justice that is love.[7]

This sounds strikingly familiar to George Fox's vision of an ocean of darkness and death lying underneath an ocean of light and love:

---

5. Notto R. Thelle, "Relation, Awareness and Energy," in Jeanrond and Lande, *Concept of God in Global Dialogue*, 58.

6. Dietrich Bonhoeffer, *Discipleship* (Fortress, 2003), 287.

7. Ilia Delio, *Clare of Assisi: A Heart Full of Love* (St. Anthony Messenger, 2007), 5.

> Yet I was under great temptations sometimes, and my inward sufferings were heavy; but I could find none to open my condition to but the Lord alone, unto whom I cried night and day. And I went back into Nottinghamshire, and there the Lord shewed me that the natures of those things which were hurtful without were within, in the hearts and minds of wicked men. . . . The Lord answered that it was needful that I should have a sense of all conditions, how else should I speak to all conditions; and in this I saw the infinite love of God. *I saw also that there was an ocean of darkness and death, but an infinite ocean of light and love, which flowed over the ocean of darkness.* And in that also I saw the infinite love of God; and I had great openings.[8]

God's immanence constantly desires human engagement, at the core of God's being: the ontic reality of the Divine Cloud is relationship both within the electron clouds of uncertain certainty and with humanity.[9] This relationship brings joy, love, and strength—for both Cloud and humanity—only if humanity willingly engages in a truthful pursuit of an interdependent relationship.[10] This interpenetrative relationship between the human and the Divine is the beginning of reconciliation, in that a true relationship leads to reconciliation on both the human/divine level and on the human/human level. Human ontology (nature of being) is thus made complete and whole in the ontology of an interpenetrative Spirit.[11]

This communal ontology of God is meaningless without a corresponding spirituality of peacemaking and reconciliation, in which rejection of the good in others will hamper union in the communal self.[12] We can become integrated individuals, with the attendant characteristics of power, control, and survival,

---

8. Fox, *Journal of George Fox*, 19, emphasis added.

9. Anselm Kyongsuk Min, "Solidarity of Others in the Power of the Holy Spirit: Pneumatology in a Divided World," in *Advents of the Spirit: An Introduction to the Current Study of Pneumatology*, ed. Bradford D. Hinze and D. Lyle Dabney (Marquette University Press, 2001), 417.

10. Howard Thurman, *Jesus and the Disinherited* (Abingdon-Cokesbury, 1949), 109.

11. G. W. H. Lampe, *God as Spirit*, The Bampton Lectures 1976 (Clarendon, 1977), 18.

12. Battle, *Blessed Are the Peacemakers*, 30.

only when we rest in the peaceful, reconciled communal self.[13] The mystical consciousness required to become aware of the interconnectedness of God with the creation can be developed only in a community infused by a pneumatological spirituality of peacemaking and reconciliation. What would that spirituality—and the community emerging in response—look like?

A *narrative* perspective understands all human life as communal, and all community as narrative. Narrative sees the self as *story*, as embedded in the story of a community that undergirds the self with a web of meaning.[14] A spirituality of narrative takes strength from the paradox of the interdependent God, finding in the Spirit a correlative and affirming narrative of diversity that reflects the diversity and confusion of human existence.[15] Stanley Hauerwas states that this diversity provides us with "skills appropriate to the conflicting loyalties and roles we necessarily confront in our existence."[16] This diversity is also essential to the self, for the self can be constructed only from the building blocks of communal life.[17]

Narrative is not only about the togetherness of community and the ties weaving it together. Instead, by aligning human wants with the true story of the communal Divine Cloud—the Presence of the Cosmic Microwave Background (Father/Parent), the Incarnation of Divine Humanity (Son/Child), and the Encounter of the Electron Cloud (the Holy Spirit/Spirit)—and by living into the story together as a community, humans gain the resources to lead truthful lives. Any togetherness gained in the community is a byproduct of living faithfully with this story. The main focus of narrative spirituality is on weaving the life of the community into the life of the Divine Cloud, rooted in the ground that makes reconciliation flourish.

A spirituality of reconciliation is *covenantal*, for all reconciliation is based on God's promise of blessing and caring for the life of the community. Friend

13. Min offers solidarity as an alternative construct to communion ("Solidarity of Others," 422).

14. Stanley Hauerwas and William H. Willimon, *Resident Aliens: Life in the Christian Colony* (Abingdon, 1989), 77.

15. Yves Congar, *I Believe in the Holy Spirit* (Seabury Books, 1983), 58.

16. Stanley Hauerwas, *The Hauerwas Reader*, ed. John Berkman and Michael Cartwright (Duke University Press, 2001), 245.

17. Hauerwas and Willimon, *Resident Aliens*, 78.

Doug Gwyn explains that the covenant is God's unconditional promise to restore wholeness to the world. This promise is both unavoidable (as it is rooted in God's will) and conditional (God's will finds its answer in the conditional human will).[18] This paradox of unavoidable/conditional continues the paradoxical nature of the interpenetrative union of the Divine Cloud.

The Divine Cloud promises *shalom* for the entire creation.[19] Community occurs through the harmony and peace of God and is healed through the reconciling presence of God in the creation.[20] Covenant is the promise of God to maintain a relationship with humanity. The fullness of this covenant can be experienced only when humanity is completely committed to being in relationship with God.[21] Covenant is integral to reconciliation, for it gives humanity *hope* for the future. Hope gives humanity a reason to remain patient and thus the strength to continue seeking unity with God through reconciliation communities.[22]

A spirituality of reconciliation is *rooted in place* in that, as all relationships occur in the place of the community, reconciliation between divided people must occur in the context of a "place." Place has contextual meaning and is thus narrative. David Stevens even suggests that reconciliation is itself a place, in which, in the words of Psalm 85:10, the necessary materials for communal relationship all meet: mercy, justice, righteousness, and peace. The interplay between these four core aspects of communal life is reconciliation.[23]

Reconciliation is *responsible*: It takes responsibility for ensuring that justice, peace, breaking cycles of violence, and ending poverty are realities for all of creation in the Divine Cloud, both in the present and for all future generations.[24] Reconciliation is thus also political, seriously engaged in the active

18. Douglas Gwyn, *The Covenant Crucified: Quakers and the Rise of Capitalism* (Quaker Books, 2006), 8.

19. Gwyn, *Covenant Crucified*, 7.

20. Lampe, *God as Spirit*, 177.

21. Gwyn, *Covenant Crucified*, 8.

22. Gwyn, *Covenant Crucified*, 5.

23. David Stevens, *The Land of Unlikeness: Explorations into Reconciliation* (Columba, 2004), 31.

24. William Schweiker, "A Preface to Ethics: Global Dynamics and the Integrity of Life," *Journal of Religious Ethics* 32, no. 1 (2004): 32.

pursuit of social change. This sense of political responsibility is based on the claim that all of life is good, with the attendant demand that life is respected and given the opportunity to thrive.

Reconciliation is *forgiving* since forgiveness is the only way to keep way open for Spirit to heal the broken relationships in the community. Forgiveness is essential and has its roots in the Divine incarnation. Reconciliation cannot occur through purely human effort, therefore. It is rooted in a willingness to overcome enmity and suffering through allowing God's mercy to fill our hearts.[25] Forgiveness is one of the actions of the Divine Cloud, for it seeks to reintegrate the unique individual while also reconciling the victim and the offender.

A spirituality of reconciliation must be *humble*: Approaching reconciliation with humility allows us the perspective necessary to ask Spirit to guide us to seek forgiveness and to grant it for the good of the Divine Cloud.[26] This humble perspective opens people to accept responsibility for each other and for the opportunity presented in humble forgiveness. We are bound together metaphysically and atomically and climatically and economically and hydraulically: We each have a responsibility to hold each other accountable to the commitment we each have made to the community, including the commitment to abide by the standards of the community. This process is not in any way designed to punish, exclude, or alienate—only to reconcile.

The consequence of being in relationship with the ground of all existence themself is alignment with the standards of "that which is life." Therefore, warmongering, exploitation, oppression, abuse in any form, greed, and arrogance are *all* off the table, along with many other activities. Sin, therefore, is creating false boundaries and divisions between the creation and acting as if one were not inextricably bound within the Divine Cloud. Discipling oneself to one's watershed involves discipline—that's just the way it goes: Sin is all that goes against flourishing in community, in which the Divine Cloud brings all of creation into a reconciled community.

We already are reconciled—now we need to act like it.

---

25. Robert J. Schreiter, *Reconciliation: Mission and Ministry in a Changing Social Order* (Orbis Books, 1992), 43.

26. Ilia Delio, *Franciscan Prayer* (St. Anthony Messenger, 2004), 117.

Theosis

Theosis is the process of transformation for humans in which, through living a life of imitation of Christ's love, humans come to an awareness of the Spirit of God residing within them and seek to gain the more complete union with God that God offers to all and desires with all.[27] Theosis thus recognizes two different forms of union with God: (1) the union with creation that has existed since the beginning of creation, manifested in the interpenetration of the Cloud with creation; and (2) the more complete union of desire and love that humanity must be open to receiving. Union with God can be realized in its full extent only on God's granting us the ability to do so. It is therefore not only possible but is actually God's desire and will for the creation.[28] There is a mutual and reciprocal attraction between God and humanity, desiring love and union, in which both are in search of the other.

The relationship between God and humanity is dialogical, expressed in the form of prayer and worship, conflict and friendship, trust, faithfulness, listening and answering. The personal encounter of Divine Presence is the most profound expression of this relationship, which can only occur when one lives a life of complete openness to God's will and is willing to have this openness change one's entire being.

Prayer is humanity's conversation with God. Prayer is seeking God's presence, resting in that presence, and placing oneself in the stream of God's life. Prayer can thus be said to be an entire outlook on one's life: in which one's thoughts and actions seek to discover the will of God, to live in a way that fulfills that will, and to spread the love of God to others. It is in this expansive understanding of prayer that we understand ourselves to be spiritual persons. Prayer is essential for theosis, for as medieval German mystic Meister Eckhart

---

27. Bonhoeffer elaborates on his view of the difference between the union of God with humans and with the rest of creation: "In this, human beings differ from the other creatures in that God is in them, in that they are God's very image in whom the free Creator views the divine self" (*Testament to Freedom*, 107).

I disagree with the distinction that Bonhoeffer appears to make here between "greater" humanity and "lesser" nature. The point in distinguishing theosis as a human process is that the choice and free will involved in theosis are exclusive to humanity. One would assume that lacking a sense of free will, nature would not need the purifying elements of theosis in order to rest in union with God.

28. Julian of Norwich, *Revelations of Divine Love* (Penguin Books, 1998), 104–5.

stresses, only prayer, our conversation with Spirit, will bring us into the silence of God: "Grace comes with the Holy Spirit, carries the Holy Spirit on its back. It is nothing static. . . . [It] makes the soul share God's own form."[29]

While every person has the capacity to achieve this union, few actually live the image of God completely. Ilia Delio suspects that our ignorance of God is the factor, as humans do not have a clear idea of what it means to be an image of God.[30] Quite possibly so: The image of God will always be incomprehensible to humans until we begin to see the image of God in every other person around us.

Union with God must therefore follow from union with others. We must first see the good in others, and then begin to see God in others, in order to see the interconnectedness of God in all creation. One cannot attain union with God while still acting as if another were devoid of the presence of Spirit. To put it another way, no one is absolutely evil.[31] There can be persons whose free will is so twisted that it has turned evil; yet even they cannot disavow the Spirit that resides within them. As Quaker philosopher Corey Beals states, Spirit (Light) permeates everything, even those who do the most evil:

> The significant factor, however, is how the person is related to the light. All have the light, but not all love the light. Those who are walking in the light can never fully escape the light for "where can I go from your Spirit? Where can I flee from your presence? If I go up to the heavens, you are there; if I make my bed in the depths, you are there". (Ps. 139:7–8) In that way, the light of Christ is in all. Anything that exists reflects God's light since God created everything. But no-one, by rejecting or hating the light "creates" a substantive evil any more than one "creates" a substantive shadow.[32]

---

29. Rowan Williams, *The Wound of Knowledge: Christian Spirituality from the New Testament to Saint John of the Cross* (Cowley, 1990), 145.

30. Delio, *Clare of Assisi*, 29.

31. Corwynn Beals, "Evil: The Presence of Absence," in *Good and Evil: Quaker Perspectives*, ed. Jackie Leach Scully and Pink Dandelion (Ashgate, 2007), 141.

32. Beals, "Evil: The Presence of Absence," 145.

We must love our enemies. In loving our enemies, we see the good in them, and eventually the God. Only by being willing to open ourselves to the Divine Love that encompasses all—and have that love transform us into people who can also love the God in all persons—will we ever be able to engage in a true dialogue with God. This true, deep, and meaningful dialogue is theosis, and it is the path to union with the Divine Cloud as well as to attaining our complete humanity.

Living Atonement

Jesus Stops a Stoning

> Then each of them went home, while Jesus went to the Mount of Olives. Early in the morning he came again to the temple. All the people came to him and he sat down and began to teach them. The scribes and the Pharisees brought a woman who had been caught in adultery; and making her stand before all of them, they said to him, "Teacher, this woman was caught in the very act of committing adultery. Now in the law Moses commanded us to stone such women. Now what do you say?" They said this to test him, so that they might have some charge to bring against him. Jesus bent down and wrote with his finger on the ground. When they kept on questioning him, he straightened up and said to them, "Let anyone among you who is without sin be the first to throw a stone at her." And once again he bent down and wrote on the ground. When they heard it, they went away, one by one, beginning with the elders; and Jesus was left alone with the woman standing before him. Jesus straightened up and said to her, "Woman, where are they? Has no one condemned you?" She said, "No one, sir." And Jesus said, "Neither do I condemn you. Go your way, and from now on do not sin again." (John 7:53–8:11 NRSV)

This passage has been marked by controversy since it was written. Most of the earliest manuscripts do not include this text, while others include it in Luke or even place it at the end of the Gospel of John. Augustine was among the first to reclaim this text from its banishment, noting dryly that it was removed initially due to the opinion of some of the writers that the text granted women the "liberty to sin with impunity," as though the woman "should not have been cured by the divine physician of that sin in order not to offend others who are equally unclean."[33] By rescuing the text from permanent exile, however, Augustine established the primary interpretation of the passage, one that is still one of the most prevalent interpretations: that Jesus is forgiving a woman guilty of the terrible sin of adultery. This text, and in turn this interpretation, has shaped Christian understanding of adultery even until the present day. The absence—in the story—of the male partner in the adulterous act has had dramatic repercussions, for the blame for adulterous acts has often been laid at the feet of the woman-as-tempter.

Recent historical-critical readings of the text have either dismissed the story, or at least marginalized it, by questioning its validity and by placing brackets around the text with a note mentioning the controversy about its validity as a piece of the original text of John.[34] The desire for historical accuracy can be seen to overset the undeniable fact that however uncomfortable historical-critical readers might be with the text, it is still located in the text and has been so since before the closing of the New Testament canon.

Both readings also fail to grasp the profound political and theological implications of the text: that it is actually a trial of Jesus's messiahship and place in the community by the scribes and the Pharisees, who were using the woman as the means by which Jesus would be forced to incite mob violence and so give the Romans the impetus to put Jesus to death. This is one of the main approaches Quakers take to atonement theology, particularly as it relates to the role of the crucifixion: Death is an inevitability when you take on empire directly and attempt to undermine its self-proclaimed power over life and death. This has similarities to Abelard's moral example theory of atonement, yet with the twist that this nonviolent approach charts the crucifixion as a demonstration of God's love only in the sense that love involves commitment, and true commitment to undermining the power of the Roman state results in a way of being that will not rest until justice is achieved.

Or death is achieved, which is the more likely outcome, to be honest.

---

33. Joel C. Elowsky, ed., *John 1–10*, Ancient Christian Commentary on Scripture New Testament 4A (InterVarsity, 2006), 272.

34. Gail R. O'Day, "John," in *The Woman's Bible Commentary*, ed. Carol A. Newsom and Sharon H. Ringe (Westminster John Knox, 1998), 628.

What is notable about this passage is that it not only offers a vision of Divine forgiveness that requires nothing—only a request to live differently—it also demonstrates the challenge that all levels of society faced when trying to come to terms with Roman imperial occupation. In this framing, the actions of the temple elite make sense from both a political and survival viewpoint. These are not the "scheming Jews" of anti-Semitic conspiracists but actually leaders with a responsibility to their people to maintain their access to the temple to perform the most important rituals of the Jewish religious calendar.

Of course, these leaders are as self-focused and flexible as politicians often are—but before tossing around allegations of collaboration, what this passage demands is empathy: Would you really do differently, when faced with the endangerment of the little public space and power that Rome still permitted Judaism to access? A closer examination of the sociopolitical context described in this passage demonstrates that this text is best read as an attempt to trap Jesus into doing something that will cause the Romans to sentence Jesus to the death penalty—and to thus save the people from yet another in what had been a long, deadly line of messiahs who riled up the people without actually alleviating their suffering.

The literary context of this passage within the overall text of the Gospel is bracketed by threats to Jesus's life that cause him to enter hiding (7:1; 8:59). Jesus enters into hiding in Galilee, which is far from the temple in Jerusalem, the power base of the scribes and Pharisees. When the Festival of Tabernacles begins, Jesus follows his brothers to the temple (7:10), while still attempting to remain in secret. Throughout chapter 7 Jesus engages in a dialogue with "the Jews" about whether he is truly the Messiah (vv. 25–31), evades an attempt by the Pharisees to arrest him (vv. 32–36), and causes major divisions among the crowd and the temple leadership (vv. 40–52). Jesus has therefore become quite a disturber of the peace. It is in the midst of this social turbulence that the Pharisees attempt to trap Jesus into condoning the illegal killing of the woman in 7:53–8:11. Jesus dodges the trap set for him—this time.

Jesus continues to engage the Pharisees in a dialogue for the remainder of chapter 8, even utilizing legal language to defend his testimony that he is the Messiah due to his connection with the Father (vv. 21–20), his impending death (vv. 21–29), and finally his argument that his disciples are the true sons of God, as opposed to "the Jews" who are actually illegitimate, due to their lack of understanding of who Abraham really was (vv. 31–58). The attack on their righteousness and status of chosenness is apparently the last straw for his interlocutors, for in 8:59 they finally take action to take his life—the same illegal action that in 7:53–8:11 they were seeking to force Jesus to do. Having turned the tables on his interrogators, and having shown the trial to be a mockery by inciting his adversaries to forget legal precedent and to take extralegal action, Jesus departs the scene. Read in this light, 7:53–8:11 fits quite well in its current place in the Johannine text—as a literary device whose function is to develop the narrative plot for the confrontations between Jesus and his rivals.[35]

In John's Gospel, the term "the Pharisees and the scribes" is used to delineate those persons with whom Jesus most often came into conflict, with the chief priests emerging occasionally, when the conflicts center in the temple precincts. The Pharisees were a sect within Judaism that emphasized adherence to the oral tradition that had developed as rabbis interpreted the Mosaic law. The oral traditions were vast and covered nearly every aspect of Jewish daily and sacramental life. The Pharisees were not as strict in their interpretations as they are portrayed in some of the stories in the Gospels, yet their modern reputation—of emphasizing adherence to a vast set of rules as the means for fulfilling the Abrahamic covenant—is quite well deserved. They were not blessed with a majority of adherents from among the Jewish people, yet they held positions of power that belied their minority status. Their status was due in some part to their willingness to collude with the Roman authorities. According to Josephus, they were active even in attempting to quiet revolutionary sentiment among the populace during the first Jewish rebellion against Rome (66–73 CE).[36]

They also often held positions of leadership in the temple. Their positions were predicated on the Romans leaving the temple alone, permitting the Jewish rites and sacrifices to continue without Roman interference. Jesus's claims to messiahship were therefore quite dangerous, for they carried with them the overt political message that Jesus was now Lord (as opposed to Caesar) and that the temple was being both mismanaged and exploitative—especially toward the common people. The first message threatened Rome's hegemony, while the second threatened the hegemony of the temple leaders, specifically

35. Jean K. Kim, *Woman and Nation: An Intercontextual Reading of the Gospel of John from a Postcolonial Feminist Perspective* (Brill Academic, 2004), 124.

36. Kim, *Woman and Nation*, 125.

the scribes and Pharisees—those whose power base was dependent on their control of the temple.

Yet, the Pharisees also saw in Jesus a threat to everything they understood to be of God's will for Israel. They truly believed that the safety and security of the Jewish people lay in remaining pure by following God's laws as closely as possible, as well as by maintaining the uneasy peace between the temple and Rome that permitted the Jews to retain control over their holy spaces and national festivals.[37] Jesus's claim to be the Messiah was a significant threat to that peace, for the Pharisees knew all too well that the Romans tolerated the temple only as long as it didn't disturb the peace. Their fears proved founded when the Romans laid siege to Jerusalem in 70 CE and ultimately destroyed the temple later that year. The Jews had upset the peace, and the Romans had destroyed the temple. The Pharisees were right to fear Jesus's message.

The Pharisees were placed in a bind: According to Roman law, the Jews were not legally permitted to inflict capital punishment, as that right was reserved for the Roman procurator. The Pharisees were also kept from directly engaging in inciting a riot that would lead to death, for they would be held liable for both the disturbance of the peace and the resulting deaths. All of which makes the aborted stoning in 7:59 more remarkable, for it demonstrates how frustrated the Pharisees must have been by that point to forget the danger that a successful stoning would have placed them in. If they were able to incite a riot while placing the blame squarely on Jesus's shoulders, they could rid themselves of the threat both to their nation and to their own power bases without risking any danger to themselves.

The method that the Pharisees employ to trap Jesus is quite shrewd. They come to Jesus while he is teaching in the temple, guaranteeing that a crowd will be present to witness what is about to transpire as well as be a useful mob—if needed. They present Jesus with a woman whose guilt is being assumed by all her accusers. Adultery was a sin in that it defiled whichever parties in the act were married, while the man who engaged in the adultery was also trespassing on the property rights of the husband. This was an emotional charge, which often incited passionate responses.

---

37. Barbara A. Holmes and Susan R. Holmes-Winfield, "Sex, Stones and Power Games: A Woman Caught in the Intersection of Law and Religion (John 7:53–8:11)," in *Pregnant Passion: Gender, Sex and Violence in the Bible*, ed. Cheryl A. Kirk-Duggan (Atlanta: Society of Biblical Literature, 2003), 144.

The Mosaic law attempts to ameliorate the danger of vengeance by requiring witnesses to the actual event, witnesses who could prove that the woman had been warned that what she was doing was a sin (which, for obvious reasons, could prove to be quite challenging).[38] The woman and man both needed to be present at the trial, which later traditions required be held in front of the Sanhedrin: Adultery carried a penalty of stoning, and only the Sanhedrin was permitted by Jewish law to declare judgment in capital cases. In other words, if Jesus declares the woman guilty, he can be accused of not following Mosaic law but can also be accused of giving the crowd the impetus to kill the woman, which it seems anxious to do.[39] Yet, Jesus cannot claim her to be innocent, for only the Sanhedrin (according to Jewish law) or the Roman authorities (according to Roman law) can declare guilt or innocence. Notably, the woman's guilt is uncontested.

The stage is set for both the woman and Jesus to engage in radical actions in defiance of the status quo imposed on them: By subverting the crowd's expectations, they diminish the crowd's power to set the agenda. Let's examine the woman first. She is unnamed and, due to the murky legality of her accusation, is obviously a pawn in the Pharisees' plot to trap Jesus. Her reasons for engaging in the act are not examined in the text. For the Pharisees as well as the Gospel writers, neither her motives nor her identity are germane to their purposes: She becomes the embodiment of sin, and thus her body becomes the context over which greater forces battle. She realizes that she has no control over the outcome of the trial occurring around her and decides instead to control her reaction to the event. She has no advocate at the public hearing, yet in a courageous move evincing a remarkable strength and resilience, she keeps her peace, forecasting Jesus's silence at his own show trial. She robs the crowd of any emotional response to feed off and so demonstrates that she can maintain her dignity even while potentially losing her life.

Jesus demonstrates that he will not be swayed by the power of the crowd—nor be cowed by the power held by the Pharisees—by refusing to respond when they demand it, even going so far as to completely ignore them, writing on the ground instead. The Pharisees are forced to recognize that they are powerless to force Jesus to respond—his response is the only way to trap him, yet their

38. Kim, *Woman and Nation*, 138.

39. Holmes and Holmes-Winfield, "Sex, Stones and Power Games," 145.

scheme falls apart if he doesn't engage. Having reclaimed the position of power in the situation, Jesus then uses that position to establish equal status between the woman and the Pharisees. The Pharisees had been using the woman's body as an object, totally marginalizing her as a person: She became nothing except for her sin. As Rene Girard theorized, mob violence depends on a "unanimity-minus-one," where the entire crowd is unified against a negative force that is embodied in one person. The mob violence that the Pharisees seek to incite depends on Jesus either getting out of the way and allowing the crowd to scapegoat the woman or somehow becoming the target himself and therefore maintain the cohesion of the crowd against the scapegoat: The one person who embodies the sin that must be purged from the body politic.

Jesus completely destroys this dynamic by forcing each person to engage their own sin, placing everyone—the woman, the Pharisees, and the entire crowd—on the equal footing of being sinners. Jesus further undermines the unanimity of the crowd by forcing individual people to step forward, showing themselves. This utterly destroys the crowd's violent facelessness, as people walk off as individuals, thus stopping the scapegoat effect right in its tracks.[40] They are also forced to recognize that Jesus made them equal to a woman—an unclean woman, at that. Finally, Jesus completely evades the Pharisees' test, leaving them without a convenient reason for the Romans to kill him.

The passage finishes with a denouement that demonstrates the extent of God's grace. Having implicated every person present in sinful behavior—no one throws a stone, after all—Jesus forces them all to publicly acknowledge their sin. In the end, everyone (except for the woman) leaves, all implicated in sin. Jesus asks the woman whether any who condemn her remain. By answering no, the woman recognizes that Jesus sees her sin and doesn't condemn her to remain in that state. Jesus then speaks the words of grace: God acknowledges our sins, forcing us to look at them but only for our betterment, so that we may "go, and sin no more." Jesus shows that God loves us exceedingly, offering forgiveness without condition or qualification.

Affirmation Mysticism

In 1917, the American Friends Service Committee was formed as a unified effort across the Anglo-American Friends world to respond to the ravages of the

---

40. Gil Bailie, *Violence Unveiled: Humanity at the Crossroads* (Crossroad, 1995), 196.

First World War.[41] Rufus Jones was only one among many who devoted significant time and attention to that effort. Jones was the person selected as the committee's first chairman, however, and remained its honorary chairman until his death in 1948.[42] Jones's prominent status among Friends internationally—both as a writer and a weighty (influential and wise) Friend—influenced this choice. While his academic work likely played a role in building his weight among Friends, much of it was also driven by the reputation Jones gained as a spokesman for Friends. This was linked to his intentional project of reunifying Friends, divided during the multiple schisms of the nineteenth century, with his theology of Divine/human interdependence through the Inward Light.

His role as chairman helped ensure that his theological work would make a significant impact on the foundational theology of American Friends Service Committee. Jones examined the ethical and practical elements underlying the founding and subsequent work of the committee during 1917–1919 in his historical work, *A Service of Love in War Time: American Friends Relief Work in Europe, 1917–1919.*[43] However, he did not actually explicate his vision of Divine/human interdependence and its implications for the interdependence of all humans within society and Quaker social testimony in general. He also did not explore the implications for informing the why of Quaker relief work specifically, while little subsequent theological work has been done examining this connection.

Affirmation Mysticism and Interdependent Incarnation

Jones insisted on delineating what he understood as a dichotomy between negative and affirmative mysticism, with mysticism encompassing all aspects of human engagement with the Divine as well as any subsequent relationship that developed as a result of these interactions.[44] Jones termed negative any interaction that focused mainly on silencing the individual's sensory experience and

41. This section is adapted with permission from Christy Randazzo, "Affirmation Mysticism: The Activist Theology of Rufus Jones," *Quaker Religious Thought*, no. 133 (2019).

42. Harry E. Fosdick, *Rufus Jones Speaks to Our Time* (Macmillan, 1951), xi.

43. Rufus Jones, *A Service of Love in War Time: American Friends Relief Work in Europe, 1917–1919* (Macmillan, 1920).

44. Rufus Jones, *Social Law in the Spiritual World: Studies in Human and Divine Inter-Relationship* (John C. Winston, 1904), 140–41.

that removed the human from relationship with human community by being absorbed in God or "swallowed up in the Godhead."[45] Jones dismissed this pursuit on both theological and ethical grounds, as he understood it to violate the Christian call to be in community. For Jones, this was an incalculable loss, with the only benefit being the individual gain of a life united entirely and only with God the infinite.[46]

Jones contrasted this with his affirmation mysticism formulation, which he understood to be the counterpoint to negation due to its insistence on uniting with the infinite God within the finite, specifically the grittiness of daily life. Jones claimed that while there were transcendent elements of affirmation mysticism, including mystical visions, these were only a starting point for affirmation mysticism and were not the end of the mystic's pursuit of a relationship with the divine. Jones instead claimed that the affirmation mystic understood that the vision was simply the beginning of a relationship: God's opening to a deeper relationship. However, he insisted that "those who would have a closer view of the Divine must seek it in a life of love and sacrifice."[47] In this way, Jones married what he understood to be the two main elements of the Quaker life: the human opening to the Divine through waiting patiently on God to speak to the individual in community, and the social action that divine engagement would compel within the human. Thus, by emphasizing both the worship/mysticism and activist/social elements of Quakerism above all others, Jones was able to frame Quakerism as inherently mystical through a definition of mysticism that affirmed the lived, human experience.

Jones reflected a concern already extant within his context and time. Liberal religion at the turn of the twentieth century was strongly influenced by the social reform emphasis of the time, including the social gospel movement, as well as a skepticism of ecstatic expressions of Divine presence. What separated Jones from his liberal contemporaries was his insistence on bracketing off an understanding of mysticism that bridged liberal hermeneutics and concerns with the mystical foundations of Quakerism—which arguably had far more in common with the negation mysticism that Jones rejected—toward

45. Jones, *Social Law in the Spiritual World*, 149–50.

46. Rufus Jones, *New Studies in Mystical Religion* (Macmillan, 1927), 79–80.

47. Jones, *Social Law in the Spiritual World*, 149–53.

the goal of establishing mysticism as the core, common, and unifying element of a modern, twentieth-century Quakerism.

While Jones's biases certainly blinded him and likely led him to develop what I argue is an incomplete understanding of the history of Christian mysticism, his understanding of how to frame Quakerism to fit his context was unparalleled. Not only is Jones's definition of mysticism the most commonly accepted one among current Liberal Quakers, but his affirmation mysticism has heavily influenced Liberal Quaker social action and Liberal Quaker theological reflection on that social action. A key element in that theological reflection has been Jones's insistence that humans are already in an interdependent relationship with the Divine, without the need to engage in any practices of self-abnegation to "clear out the human" in order to connect directly with the Divine.[48]

Dialogically, this both shaped and was shaped by Jones's strongly incarnational Christology. As a Quaker, Jones's theology had been shaped by the consistent theological conviction that "every human life partakes of God."[49] Jones's liberal reading of Quaker tradition led him to understand George Fox's experience of the Divine as what he termed a "continuous sense of the Divine life enfolding his own." This is an experience that, as Jones admits, is never stated as such anywhere within Fox's journal but is certainly strongly implied—or so Jones argues.[50] This "continuous state" of God's enfolding presence within human life is not entirely without warrant in Christian theology, however, especially when one takes seriously the Christian claim to Christ as the Divine incarnate within humanity.

Jones did indeed take this claim seriously and took this incarnation to its logical conclusion, or at least logical to a Quaker formed by a vision of the Light of Christ actively present within every single human, continuously inviting the human into a deeper relationship.[51] Jones strongly emphasized a close reading of the apostle Paul, particularly Paul's imagery of the closely interconnected relationship between Christ and humanity within 1–2 Corinthians as well as

48. Rufus Jones, *The Testimony of the Soul* (Macmillan, 1936), 152–53.

49. Jones, *Social Law in the Spiritual World*, 165.

50. Jones, *Social Law in the Spiritual World*, 163.

51. Rufus Jones, *The World Within* (Macmillan, 1918), 33.

Ephesians. This reading gave Jones scriptural warrant for his understanding of the interdependence between the incarnate Christ and humanity.

Christian tradition emphasizes that through Christ's human nature all of creation is capable of being in relationship with the Divine. This establishes the path along which Jones can create a doctrine of God as interdependent with humanity. In many ways, Jones can be said to be a confessional theologian and an apologist: Not only was his reading of Scripture and Quaker theological history deeply bound by his identity as a Quaker in a specific context, but he felt a very insistent calling to develop theology to serve that context and community. Jones needed to locate a very specific definition of mysticism within the Christian and Quaker traditions in order to serve the confessional framework he was developing: With affirmation mysticism, he found exactly what he needed.

Interdependent God

Through the image of Christ, the being who encompasses both Divine and human, Jones offers a vision of the process through which God develops an interdependent relationship with humanity. First, Jones demonstrates that, by straddling the seemingly insurmountable divide between Divine and human, Jesus establishes himself as the channel through which God reaches out to humans and through which humans are pulled into an intimate relationship with the Divine. As incarnation transforms human existence into something that is capable of being completely inhabited by the Divine, humans are incomplete until they can live in relationship with the Divine.[52]

Next, through Christ, the Divine experiences everything humans experience, including and especially the suffering of human existence in its entirety.[53] This establishes the foundational aspect of interdependent relationship: What one experiences, the other experiences, and thus both are bound in mutual experience. This roots Jones firmly in Quaker tradition, which has always emphasized the personal experience of the Divine as the primary element of Quaker theology and practice.[54] Finally, through the working of the Divine within the human person, the human is perfected through the process of the

52. Jones, *Social Law in the Spiritual World*, 253.

53. Jones, *Social Law in the Spiritual World*, 101.

54. Rufus Jones, *The New Quest* (Macmillan, 1928), 125.

Divine changing the human into the image of God, the inward self that is from henceforth "always at home with the Lord."[55]

The theological implications of this progression are profound. For one, Jones claims that God suffers as humans suffer, meaning that eliminating human suffering is both a human *and* a Divine imperative. Second, Jones argues that humans are created to be incomplete without the presence of God. Yet, this does not presume that humans are capable of ever *actually* existing without the presence of God within. Instead, they are in relationship proleptically with the Divine, their relationship being existent foundationally in that to be human—ontologically—is to be in relationship with the Divine. This is explained in Jones's formulation that "it is impossible to make immanence intelligible without *transcendence*, even in the case of our personal spirits." In this case, the spirits Jones appears to refer to are individual human souls: that which makes the human recognizably human—as opposed to the Spirit of God.[56]

Third, Jones envisions a panentheistic Divine, a Spirit who is both immanent within and transcendent beyond the world, who is, as Jones states, the "Ground and Source of all we can call Mind or Reason in the universe."[57] A God who experiences everything that humans experience is a God who experiences what *every* human experiences. If all humans are bound to a God whose incarnation in the world makes the world closer to God, this binding also makes God's self closer to the entire world, enfolding the entire world within the Divine. Thus, the panentheistic God brings all of humanity into relationship with the entire creation, destroying boundaries and opening the horizon for new possibilities for humanity. This brings with it a rippling of consequence for humans individually, however: human interconnection.

Social Theology

The ethical implications to this interconnection are clear: When you make any human suffer, you also make God suffer, an untenable situation crying out for remedy. Yet, as God is present throughout the entire creation, and within humans as the Inner Light (the term Jones preferred and through his

---

55. Jones, *World Within*, 35.

56. Jones, *Testimony of the Soul*, 110.

57. Jones, *New Quest*, 186.

continuous use aided in its spread among Liberal Friends), then harm to any one human is untenable, as it carries with it a tripartite harm: to the human as themselves (human), to the human as a part of the Light (Divine), and to the human as a member of humanity (human and Divine). Jones understood the human person to be an individual only as they were a member of the created order, and thus only as they were a member of the interdependent community of God and the creation. Their personhood existed through connection to others, or as he stated, "Personality at every stage involves inter-relation."[58]

This is the final step of the process that begins with God's creation of a human who *requires* relationship with God, and a God who in turn *desires* relationship with every human. Through God, humans are interconnected to each other. As humans cannot be truly human without a relationship with the Divine, through Spirit humans cannot be truly human unless they are in interconnected relationships with other humans.[59] In other words, following Jones down the rabbit hole here leads to the inevitable conclusion that humans do not seek to free humans from oppressive structures of war, famine, and homelessness—the work that American Friends Service Committee initially did for millions of refugees of the war—simply out of obligation to God or even only to aid other humans in need. In fact, I argue that the most radical implication of Jones's theology is that humans do relief work *because they are human*, because failing to serve the other is to fail as a human person, and it is only through service to the other that the self truly becomes the self.

Jones therefore requires an affirmation framework of mysticism because it allows no room for any miscommunication about the intent of the human engagement with the Divine: to force the human to always understand themselves as in community, of community, and as bound by the needs of community.[60] Whether Jones actually failed to grasp the true intent of the mystics he termed negative—to leave nothing between the human and God in order to then return back to the world ready to do the work of Christ within the world—is certainly debatable. However, I think that it is obvious that Jones wanted to leave very little doubt about his theological anthropology and its implications in the world. He was quite willing to frame his arguments to

58. Jones, *Social Law in the Spiritual World,* 58.

59. Jones, *New Studies in Mystical Religion*, 170.

60. Jones, *New Studies in Mystical Religion*, 171.

achieve that end. Jones's understanding of Quaker testimony, and the social responsibilities of Quakers, was rooted in this anthropological foundation and stemmed from it. Jones thus establishes a vision of Quaker ethics that is neither deontological nor virtuous but is instead ontological: an ethic that is actually an outgrowth of the human person living the most complete human life possible.

The Ever-Present Now: Divine Immanence and Time

The Liberal Quaker experience of God as a present reality extends to their understanding of the kindom of God as a present reality. This reality is embodied in the community of Quakers, particularly in their lives and in the Quaker insistence on an ethic derived from lived experience, as opposed to derived from a doctrinal formulation.[61] The kindom is realized, therefore, in that it exists through the presence of God in each person.[62] For some Liberal Quakers, the focus on God's immanence leads to a diminished insistence on the necessity of an eschatological reality outside the present moment, as the eschatological promise of union with God is not required when God is already in union with creation in the present time.[63]

Jones's construction of a *realized* eschatology is somewhat controversial, especially in light of the fact that evil and suffering still exist in the world.[64] An alternative framework could be the vision of a *realizing* eschatology, in which the eschaton exists (and is thus *realized*) but which also acknowledges that suffering and pain exist in the present temporal reality for Liberal Quakers (and is thus also incomplete). The bridge between the realized-ness of God's immanent presence in the world and the realizing-ness of a broken world is the hope that, through God and the actions of humans, the world can achieve a reconciled state.

This is a dual reality: The kindom as an ultimate goal is transcendent and dependent on God's actions; yet, the stages that must be followed to bring

---

61. John A. Hughes, *The Light of Christ in a Pagan World* (Allen & Unwin, 1940), 76.

62. Rufus M. Jones, *The Nature and Authority of Conscience* (Swarthmore, 1920), 22.

63. Howard Brinton, *The Religious Philosophy of Quakerism: The Beliefs of Fox, Barclay and Penn as Based on the Gospel of John* (Pendle Hill, 1973), 64.

64. William Littleboy, *The Day of Our Visitation* (Headley Brothers, 1917), 34.

about the kindom are both immanent in history and dependent on human agency. An incarnational approach roots the duality of eschatology specifically within Jesus's person, in which Jesus's human aspect reflects the present immanence of the kindom, while his divine aspect reflects its ultimate transcendence. As Jesus was unable to separate the twin elements of the kindom, humanity cannot either.[65] While the kindom depends on human agency, it will come into fruition only through the will of God.

A universalist perspective on the kindom argues that an eschatological viewpoint can bring about a radical discontent for the present state of the world and foster either a complacency toward the inevitability of God's action to improve the world or an apathetic acceptance of the present. While we can have hope in the grace of God to achieve a future reconciliation, Quaker universalists argue, we cannot allow ourselves to become complacent in awaiting the action of the Divine. Humans must take responsibility for their role in the process of bringing about this future. One potential consequence of this elevation of human potential and responsibility is the transformation of the intimate relationship Liberal Quakers share with the immanent/transcendent Divine into an intimate relationship with a Divine who is immanent to such an extent that some Friends accept a form of self-divinity.[66] This loss of relationship with a transcendent has translated into a loss of future eschaton, or even, for some, a loss of an eschatological perspective altogether.[67]

This leads to a dominant present, in which all of time exists now, with the immanent Divine infusing every individual moment. If all of time is the present, and God is intimately immanent in the creation that is always present in the now, this could lead the Divine to take any form that meets someone's present experience, with a theology of "ever-present now" that flows from that experience.[68] Unity in the group must be rooted in something other than common belief, therefore, especially common beliefs that depend on any vision of the transcendent, whether that be a sense of end time or a transcendent God.[69]

65. George B. Jeffery, *Christ, Yesterday and Today* (Allen & Unwin, 1934), 31.

66. Dandelion, *Liturgies*, 6.

67. Dandelion, *Liturgies*, 71.

68. Dandelion, *Liturgies*, 116.

69. Dandelion, *Liturgies*, 115.

This claim has a great impact on Liberal Quaker kindom theology, for it would mean that the kindom is completely present now, and may not involve a "kingdom" or even a "God." If true, then this perspective must be seen as hopeless, for it does not allow for any future state of the world that is better than the current state, nor for the hope that such a future state could ever exist, whether through human agency, divine agency, or a combination of both. The loss of the insistent language of a God actively invested in bringing about an apocalyptic kindom could lead to a loss of urgency in the necessity for change. The radical in-breaking of the kindom quietly calls for gradual "social adjustment" and the eventual fading away of the passionate drive for change that fueled Christian social action in the past.[70]

I argue that while this perspective may reflect a general trend in current Liberal Quaker thinking on time, this does not need to be the accepted trajectory of Liberal Quaker kindom thought. Instead, a renewed focus on the Liberal Quaker theological heritage can lead to a development of an eschatological sense of hope. The current focus in the academic study of Quaker theology on the theology of the early Quakers, especially their apocalyptic viewpoint, is not entirely without precedent in Liberal Quakerism. George Jeffery, William Littleboy, and Henry Hodgkin are all examples of early twentieth-century Liberal Quakers who utilized the apocalyptic language of early Quakers and their focus on the kindom of God to develop theologies of presence, hope, and a strong social ethic.

Present-day Liberal Quaker thinkers echo these earlier Quakers in their development of theologies of hope to address the challenges of facing a broken world and of bringing about the kindom in the form of peace and healing. In the twenty-first century, Simon Fisher explains that the hope that things can improve in the future is the one essential element in the practice of peacemaking in postconflict situations. Both belief in a future better than the present and hope that such a future is possible are essential elements in giving people the strength to push past the overwhelming oppressiveness of the current situation—and to take a risk on an uncertain future.[71]

Quakers are not alone in constructing this realizing/realized eschatological vision of the kindom of God. Hauerwas argues that the kindom of God, as

70. Hughes, *Light of Christ in a Pagan World*, 76.

71. Simon Fisher, *Spirited Living: Waging Conflict, Building Peace* (Quaker Books, 2004), 101.

preached by Jesus through both action and words, informs a social ethic and that much can be learned about the nature of the kindom through the example of Jesus. This is similar to positions held by Liberal Quakers, as noted above. Hauerwas insists that a view of the kindom as ethical framework—divorced from a view of the kindom as eschatological reality—is incomplete and is therefore doomed to be unfulfilling.[72] He does recognize that there does not exist a coherent scriptural view of the temporal framework of the kindom and acknowledges that the kindom is both present and future reality.[73] Future is ill-defined, however, and Hauerwas allows that the future of the kindom could occur both in the temporal, human future and in some reality defined by God's expansive awareness of time. The kindom would only develop through the initiative of God, occurring in a manner and on a time frame that God alone would completely comprehend.

Hauerwas argues that the incarnation gives humanity a foretaste of how the story of the kindom plays out. In this, Hauerwas finds common cause with Liberal Quakers. Hauerwas states that Jesus demonstrated the immediacy and nature of God's kindom through his actions and teachings, and even through his body itself on the cross.[74] Jesus thus provides the primary exemplar for the kindom, meaning that to view the world eschatologically is to view the world through the lens of the life, death, and resurrection of Jesus. Those who live as followers of Jesus are people living in the last days, as literally eschatological people. This kindom rejects the boundaries between people created by the values of the empire, instead insisting on a radical community with one's enemies and those who require forgiveness. The kindom also demands total devotion and a complete release of all measures of security, including wealth, possessions, and power. The kindom exists only in a life lived in complete solidarity with the oppressed. Hauerwas calls this complete commitment a life of discipleship, which is simply "extended training in being dispossessed."[75]

---

72. Stanley Hauerwas, *A Community of Character: Towards a Constructive Christian Social Ethic* (University of Notre Dame Press, 1981), 44.

73. Stanley Hauerwas, *The Peaceable Kingdom: A Primer in Christian Ethics* (University of Notre Dame Press, 1983), 82.

74. Hauerwas, *Peaceable Kingdom*, 73.

75. Hauerwas, *Peaceable Kingdom*, 86.

A spirituality of kindom-shaped reconciliation requires a "post-exilic stance," reflecting the creation of a new society after Israel's return from exile in Babylon.[76] In this vision, the new society is chastened from the experience of exile and will thus impart a humble and compassionate sense on the outlook of those seeking to be reconciled. *Postexilic* implies an eschatological perspective, as the new society formed from the reconciliation of the returnees is realized due to the reality of their return but is also realizing due to the inherent incompleteness of the new society and the necessity to continually form the society. This eschatological edge forms reconciliation into a quest whose final destination—complete reconciliation—will always be just over the edge of the horizon and thus always be realizing, never fully realized.[77]

These perspectives all reflect the Liberal Quaker insistence on rooting the plane of reconciliation in the dual perspective of the experience of the immanent God, present among the creation, and the work of the community of Quakers that results from that immanence. This is sharing "the task of God," in which humanity becomes the mediators through whom God's love for—and solidarity with—the creation becomes known, and how God's reconciliation takes on practical shape.[78] Therefore, a Liberal Quaker theology of reconciliation requires that the kindom of God be the place where the experience of God becomes a lived experience of performing the act of reconciliation in the world. This would necessitate both a return to previous Liberal Quaker thinking on the kindom and an engagement with the kindom thinking of political and reconciliation theologians—all of whom share with Liberal Quakers an emphasis on a very active social engagement for the achievement of a peaceful and just world.

This experiential theology presents Liberal Quakers with several implications in terms of this engagement with the world. Liberal Quakers have a dynamic understanding of experience, which encompasses the human relationship with both the "outer world" and the "inner world." These two worlds combine to give human experience a dialogic emphasis. Thus, in this construction, humans do not simply passively receive experiences from the

76. Schreiter, *Reconciliation*, 73.

77. David Stevens, *The Land of Unlikeness: Explorations into Reconciliation* (Columba, 2004), 40.

78. Scott, *What Canst Thou Say?*, 46.

sensory input of the world, but they also interact with their environment. This applies to the human experience of God, meaning that we are also in dialogue with God through our experiences both of the world and of God in the world. Liberal Quakers apply a few key caveats to this understanding. First, there is no one authoritative experience for all humans: This experience is both individual and communal, and the individual must be interpreted through the communal. Second, the experience is a-rational, meaning that Liberal Quakers reject the valorization of the rational interpretation over the emotional and spiritual experience.

Liberal Quakers demonstrate a strong preference for experiencing the presence of God unmediated by any other human interpretations of their experiences. This has included a rejection of priests, sacraments, and explicit theological formulations that might bracket the experience in such a manner as to cut off "unruly" experiences or those that do not conform to the established norms.

The Liberal Quaker view of the kindom of God is an extension of the Liberal Quaker experience of God as a direct reality as well. As the experience of God is a current and present reality, kindom is also a current and present reality. This is demonstrated in a very embodied fashion in the community of Liberal Quakers, in the very bodies of the gathered community itself. This reflects the Liberal Quaker emphasis on lived ethics as opposed to an ethic derived from doctrine.

There is some debate over how optimistic Liberal Quakers should be toward the extent of God's union with the world. This is not to claim that Liberal Quakers reject the existence of evil and suffering in the world; instead, their acceptance of the existence of such evil compels them to act toward the elimination of suffering in the current world, as opposed to waiting for the next world to achieve liberation from evil and suffering. Thus, Liberal Quakers place a high level of importance on human agency and responsibility, in each person's current moment and time.

Mustard Seeds

The parable of the mustard seed (Luke 13:18–19) compares the kindom of God to the tiny seed of the mustard plant, which was considered a dangerous weed. The essence of the parable is that the seed lands in the ground and takes root, growing to an impressive size in order to provide shelter for birds. The parable of the mustard seed informs us that Jesus had a vision of the kindom of God as something that would defy human expectation, even Jewish prophetic expectation, and that would grow from its humble beginnings in the contemporary historical movement into something so dominant that it would draw all of creation toward it.

Luke, however, places his parable in the context of a series of teachings, healings, and parables that speak to the reversal the kindom of God will bring on the established order of the world—barren fig trees will bloom, the crippled will be healed on the Sabbath, yeast will transform plain flour into leavened bread, lifelong friends will be denied, and as 13:30 states, "the last shall be first, and the first shall be last." Within this context, the parable of the mustard seed speaks more to the reversal of what would be expected: a person intentionally sows the tiny seed of a pernicious weed in a small garden, probably a quite well-ordered garden, which eventually becomes a mighty tree that dominates the entire garden. This reflects Luke's overall theme of a revolutionary gospel that will defy expectations about power and Messiah and that places the undesirable, whether poor, broken—or even a dangerous and pernicious weed—in the position of greatest honor.

By placing the context of the parable in a garden (which is more likely to be grown in an urban setting) as opposed to a field (obviously an agricultural image), Luke may have been speaking to a more urban audience for whom overtly agricultural images did not carry much weight. This is consonant with the more erudite and refined Greek employed to compose the text—Luke was well-educated and may have been intending his Gospel for educated, urban readers, such as those who would have lived in the urban centers of the Roman Empire where much early Christian missionary work was focused.

These aspects are all consistent with Jesus's overall message. He proclaimed a kindom that would take root in the lives of those who were open to the message and would transform not only their lives in dramatic ways but also the lives of those with whom they shared the message. He spoke in apocalyptic terms of a time when God would judge those who had not taken his message to heart, who would be forced to deal with the consequences of their inability to let the message of the gospel consume their lives. Finally, Jesus understood the message of the gospel to be one that reversed all common understanding of what God's power and might actually looked like, proclaiming that the coming kindom of God would grant power through weakness—and only in humility and in service to the other would true life be found.

The death-and-resurrection nature of the seed and plant has an obvious connection to the understanding Jesus had in all four canonical Gospels: that, for whatever reason, in order to bring the kindom of God to life, he would need to commit to a way of being that would result in his inevitable death, in a humiliating manner, which would reduce him to a state of complete powerlessness and unimportance before the Roman authorities. The historical Jesus believed that through his death, the kindom of reversal he preached would be born in a surprising and nearly irresistible way.

One of the questions that this realization brings immediately to mind is: If Jesus understood the kindom to be a dramatic and revolutionary restructuring of the social order that might result in his death—and he preached anyway—then who are we serving when we fail to allow this message to implant into our hearts and grow as exponentially as the mustard plant? The other question is like unto it: If we take as fact that the kindom of God has not grown to its full size, for the world order has not been completely overturned, then what are we doing if we're not doing everything in our power to cast mustard seeds far and wide, wherever we are, with whomever we meet?

CHAPTER SEVEN

Seeds/Hope

How Do We Live in Hope and Prepare for the Future?

> And the Lord let me see atop of the hill in what places he had a great people to be gathered. . . . And the Lord opened to me at that place, and let me see a great people in white raiment by a river's side come to the Lord.
>
> —George Fox's vision on Pendle Hill, 1652

Apocalypse in These Modern Times

Climate—*Cooper River Watershed, Lower Delaware River, All Hallow's Eve 2024*

In June 1652, George Fox ascended Pendle Hill and saw a vision of a gathered people: the axis around which the community of early Friends would revolve for at least the next generation. On June 16, 2015, Donald Trump descended an escalator in a gilded atrium of Trump Tower in Manhattan and revealed the axis around which the world would revolve for at least the next decade.[1] What these disparate events have in common is that they were both apocalyptic. We've already explored the apocalyptic context of Fox's vision in chapter 3, so I'll focus my attention on the apocalypse of Trump's speech instead. Between his vicious xenophobia and racism, his consummate braggadocio, his complete incapacity to speak without lying, his rambling nonsense (and his rambling, stream-of-consciousness conspiracy theories), his delusions of strength and grandeur, his soon-to-be-infamous "American carnage" imagery of a nation betrayed and hollowed out from within by shadowy forces, Trump

1. Michael Kruse, "The Escalator Ride That Changed America," *Politico Magazine*, June 14, 2019, https://www.politico.com/magazine/story/2019/06/14/donald-trump-campaign-announcement-tower-escalator-oral-history-227148/.

revealed everything that would define the experience of being alive during the Trump/MAGA era.[2] Trump had already captured the nation's attention due to his reality television stardom, where he performed his magic act of business acumen with such skill and authenticity and sleight-of-hand that everyone forgot how his "skills" had bankrupted nearly every business endeavor he ever attempted—Trump as David Copperfield, but magic tricks with real-life consequences for real-life people.

Donald Trump had existed in the public eye for decades before then, particularly in his native New York. My grandfather George—an accountant and finance expert who once worked for the office of the borough president of Brooklyn during the 1960s and 1970s—would tell me stories about his interactions with Fred Trump, when his son Donald would accompany his father on trips to secure approval for the numerous building projects the elder Trump was developing in Brooklyn. My grandfather was a man of his time, and while he appreciated Fred Trump's "gentlemanly" treatment of city workers (and gently chided his racism, xenophobia, and slumlord approach to building maintenance), he had nothing positive to say about Donald Trump, dismissing him as a crass boor and a playboy. George Metcalfe could bear many sins, but he drew the line at being lazy and rude. (I agree, Grandpa. Thank you!)

Donald Trump was unavoidable if you lived in New York during the 1980s and 1990s. His smirking face peered out at you from the tabloid rack crowding the grocery checkout line, usually wearing a tuxedo, with his arm around someone famous for being beautiful, rich, powerful . . . or simply famous for being famous. Anyone surprised at how much Trump's worldview is shaped by American celebrity culture obviously wasn't shopping for groceries at King Kullen in 1985 in St. James, New York. I spent ten years living in St. James, a small town on Long Island filled to the brim with police officers, firefighters, and ex-military—that is, an assortment of men (and their families) shaped by the particular kind of masculinity Trump praises and centers and seeks to embody for his followers. Even then, Donald Trump was seen as an exemplar of a particular kind of dominant masculinity, attractive because of its access to a world of success, money, power, influence, and beauty—the same milieu (and attendant worldview) Trump still purports to represent and that is still one of the cornerstones of his appeal.

---

2. Donald Trump, "Presidential Announcement Speech," *Time*, June 16, 2015, https://time.com/3923128/donald-trump-announcement-speech/.

None of this—the authoritarian ranting, the blustery rhetorical bludgeoning—is new. This is the same man who bankrupted Atlantic City casinos and with them Atlantic City, New Jersey, itself—and never apologized for dropping an economic bomb on the city. The same man who put a full-page ad in *The New York Post* in 1989 advocating for a return to the death penalty in order to punish a group of young Black and Latino men (known as the Central Park Five) falsely convicted of assaulting a white woman—and never apologized when they were exonerated. The same man who ordered the separation of migrant children from their parents (some permanently)—perhaps one of the most cruel policies to emerge from his ineffectual and divisive administration. Finally, this same man advocated, just a short few weeks ago, for the government to inflict retaliatory violence on his political enemies—should he be reelected.

The last decade has been a surrealist and terrifying Orwellian delirium in which the world is cracked and capsized. Yet, little of this is new, and none of it is unique to Trump. Racism, xenophobia, authoritarianism, structural injustice—some of this is written into the very fabric of the United States, even included in our founding documents. Many of the divisions sundering our society, and the charlatans manipulating these rifts in order to benefit from whipping people into a frothy frenzy, have been present in our country since time immemorial. Huey Long was the Trump of his era and place—1930s Louisiana, which Long ran as his personal fiefdom, through a mix of authoritarian populism and demonization of the usual suspects. Oh—and critics: He hated those. In the same decade, Father Charles Coughlin was both Rush Limbaugh and Tucker Carlson at once—a demagogue who used mass media *masterfully* to promote a message of fascist anti-Semitism. At the height of his influence, nearly one-quarter of the country would tune in to listen to this guy rant.

In the 1970s, singer Anita Bryant spearheaded a movement to enact antigay legislation in Florida, kicking off a national conversation that did not go at all well for queer people. Eerily reminiscent, the current antitrans panic being whipped up by legislators at every level of government began around 2015 but really kicked into high gear in 2020 with 85 bills considered, 155 in 2021, 174 in 2022, 615 in 2023, and finally, a staggering 661 specifically antitrans bills proposed so far in 2024.[3] At this moment, the right is dumping tens of

3. Trans Legislation Tracker, https://translegislation.com/learn, accessed January 30, 2025.

millions of dollars on antitrans ads—it's such *fun!* when your media market is Philadelphia, the largest city in Pennsylvania, a swing state of *overwhelming* significance in this election. I try to avoid looking at billboards, let's just put it that way. These ads aren't actually effective. The majority of people who see these ads think that they are meanspirited and unnecessary—a breath of relief that most people still think that it's not cool to mock and belittle trans people. Yet, the real intent of the ads is to plant, in the souls of as many people as they can, a tiny seed of disgust and revulsion of gender fluidity—one day it might take root and germinate, and grow tall, bloom, reproduce, and feed the next generations while planting seeds in another soul, and on and on: a life cycle of hate.

Everything old has become new again.

I am writing these words in these last few days before the 2024 election, an election whose outcome I do not currently know. I am irrevocably embedded within this context, as is my worldview—and thus my theology. I began writing this book back in the spring, when this election—and this book's deadline—were still seven months away and my fears about my trees were keeping me awake at night. Now, I am still focused on climate change, as this last month two hurricanes, Helene and Milton, ravaged the states of North Carolina and Florida, respectively, mere weeks apart from each other. Their overwhelming ferocity brought shocking devastation that literally wiped entire towns off the map.

The weather is bizarre—wrong, somehow, but for most of us also fantastic. I, along with most of the country, have for the last month-plus been enjoying the most *fabulous* weather possible. Well, it's not that I have been able to enjoy more than what filters in through a window, as I have done little these past few weeks but wake, eat, clean, write, eat, write (till sleep commands), wake. I am rooted in this one spot, this one house, this one yellow and eclectic library/office, this "ancient but holding their age well" maroon recliner.

I have become a tree, rooted right *here*.

Anyway, this astonishing run of the most perfect autumn that anyone can remember has been a gift. But at what cost? My trees have been suffering—you can see the green shrinking in, the life being sucked dry. I have images of vampires sucking away at the roots, draining away the life force. Really, it's just the risk of rootedness showing its true color—whatever the climate is where you live is the climate where you live. These trees are fighters, though, and are likely keeping tabs on one another across the mycorrhizal web. I strive to have hope for them—but this is the new normal, and we all must adapt to it: not accede, adapt (dance). The election is only days away, and all other concerns seem to pale in comparison to what has become an existential choice between two vastly different visions of this country's future—one where my right to exist as a trans person will be protected by those in power and another one where it's guaranteed to disappear.

Again, none of this is new. I have lived through a few elections that felt existential and have survived to tell the tale. The United States has endured even more existential elections—1860, anyone?—and also still exists. The only thing different about this election is that it's occurring now, in this exact moment in time, when I am concurrently writing a book about the theology of a religious group that was formed during a time of apocalypse and shaped by several subsequent times of apocalypse. I can certify, with absolute certainty, that I have gained a new depth of understanding about the early Friends by living through the past seven months with their stories in my head and my heart.

A new world is being birthed at this moment, one in which adaptation will be among the key virtues. Again, adapt does not mean accede, as anyone who has ever danced with bamboo, honeysuckle, English ivy, mint, or any of a number of highly adaptive, tenacious plants will know. Drive on long stretches of empty road in the South, look out your window and marvel at the strength and persistence of kudzu. Bamboo is among the most flexible materials that can also be used to build a bridge for massive equipment; you can grow it nearly *anywhere*, and it will break your tools—and you—should you try to extract it somehow from where it has decided to root. A theological perspective open to adaptation is *not* weak.

In this chapter, I tell the story of how encountering apocalypses—immense and individual—rooted my perspective on apocalypse generally, and specifically in relation to Quaker theology. As I explain in chapter 4, the foundational emphasis on God's continuing revelation to humanity has profound impact on Quaker theological development in this way: If the Divine is continually revealing themself to humanity, adapting to the inevitable change that is inherent in life's evolutionary process, then humanity's words about God need to adapt to respond in kind. Therefore, Quaker theology is dynamic, adaptive, responsive, participatory, and fully engaged with the world.

As this book demonstrates, the construction of Quaker theology is a "way, not a notion," a common phrase in Quaker circles that reminds Friends that Quaker theology is a way of life embedded in a communally understood framework, not a rigid belief and ethical structure bound by adherence to "notions," or specifically defined theological statements. For example, I explain in chapter 5 that while the *pollen* of enacted testimony must evolve as the world evolves (the testimony to hat-honor gave way to the testimony to equality, for example), the central, core framework of *testimony* as a structured framework of embodied theology will always be central to the Quaker way. Quaker theology evolves . . . or it rapidly becomes lifeless. The stories I tell here are stages in the evolution of my perspective on and approach to the complex interactions between endings/deaths and beginnings/births—what I call apocalypse theology—that I have been exploring throughout this book.

That's why I begin with a story establishing the context within which I am living and to which my theology responds. I connect each story to an element of the ecosystem and demonstrate the way that my response to an apocalyptic moment (or my attempt to understand the response of others to an apocalyptic moment) evolved my thinking. The story connected to *seeds* here ("Cooper River Watershed, Lower Delaware River, Late October 2022") actually occurred mere days before I completed the proposal to write this book and emailed it to Fortress Press—in 2022. In other words, I am not going to provide a summary of the book that reminds you of what I wrote in each chapter and instead will simply demonstrate the method by doing it.

Bodies—*Jones Falls, Chesapeake Bay Watershed, October 2007*

> I repeat: Theology is always done for particular times and places and addressed to a specific audience. . . . God does not do theology. *Humans do theology.*
>
> —James Cone, *A Black Theology of Liberation*, emphasis original

I remember the first class I ever took on systematic theology in seminary. It was 2007, my daughter had just been born a few months prior, the Great Recession was beginning—quietly—to gather steam, and I was years away from being convinced as a Friend. I learned about the "great questions" of theology: the questions that seemed universal and the answers that seemed objective—at the time. I remember threading my way through the dense arguments of Karl

Barth, a Reformed minister and theologian who is widely considered to be one of the defining Christian theologians of the twentieth century. Barth is best known for his vigorous critique of liberal Christianity (the very tradition which had such a profound influence on Liberal Quakerism), his radical centering of the Trinity as the foundation of a theological framework built entirely on the figure and act of Jesus Christ, his biblical commentary (especially in *The Epistle to the Romans*), and finally his magisterial—and highly influential—multivolume systematic theology *Church Dogmatics*.

At the same time, I was also taking a course on contextual theology, which can be understood as theologies that emerge from and speak to the theological concerns of a specific community and its context. Some examples of contextual theologies include Black theology, feminist theology, queer theology, and disability theology, among many others. It was in this class that I was first exposed to the work of James Cone, one of the founders of Black theology and widely considered one of the most influential liberation theologians of the twentieth century. I distinctly remember reading his argument about all theology being contextual, and particularly the role that white supremacy played—and continues to play—in the fundamental stories white churches tell when they engage in the work of theology (stories that center white experiences and dismiss the experiences of any other community). I felt convicted and affirmed at once. His argument about "white theology" stung because it was true and healed because its truth resonated so profoundly with my own experience of constructing theology.

The impact this had on my understanding of theology was apocalyptic, as it tore open my previous theological vision and planted in my heart, mind, and soul the seed of a radically different approach—one that would eventually lead me away from the Anglican identity I held in 2007 and toward my Quaker convincement. Cone gave me permission to find theological meaning in every aspect of my own theological experience by demonstrating how he did the same: through music (*The Spirituals and the Blues*), poetry and metaphor (*The Cross and the Lynching Tree*), the centrality of liberation and freedom to the Christian life (*A Black Theology of Liberation* and *Speaking the Truth: Ecumenism, Liberation, and Black Theology*), Christian theology as inherently political (*Black Theology and Black Power*), and on. Cone engaged in the central questions of theology, especially systematics, and the list is staggering, including the sources of theology, Christology, theological anthropology, hamartiology (the theology of sin), the impact of context on theological construction—again, and so on and so forth. I found a fully realized theological world in the writings of James Cone, and was inspired to ask the same kinds of questions of my own context—one of the roots of this current project.

I distinctly remember asking my professor why James Cone was considered a Black theologian, while Karl Barth was simply a theologian. The answer was a recitation of the exact argument that I had just read Cone dismantle: Cone engaged theology as a "contextual theologian" whose views on the great questions were specific to the Black community, whereas Barth was considered a capital-*T* Theologian, whose views on the great questions were considered universal. Of course Cone's experience as a Black man living in the United States during the twentieth-century civil rights era would render his work irrevocably contextual, as only Black people are Black, and only Black people can understand how God presents themselves to Black people. Barth's experience as a white Swiss man living in Germany during the lead-up to the rise of Nazism and its conquering of the German Lutheran church colored his theology, I was told, but his theology was still seen as Theology, however, and thus somehow still universally applicable to Christians everywhere.

I'm with Cone on this one: What absolute, utter nonsense.

Barth's refusal to sign an oath of loyalty to Hitler in 1935 led him to be deported (as he was a citizen of Switzerland) and not imprisoned, as happened to many other Germans who similarly refused to sign. You simply cannot argue that Barth saw the ways that the Nazis manipulated liberal theology to shrink God down to the role of Nazi supporter and say that this had no effect on his consistent emphasis on the absolute otherness of God. If James Cone's Blackness inspired him to write his searing *The Cross and the Lynching Tree*, the first book I read where I truly *felt* the utter injustice and astonishing cruelty of the crucifixion, then Barth's Swissness inspired him to help write the Barmen Declaration, the first theological statement that made me *feel* the courage required to stand against the mighty power of the state.

Barth didn't write Theology, therefore, but instead engaged in the work of contextual theology—same as Cone, and the same as me. Paraphrasing Mos Def, theology isn't some giant in the hillside who sometimes comes down and visits the people. Instead, I agree with Cone that theology is *always* contextual, *always* particular, *always* human. I'm also pretty certain that Barth would agree with Cone and me. Regardless of how people teach his thought now, Barth always retained a pastor's concern for writing theology that preaches.

I cannot extricate myself from this specific context any more than any other person can extricate themselves from their own context, for objectivity is a lie told by those who frame the experiences considered universal for a time, a culture, a society. I cannot view the writings of the early Friends dispassionately or objectively, as they were written by people who were themselves incapable of objectivity. Similarly, I cannot engage with these writings objectively, as I will always be engaging anything from within the inherent uniqueness of my own, individual, human consciousness. Yet, paradoxically, it is this very same particular individuality that is the cornerstone of universality: The one common experience that all humans share is the unique experience of being an individual.

Individual subjectivity *is* universality. I do not experience the world as a Black man, and James Cone did not experience the world as a queer person. Yet, we both experience(d) the world as *humans*, with emotions and dreams and a body that *feels*. This is the beauty of Christianity, actually: God understands the universal experience of *humanness*, having already experienced the particular experience of *being human*. Why is Cone's Christology taught as contextual, while Barth's is taught as universal—as Theology? Wasn't Jesus irrevocably contextual? I've yet to meet a person who studies Theology who has lived life as a first-century Jewish man living under Roman occupation. Particularity is the point of Jesus: Universal humanity wasn't crucified—Yeshua bar Joseph was, the son of Miriam, the friend of Martha and Mary, the teacher of Peter, the holy man whose message frightened particular people in specific contexts because of their potential influence on other particular people in the specific context of that time in that place. And so, I am now writing on the eve of a potentially life-changing election, and my work will inevitably reflect that—especially my continued emphasis, throughout this book, on the theme of apocalypse.

Apocalypse need not mean the end of the world for everyone everywhere. The word itself does not mean anything other than "revelation"—again, the word in Greek literally means "revelation." This isn't simply a realization, or a moment of enlightenment, or even an epiphany: What is revealed must speak to something fundamentally true about the world, a revealing of something that cannot be unseen, cannot be unknown, and whose impacts cannot be reversed. In this way, apocalypse can absolutely be the end of the world while also encountering individual people very differently: The world Margaret Fell knew before she heard George Fox preach ceased to exist the moment she was born anew, in this new world of the direct human experience of Divine Presence.

Similarly, the last decade has been apocalyptic not because of the turmoil and strife but because of the ways they have revealed truths about the world that cannot be unknown. The rise of Trumpism ended the world as we knew it and birthed two worlds, two entirely different universes within this country, with people who experience the world around them in fundamentally divergent ways. What is true in one world is almost guaranteed to be seen as lies in the other, and what is seen as right in one world is almost guaranteed to be critiqued as wrong in the other. Both worlds have their own understanding of truth, publicized by their own media universes. People in one world may not just fail to understand the perspective of folks in the other world; they may not even consider people in the other world to be *fully* human. This level of extreme polarization usually accompanies some form of civil war—even if it is a cold war, as our current situation seems to be.

These divisions aren't strictly geographical, despite the common invocation of the red state/blue state categorization as applicable to an entire state or region. Both worlds are as present in red states as they are in blue: Out of nearly eight million votes cast in New York state in the 2016 presidential election, nearly three million were for Trump. Out of three million votes cast in New York City in the 2020 presidential election, nearly seven hundred thousand were for Trump. No one can argue that New York City is red, by any stretch of the imagination, and yet nearly one-quarter of residents approved of Trump and agreed with his vision of the country's present and its future. You could live directly next to someone from the other world and even send your kids to the same school, and you'd still be experiencing two vastly different realities. How does a society begin to heal when your neighbor feels entirely justified in questioning your right to exist?

While in seminary, I found one way of responding to this question in reconciliation theology, and in 2009 I decided to study the religious responses to apocalyptic circumstances by moving to Northern Ireland and studying reconciliation practice and theology in a community devastated by the apocalypse of civil war, where religious actors were both violence-makers *and* peacemakers. I was not yet a Friend, but I became enamored with the idea of testimony and began to see analogues of it scattered across the Christian theological landscape. I was also seeking to find tools for coming to terms with being disowned by my family just two years prior—only a few months before my revelation about Cone and Barth—an apocalypse in its own right.

While Quakers had their own unique approach to reconciliation work and continued to demonstrate the effectiveness of Quaker social action, I was most intrigued by the concept of "reconciliation community"—a religious community with a specific call to and charism for reconciliation, who committed themselves so wholeheartedly to reconciliation that they lived in community with others who had made the same commitment. This is how I came to first understand testimony through a non-Quaker community, enabling me to see more clearly this community of Friends I was slowly moving toward embracing.

Flowers—*Belfast Lough, River Lagan Watershed, April 2010*

I want to offer one example of two worlds sharing the same land: the civil war in Northern Ireland, known as the Troubles. I won't spend much time explaining the history and context of the Troubles, as the bewildering complexity of its roots contributed to the overwhelming complexity of its body—a past, I will remind you, that has not even passed. What is essential to know at this stage is that by the time that the Troubles began in the late 1960s, the two main communities had long split over whether the province of Northern Ireland should remain united with the rest of the United Kingdom or should unite with the Republic of Ireland. These two communities—respectively, Protestants/Unionists/Loyalists and Catholics/Nationalists/Republicans—were often neighbors, yet experienced two vastly different realities when it came to the institutions of their daily lives: schools, policing, employment opportunities, and even health outcomes.

These positions were connected to two sets of broad cultural, religious, and political communal ties, but not exclusively. Not every Protestant considered union with the United Kingdom an existential issue, nor was every Unionist absolutely committed to ensuring a Protestant hegemony in Northern Ireland—and the same applies to Catholics and Nationalists, but from the perspective of the Republic of Ireland and the Roman Catholic Church. The context made for many strange bedfellows, but when the Troubles began, the walls came up (figurative and literal, as Belfast is riddled with miles on miles of tall "peace walls"—massive fences that run through backyards and across side streets, carefully and oppressively dividing these two worlds from each other), and neighbors who used to share their lives across their back fences were now as separated as if they each lived in entirely different cities.

The religious community that most inspired me—at that time—was the interdenominational (and increasingly interfaith) reconciliation community known as the Corrymeela Community, one of the oldest and most respected religious communities on the island of Ireland, focused on reconciliation. The Corrymeela Community was formed in 1965 when the Rev. Ray Davey, the chaplain at Queen's University Belfast, as well as several friends and students, became interested in bringing reconciliation to the divisions within Northern Irish society. Ray Davey was inspired by his experience working at a YMCA center in North Africa during World War II, as well as by the emergence of the Agape Community in Italy, to root his vision of a reconciling community in an "open village" concept. The open village would be a place of openness and hospitality, "open to all people of good will who are willing to meet each other and work together for the good of all."[4] The open village would be located in a specific place, yet would focus its work on bridging differences between people. The work of the community would focus most especially on the religious, cultural, and national differences between the Roman Catholic and Protestant communities, the two main religious communities in Northern Irish society at that time.

Davey was deeply moved by the ecumenical nature of the work of the YMCA in North Africa, where Davey met and served servicemen from a far wider diversity of backgrounds than he had experienced in Northern Ireland.[5] He became convinced that the root of much of the strife and division in Northern Irish society stemmed from the effect that the segregated nature of the society had on the hardening of boundaries and views of difference between the communities, and that only encounter with difference, in a safe and hospitable environment, would begin to bring healing and reconciliation to the two communities.

---

4. Ray Davey, *A Channel of Peace: The Story of the Corrymeela Community* (Marshall Pickering, 1993), 77.

5. Davey, *Channel of Peace*, 32.

The founding members of Corrymeela decided to root the nascent community along several planes of place, including Christianity, Celtic traditions, and the physical places of the Corrymeela Center in Ballycastle, County Antrim, and the Corrymeela House in Belfast. As Christians, the members felt it necessary to root their reconciling work in the narrative of the Gospels, as an attempt to live into the kingdom of God preached by Jesus. This Christian foundation has rooted its work in a highly contextual theological framework, in that the divine work of reconciliation must be complemented by practical human efforts toward reconciliation rooted in a very specific place, context, and tradition.[6] This framework revolves around the themes of place, people, and relationship, in which the work of the community would seek to bring people to a specific place in order to build relationships. This progression is intended to be a continuing cycle, in which once relationships are developed between people of different places, the people would then use the relationships to bring new people to a specific place in order to build relationships, and so on. The vision of Corrymeela is based on the conviction that if the community remains committed to the work, the cycle will continue to spiral out into the greater community and slowly lead to reconciliation across the island of Ireland.

These themes hold a multiplicity of definitions, most especially *place*. Each theme is present on both a physical as well as a metaphysical plane, with the metaphysical rooted in the concept of the kingdom of God, in which human interaction is meant to serve the greater purpose of eventually bringing humanity to reconciliation with itself, in order to join with the reconciliation that God has already made with humanity through the life, death, and resurrection of Jesus Christ.[7] *Place* is understood as rootedness in a Christian, Celtic tradition as well as the specific locales of Ballycastle, Belfast, Armoy (Knocklayd Retreat Center), and wherever Corrymeela members are at work on reconciliation.[8] *People* can be understood as both the entirety of humanity as created by God, joined together through Christ, and the people who visit and inhabit the spaces connected with the community. Reconciliation in this

6. Emmanuel Katongele and Chris Rice, *Reconciling All Things: A Christian Vision for Justice, Peace and Healing* (IVP Books, 2008), 25.

7. David Stevens, *The Place Called Reconciliation: Texts to Explore* (Corrymeela, 2008), 9.

8. Davey, *Channel of Peace*, 109.

context is highly concrete, as a specific action to specific people.[9] *Relationship* is understood as the commitment of God to a humanity interdependently joined together through Christ, as well as the relationships between people who are affected by or engaged in the work of the community.

Corrymeela understands the efficacy of this committed, embodied, contextual theology (based on the triple concepts of people, place, and relationship) on the efforts at reconciliation in Northern Ireland to be visible in the testimonies of individual people transformed by their interaction with the work of Corrymeela, as well as in the invisible reconciliation achieved by God.

Place

On the campus of the Corrymeela Center in Ballycastle sits the Croi, the locus of worship, prayer, and liturgy for the center. It may also accurately be termed the heart of prayer at the Center, for Croi in Irish means "heart."[10] Across the entrance to the Croi is written the Prayer Attributed to St. Francis. Out of all potential verses to greet every person who enters the heart of the community at least twice a day for daily prayer, the commission of the peacemaker was chosen. If worship and prayer are the heart of the community, in both a physical and spiritual sense, then the spirit of the community must be the active peacemaking advocated by both St. Francis and Jesus. These words, inscribed on the door of the Croi, signify that place, for Corrymeela exists as both the rootedness of the physical location of Corrymeela and a rootedness in the narratives, philosophy, and traditions of Christianity.

The physical place of Corrymeela provides an essential aspect of reconciliation—by the very fact of its permanence as a specific location, Corrymeela demonstrates its rootedness in the Northern Irish context and experience as well as a commitment to improving that context. This commitment to peacemaking has been proven over time, in part, as Ray Davey states, simply because "of the existence of the Center from the very start [of the Troubles]."[11] Davey

---

9. Murray Rae, "Remnant People: The Ecclesia as Sign of Reconciliation," in *The Theology of Reconciliation*, ed. Colin E. Gunton (T&T Clark, 2003), 97.

10. Alf McCreary, *In War and Peace: The Story of Corrymeela* (Brehon, 2007), 167.

11. Davey, *Channel of Peace*, 131.

also quotes the succinct explanation, given by Lord Billy Blease of Cromac, of the effectiveness of Corrymeela: "Corrymeela means trust."[12]

Place for Corrymeela is also rooted in its commitment to living a witness to a Christian vision of peace as explicated in the Gospels, with a particular emphasis on the traditions of Celtic Christianity—most specifically the focus on hospitality. In this way, Corrymeela is rooted in the place of the narratives and traditions of Christianity. This is achieved not only through the work of the community in embodying the reconciling work of Jesus but also in the emphasis Corrymeela places on studying the biblical narrative and gleaning insights about the will of God for reconciliation, and the form that human work for reconciliation should take.

Rootedness in the place of Christianity is demonstrated by the emphasis placed on worship. The Croi has already been mentioned as the physical heart of the Corrymeela Center, placing worship and prayer at the physical heart of Corrymeela. The twice-daily call to prayer in the Croi further establishes worship as a priority. This highlights the explicit link between praxis and prayer as well as between the narratives of the Christian life, both in the Bible and in church history, with the present day, demonstrating how the contemporary community can draw strength from these narratives as they engage in the work of reconciliation.

Corrymeela makes an explicit link between the contemporary community and the traditions of Celtic Christianity, stating how such traditions can serve to bind the two divided communities in Northern Ireland by drawing from the Celtic Church tradition, which is the common heritage of Catholics and Protestants in Ireland. This is an intentional attempt to utilize history as a tool for reconciliation by demonstrating the falsehood of the divided-history myth perpetuated in both communities.

This rootedness in the place of Celtic Christianity not only provides a tool for bridging gaps between the Protestant and Catholic communities in Northern Ireland; it also serves to root the work of the community in a contextual tradition: that of ancient Celtic retreat centers and centers of hospitality. The rule and ethos of hospitality was central to the Celtic community ethic.[13]

---

12. Davey, *Channel of Peace*, 131.

13. Johnston McMaster, *A Passion for Justice: Social Ethics in the Celtic Tradition* (Dunedin Academic Press, 2008), 106.

Hospitality to the members of the community as well as travelers was foundational in the Celtic cultural ethos and was made an institutional reality by the existence of laws regulating how travelers were to be treated. This was rooted both in the Judeo-Christian tradition of hospitality toward the stranger and in Celtic honor culture. Not only was a failure to show hospitality both an infraction of the law as well as a sin, but it would impute dishonor on whomever made such a mistake. In Celtic Christianity, this ethic found a specific practical expression in the hospitality offered by Irish monasteries to any in need of food or a place to stay. By rooting itself in Celtic Christianity, Corrymeela roots itself in the traditions and ethic of a form of Christianity that demonstrates potential for achieving reconciliation across Christian communities in Ireland.

People

Corrymeela claims a call to serve as a prophetic witness to the need to change the status quo of institutional preservation in both the church and society and to engage in the mission of the gospel in the world.[14] This call encapsulates the Corrymeela concept of people: both individuals and a community that are actively engaged in changing the current climate of fear, division, and misuse of power that seems to define the culture, institutions, and interactions of individuals in Northern Irish society. In order to achieve reconciliation, therefore, a religious community must be actively engaged in the political and social life of the wider society.[15]

This emphasis on the individual and corporate aspects of people permits individuals to become involved in the work of Corrymeela without necessarily becoming a full member of the community or to relinquish their own, separate, community identity. *People* could therefore just as easily mean the individual who attends a Corrymeela conference as it means the long-term Corrymeela volunteer who is coordinating the conference. This distinction can prove to be very helpful when engaging in reconciliation work in a divided postconflict society, in which community identity is not only an epistemological reality, but it is also an unambiguously concrete one affected by segregated patterns of living, work, and housing. These patterns can be dangerous to

14. Alf McCreary, *Corrymeela: The Search for Peace* (Christian Journals, 1975), 33.

15. Frank Wright, "Reconciling the Histories of Protestant and Catholic in Northern Ireland," in *Reconciling Memories*, ed. Alan D. Falconer and Joseph Liechty (Columba, 1998), 134.

intersect, as the boundary walls are often enforced by the dangers of physical violence and the consequences of the transgression of community norms and rules. Allowing space for individuals to engage in the work of Corrymeela, to take advantage of its resources, reputation and philosophy, without actually having to relinquish their place in a single-identity community permits people who are rooted in a community to retain their roots while also granting them the ability to slowly undermine the barriers that separate them from the other community.

Corrymeela sees itself as both individual people and as a corporate people who, in both guises, are involved in working to bring about the kingdom of God on earth. This is a highly charged political stance, for it places loyalty to any other kingdom behind loyalty to Christ as King and to Christ's work as reconciler of the entire world to himself. This theological stance by necessity rejects any claims of superiority or primacy for any one specific group within Christianity. This by no means rejects the particularity of difference embedded within the identities of separate religious communities, however, nor does it call for a pan-Irish Christianity that would eliminate the differences between the Catholic and Protestant traditions. Instead, Corrymeela views itself as a reconciling community of the Holy Spirit, firmly based in the person and work of Jesus Christ, called to be witnesses of God's love.

This emphasis on their status as a community focused on reconciliation permits them to claim universality and particularity simultaneously, and as such to empower its members to retain their separate denominational identities. Corrymeela is a community of reconciliation as its primary purpose, with worship as an outgrowth of that mission, whereas members are expected to participate in their own local church communities, whose primary focus would be on communal worship.

Corrymeela views its role as a people of prophetic witness both to the church and to the political structures of society. The witness to the church places Corrymeela on, as Alf McCreary notes, "a frontier position, interpreting the church to people outside, and trying to make the churches and church people aware of and sensitive to the attitudes and ideas of those outside."[16] Corrymeela is thus a protest group that is distinctly rooted in both the church as an institution in Northern Ireland and individual parish communities

16. McCreary, *Corrymeela*, 92.

scattered throughout the province. Corrymeela insists that it is not a separate church community; therefore, the individual people of Corrymeela are members of separate church communities throughout the world. Yet, as a corporate people, the Corrymeela Community channels the reconciling work of God to the world.

Corrymeela's identity as a religious people is integral to its work, both in granting its work legitimacy and in giving it a unique place from which to speak to members of both religious traditions in the Northern Irish conflict.[17] This mixture of religion and political activism is by no means unique to Northern Ireland or to Corrymeela. The gospel is a highly political work, and Jesus was crucified for his highly charged political preaching when he advocated dramatic changes in the structures of society, especially in the realm of governance and economic life. The work of reconciliation, as an effort to ensure the healing of divisions in society, is an unavoidably political activity.[18] If one accepts that reconciliation is central to Christianity, then one could easily claim that Christianity is an active, political religion.

Relationship

David Stevens places Corrymeela's understanding of a Christian vision of reconciliation directly on the person of Jesus Christ. He uses Ephesians 2:14 to demonstrate the manner by which Jesus is able to end division and as such to create relationship among all people: "For he is the peace between us, and has made the two into one and broken down the barrier which used to keep us apart."[19] Christ has mended the breaks in our relationships with each other, through his own initiative, and offered this reconciliation as a free gift to us all. Through emptying himself, Christ has created a space within himself for all people, Jew or Gentile, Catholic or Protestant, to join together and share in the life of Christ.

At the spiritual level, the work of reconciliation has already been achieved through the work of God, and humans need only acknowledge this reality

17. Duane K. Friesen, "Encourage Grassroots Peacemaking Groups and Voluntary Associations," in *Just Peacemaking: Ten Practices for Abolishing War*, ed. Glen Stassen (Pilgrim, 1998), 196.

18. Gabriel Daly, "Forgiveness and Community," in Falconer and Liechty, *Reconciling Memories*, 213.

19. David Stevens, *The Land of Unlikeness: Explorations into Reconciliation* (Columba, 2004), 55.

and begin to shape their attitudes, behaviors and actions accordingly. Jesus is the peace between us and the basis for all Christian comprehension of relationship, especially the Corrymeela vision of reconciliation among people who have historically not seen themselves even as all members of the same one body of Christ, let alone as partners in the work of reconciliation and peace commanded by Jesus. For Corrymeela, therefore, the allegiance to Christ supersedes any and all other loyalties and as such destroys any barriers that difference may create.[20]

All relationships among people, according to Corrymeela, lie within the embrace of Christ. As such, Corrymeela does not pursue any political agenda other than the work of reconciliation, working toward the eventual arrival of the kingdom of God. This may appear to be a contradiction of the statement made above about the political nature of Christianity. Accepting such a proposition would forget the distinctions between the various definitions of political. If the Christian's allegiance is primarily to the kingdom of God, then all "political" work would be done for the good of the kingdom of God and based on the values of the kingdom of God. These values would include social justice, equality, peace, reconciliation—all values that could ostensibly be claimed by those seeking either a United Ireland or maintenance of a United Kingdom. Yet, the difference lies in the locus from which those values stem. Those seeking to resolve constitutional questions of statehood would place the concept of equality, for example, in terms of equality for all in the borders of a nation-state, while the kingdom of God would place equality in terms of equality for all people in all places, as all are joined in the body of Christ. This grants Corrymeela a freedom to join in partnership with any and all who are truly seeking peace and reconciliation, including people and organizations on either side of the divides between Nationalist and Unionist in Northern Ireland, as well as between the Republic of Ireland and the United Kingdom.

For Corrymeela, relationship exists on a multiplicity of levels, ensuring a wonderful confusion of communities for any who are involved in any aspect of the community's work. One such example is the relationship that exists among Corrymeela's three physical locations. Attending a residential session at Ballycastle may bring a unionist into direct contact with a Nationalist, or participating in a program in Belfast coordinated by the Corrymeela House may

20. Timothy Kinahan, *A More Excellent Way: A Vision for Northern Ireland* (Corrymeela, 1998), 22.

bring an evangelical Protestant into direct contact with a Muslim long-term volunteer from Ballycastle who drove to Belfast to assist with the program. These interactions, and the relationships that may develop from them, are the core of Corrymeela's reconciliation work.[21]

This certainly sounds like a theology of *flowers* to me.

Leaves—*Wye River, Chesapeake Bay Watershed, Late March 2020*

In early March 2020, the world stopped. The seeds dropped by the Covid-19 virus all over the world took root, and rapidly an epidemic—originally centered in a few locations in China—bloomed into a pandemic that would eventually infect nearly eight hundred million people, kill seven million people, and utterly transform the lives of every single person in the world. A ruthless, deadly plague that infects the entire world, disrupting entire societies, while dismantling some governments and creating new ones? That's a textbook apocalypse.

My spouse's work was categorized as essential (she is a first responder, after all), and in these terrifying early weeks my daughter and I were encouraged to spend time away from our home to avoid infection. We spent a few weeks with my in-laws at their house in Maryland, while my daughter adapted to virtual learning and I adapted to virtual teaching. The virus was an unseen gas, creeping into all the spaces and crevices of our lives so that even when we were intentionally avoiding thinking about the pandemic, it was the only thing on our minds.

By this time, I was one of the editors of a project called the Politics of Scripture, which weekly publishes an informed and reflective political interpretation of one of the passages selected by the Revised Common Lectionary—the calendar of Jewish and Christian Scripture readings that millions of Christians worldwide follow for their weekly worship services. I was struggling to find a way to make sense of everything happening around me and eventually wrote the following reflection for Ezekiel 37:1–14. What this passage and my response to it provided for me was the turning of a new *leaf*: a way of interpreting apocalypse from the perspective of the liminal space between death and life, opening me up to experiencing apocalypse as a journey between these two points, and in

21. John Morrow, *On The Road of Reconciliation: A Brief Memoir* (Columba, 2003), 71.

turn opening my awareness to the presence of apocalypse as an experience that is simultaneously, immensely communal and intimately individual.[22]

~ ~ ~

There are moments when, akin to a waking dream, we are fully aware of ourselves in the grand sweep of history, when we can feel, viscerally, that we are in the midst of seismic shifts in our lives. Right now, we are standing side by side with Ezekiel, desperately trying to process exactly how we wound up in a world we don't recognize and over which we have no control. This is truth: The world, as we know it now, has irrevocably changed. Our measures for normal are all broken, and we will not be returning to any sense of stability and balance any time soon. We have no clue when this crisis will subside, and we are completely in the dark about what the world will look like when it does. We are moving at breakneck speed through an impenetrable fog, without any sense of direction and completely bereft of landmarks. We have precious little control over the future, and we feel powerless to stop the forces at play, which seem to be working to transform even the smallest aspects of our lives.

These moments are when I feel the most connection with the past, because they seem to create wormholes that bring together numerous moments in time, gathering us all together in one place so that we can all stand next to each other and see into each other's realities with new eyes. This phenomenon could also be termed a "thin place," that liminal space where what was, what is, and what may come to be all coalesce, and we experience the surreality of having God's time and physical time meet and embrace. This is a place where we encounter prophetic visions, where we can see the spread of history laid out in front of us, and where we encounter the Spirit of God, literally "inspired" by God as the Spirit of God fills us, shows us truth, and gives us life.

At this moment in time, we are in a place where the Babylonian exile, the impending worldwide ecological collapse, the slow-motion unraveling of national economies, the 1918 flu pandemic, and the tsunami of the Covid-19 pandemic are all occurring at the same time, this one time. We are Ezekiel in Babylon, struggling to come to grips with living in exile. We are the Israelites, grieving the loss of control over their lives, the sense that everything they had always known was lost and, most terrifying, the worry that they would be cut

---

22. Christy Randazzo, "The Sleepers Must Awaken," Political Theology Network, March 23, 2020, https://politicaltheology.com/the-sleepers-must-awaken/.

off from God, living so far from their homeland. How are they to be comforted? How are we to gain any sense of hope? Is there any future for us both?

In response, Ezekiel provides us with a vision distressing in its implications for our immediate future. In 37:1–2, Ezekiel is grabbed by God's hand and carried in God's wind to a desolate valley. God ensures that Ezekiel misses no detail, leading Ezekiel through the entire valley. The prophet sees a place of utter desolation, filled with the bone refuse of an unknown multitude of bodies so far past decay that they are solely the minerals that comprise them. This place is completely, absolutely, and utterly devoid of life. It is dead, with no hope of life ever returning. Their bones are dried up, their hope is lost, they are cut off completely, and they are buried in graves far away from their home (Ezek 37:11–12).

The power of this vision must be rooted in this reality, one that cannot be rejected or dismissed. We must not shy away from accepting that we are facing the death of something fundamental to our lives and our society. Whether it is this pandemic or the climate crisis, we must face the reality that we cannot maintain our society exactly as it was anymore. We have passed a tipping point, and we are already seeing the effects of that all around us, whether massive population die-offs, extreme weather events, or the rise of microbes that leap from animals to humans and cause pandemics. There is no hope for us if we do not stare hard into the valley and realize that this is our future.

This is a time for excessive humility, for acknowledging that our need for power and control has not only brought ourselves to this point but will ultimately lead this vision of our future to become our present reality. When God asks us whether these bones can live, we must be able to accept that, as Ezekiel states in 37:3, only God really knows. All our models and all our projections (especially our economic ones) are fundamentally flawed, and we need to fundamentally reassess the assumptions on which we have based our entire society. That's the bad news.

Before we leave this place, we need to also acknowledge that death is an irrevocable change. What was before death has died and will never return. What is reborn by God's hand is now different, fundamentally. Nothing can cease to be without causing tears in the surrounding fabric. This is easy to see in ecosystems: Death ripples out in ever-expanding spirals, causing damage wherever it hits. This also applies to smaller cycles of death and rebirth, however, such as those moments that changed us forever: the death of a loved one, the realization that we have been betrayed, or the death of a career.

Death does not need to be a tragedy, though: The moment when we become caretakers and lovers of new life is also a moment of death, when we die to our previous lives and are reborn as parents, grandparents, family. We can never return to what once was because we are now different people. Something in us has shifted profoundly, and we will never be the same as we were. We will heal, we may even become stronger, but we will never be the same. Once something ends, it is ended and is no more. Even when God grants life, God does not recalibrate time or its effects on who we are.

We must mourn what has died and accept its death before we can move on into the new life God brings. If we don't mourn and accept, and allow ourselves to feel the passing of something essential to ourselves, we won't be able to accept the new life God will inevitably bring. This is the good news, and it is also truth: God always brings new life after death. God is always following behind us, bringing life and healing after death and destruction. As Ezekiel prophesies in 37:5–6, God will cause "breath to enter you, and you shall live," bones to rejoin, sinews to be regrown, skin to stretch, bodies to heal.

Yet, if we are stuck in our previous ways of being, bound by the dead ways, then we will be incapable of recognizing new life when it sprouts among us. We will experience this new life as dangerous and instead cling to our old ways with such ferocity that we cut ourselves off from life, slowly consuming our own selves in a frightening self-mutilation of fear and greed. We *must* prophesy when called to do so, even to the driest of bones and the greediest of capitalists, and call on all to "hear the voice of God" (37:4).

God does not bring healing without partnership with humanity. We *must* be willing to give up our need to hoard power, wealth, and any other good (whether through greed or fear) and live into the role God desires for us, whether prophet, health care worker, or transit worker, faithfully fulfilling our place in helping to bring healing and life back to the dead places in our ecosystems and our economies. Ezekiel knows this, and when he does as he is commanded, healing begins to take place (37:7–8).

We might even be asked to do the impossible, to do that for which we think we are unworthy: to prophesy directly to God and to ask God to bring life into that which was once dead (37:9–10). This too necessitates a death: a death to our human measures of importance and value. In the eyes of God, all are valuable and precious. In the scale of God's creation, size is no measure of power (as we're discovering), and age is no measure of wisdom, as teenagers such as Greta Thunberg demonstrate. Even the mightiest economy can be felled from the tiniest microbe, and the fiercest social movement ignited from the tiniest prophetic flame. We will call to the Lord out of the depths (Ps 130:1), and the Lord will be attentive to our pleas, even and especially the pleas of the most vulnerable, the oppressed, the dying, or those suddenly out of work and afraid of what the future will hold.

This is truth, both for pandemics and the restoration of a people/ecosystem: Things will seem to happen very slowly, until suddenly everything seems to happen at once. From a long time of banishment, which seemed like death, God promises to drag the people of Israel from the graves of their exile and to restore them to life in their homeland. In an echo of Genesis 2:7, God will fill their mouths with God's own Spirit, giving them the gift of God's own life (Ezek 37:13–14).

What separates this vision from other miracle stories (such as John 11, for example) is that it does not place the focus on the individual human being healed or reborn. Instead, this is a collective healing, a rebirth of the entire community, and as such is both a physical healing and the rebirth and reimagining of the people, a new understanding of what it means to be a people. Staring out across the dead valley of their exile, Israel was faced with the death of themselves as a people and the utter, desolate certainty that they would never return to their lives as they had lived them. They needed to mourn their previous frameworks, for they would never return. They needed to learn how to be a people faithful to God's call in a foreign land, a place they did not understand and that would change them in profound ways.

We see through the eyes of Israel. We see through the eyes of Ezekiel. How will we mourn our previous certainties? How will we reimagine ourselves in this strange country? How will we prophesy? How will we call on God to bring healing? Will we accept it when it comes, in whatever form God desires it to take? We are a people once asleep, now waking to a new world, in which our forms of life have done irreparable harm to our earth and helped to unleash a deadly pathogen on ourselves. We must ask, How will these bones live? O Lord God, only you know.

Fruits—*Schuylkill River Watershed, Lower Delaware River, July 3, 2022*

The pandemic took a profound toll on religious communities, forcing them to either adapt to the challenges and opportunities that defined that period of time, ignore them and insist on special dispensations, or die. By May 2021, in the face of division within my Friends meeting as well as the fissures and chasms in society exposed and exacerbated by the loneliness of the pandemic, I'd awoken to a leading to find a religious community that embodied the themes and theology of reconciliation communities. I was inspired to reach out to Circle of Hope, a Christian community in Philadelphia with notable Quaker connections and an explicit call to be Christ in the specific context of the Delaware Valley. My leading was confirmed in a number of quiet, barely noticeable ways that added up to a conviction that this was the place the Light was leading me toward. I felt at home among this community of people to a degree I'd not felt in an extraordinarily long time. What I didn't know was that the church was actively dying.

The story of this remarkable community—its birth, its life, and its eventual death—has already been told truthfully and beautifully; besides, I don't have space here to even offer an effective summary. The most important thing to know is that the Light had led me to this community, and while I was feeling rebirth and new life in my relationship with the Light among this family I had found, simultaneously the community was fracturing from within, with the previously tightly woven fabric of relationships (friendships, marriages, families) that defined the life and ministry of Circle of Hope tearing apart in ugly, ragged strips. This was a breakup, but it also felt like a civil war, in which sides were drawn, walls were built, fortresses were manned, and the bonds that had been woven across decades between each branch of the Circle family tree were questioned and undermined, and eventually began to die as life leaked away. Concurrently, the legislative war against trans people had begun to seriously gain steam. Finally, the Supreme Court of the United States of America handed down the decision in the *Dobbs v. Jackson Women's Health Organization* case on June 24, 2022, the week before this sermon was delivered—an earthquake whose aftershocks we are still feeling, as I type these words. On July 3, I preached to two of these branches of Circle of Hope, attempting to find a way to reconcile these divisions while also responding to the war that had begun against trans and queer people. I began to develop a doctrine I called nonbinary theology and sketched out the outlines in this sermon.

~ ~ ~

The Scripture passage for today is among the rare few stories that Jesus not only explains but even offers a very specific series of lessons he wants people to gain from it. Jesus explains the parable himself in Matthew 13:36–43: straight from the mouth of God. From one perspective, therefore, this should be an incredibly quick sermon, with my only duty being to explain who both the wheat and the weeds are, with the core lesson being that those who consider themselves the wheat have the duty—granted directly from Jesus, so you know it's true—to patiently bear being mixed in with the unrighteous until the end of time, when they'll be freed from being forced to live among the impure, gathered up into heaven, while the weeds will be thrown into the fire to suffer along with the evil one.

Open-and-shut case, no?

Somehow I just can't leave it there. I can't help but wonder about what's not in this story and its interpretation: Whose voice isn't being heard? What potential interpretations are we missing when we focus on what appears to be the literal meaning of the passage? Allow me to digress a bit and tell you three other stories that might help explain what I mean. Two will be from my childhood, ones that taught me the power of stories to hurt. I'll then tell a final story that taught me the power of stories to heal.

When I was a child, my parents would often tell me two stories relating to my mother's pregnancy and my birth. One was absolutely hilarious and actually demonstrates a significant aspect of my personality. The other story is far more complicated and painful. A few necessary details: One, I was born eighteen months after my brother. Two, my mother suffered a burst appendix as a child, which led to some rather significant organ damage, including to her reproductive organs. Three, as a result of this damage, she was cautioned against birthing children. Four, and perhaps most importantly, my mother was quite ill while pregnant with me. Now that we've set the scene, let's begin.

Every year, my parents would relate to me the story of my birth. The details never wavered. My mother would always begin by saying that she went into labor with me rather suddenly, without any of the slow buildup that many other people experience, and especially none of the warning signs that she experienced with my brother. As my mother tells it, my parents were putting my brother to bed, preparing him for what might occur over the next few days: Mommy beginning labor, family driving in to help with the first few days, how a sibling might change his life, and so on. After they finished getting him ready for bed, my parents cleaned up from dinner, put the house back in order, and started to settle down for the evening. Suddenly, my mother felt intense, sharp labor pains, with contractions coming right on top of each other, and then she felt her water break. At this point, at 9 p.m., my parents had to figure out several things, all at once, with the two obvious ones being (1) who they could ask—last minute, mind you!—to come over to our house and, most likely, spend the night with my brother, and (2) how they would get to the hospital in the absolute quickest time possible.

They solved the first by knocking on their neighbor's door and basically begging, and they resolved the second by my mom waddling over to the car and my dad driving like a bat out of hell. My dad—ever the rule follower—always made a point of noting how very fast he drove, all the while terrified that he'd either get a ticket or have an accident. My mother then derived great pleasure in relating how she burst into the emergency room, took one look at the person at the desk, and just screamed, "*Baby!*" A nurse ran over with a wheelchair and had barely finished wheeling my mother past the doors when I began to crown. The nurse stopped pushing the chair, dashed around, and apparently had to leap into a diving catch in order to keep me from going splat all over the tiles. As I said: sitcom material galore!

Now, I want to note here that my parents never told my brother what his own thoughts were about all of this at that time, even when he asked. He begged to know where he fit into this foundational story of his own family. The main characters in this story were my parents, with even me—the baby in question—just being the initiator of the plot . . . and everyone else simply window dressing.

This second story involves a series of visits my parents made to the obstetrician during the first few months of my mother's pregnancy. It's vital to mention that my mother was warned—regularly—about the potential health challenges pregnancy would bring for her. As she'd carried my brother without any difficulties, however, she was certain she could easily carry me. She soon discovered that this was not going to be the case. As my mother told the story—and believe me, she told this story over and over and over, seemingly to anyone who'd listen—every doctor she spoke with during the first two trimesters urged my mother to consider aborting me, as I was tearing my mother's insides apart. My mother would always insist that she couldn't even conceive of making such a decision and that she was going to do everything in her power to bring me into the world, even if it cost her life to do so. Now, whenever my mother told this story, she was the star of the show—no one else spoke, most notably my father, who always chose to remain silent and to keep his own thoughts about this health crisis unspoken. I actually never learned how my father felt about any of this. My mother's narrative was *the* narrative, entirely.

Let me pause here to state that this story is *not* an antiabortion narrative. My mother suffered from significant physical and psychic pain for my entire life, and I've often wondered whether her life would actually have been easier had she chosen to abort me instead of choosing to have me and then passing her pain and suffering onto my brother and me for decades. But I digress.

These two stories were two foundational pillars of my parents' perception of who I was, what they understood their role as parents—and my role as child—to be, and what responsibilities I had to my family as a result. You see, these stories—even the first, amusing one—were never *just* stories. For my parents—and especially for my mother—they were a means to remind me on an annual basis about my place in the family, my duties to the family, and the inherent aspects of my personality that I would need to curb in order to fulfill these duties. With these stories she continually reminded me that I was impulsive, I was inherently selfish, and that my independent and rebellious streak was a danger to myself and to my parents. My mother certainly was a hero who would defend my right to exist at all costs . . . but she'd never let me forget it. My life was a gift given to me by my parents, a gift I had a duty to repay by fulfilling their vision of how I should live. For years, I accepted their framing of the narrative as definitive and acted accordingly. It was only when I began to wonder whether there was something missing from the narrative that I began to truly see myself for the first time. And there is so much missing, not only from her narrative of the story, but also from her interpretation of the story and its meaning.

This final story is about the first time that I realized I was nonbinary. Now, I had always known that I approached the world a little differently, but I always accepted my parents' two-pronged explanation for why I viewed the world so differently: (1) I was a Christian, therefore God demanded from me a different approach to the world as a result, and (2) I was a fiercely independent, knee-jerk antiauthoritarian who needed to rebel against everything and anything simply because it was there. Everything that went against the "world's" values was either explained by the first—such as the feminism and intense focus on social justice my mother drilled into my head as being inherent in the nature of God—or dismissed as the second. For example, I explained my inability to make sense of gender by stating that as God had both feminine and masculine qualities, all the ways that women were oppressed were simply sins that went against the nature of God. Gender, therefore, made sense only if it followed God's desire for the world. Therefore, I thought it was obvious I couldn't understand gender: It had only been presented to me in ways that rejected God's vision of justice! Problem solved! My need to push against the masculine roles expected of me by my family, however, was simply dismissed as me being a selfish rebel.

On one level, I still think the first statement still makes sense: Nearly every framing of gender ever constructed fails to meet God's desire for the world. Yet, there was always something... else, which only clicked into place when I finally heard about the concept of nonbinary genders. Suddenly, it was as if I had the key to the map not only of my own life but of the world itself. I wasn't just someone wedded to rebellion and resistance for their own sake, like some moody teenager, but I actually, truly, did think and relate to the world quite differently from others around me. It was a truly transformational moment for me, which unexpectedly rippled out into every other aspect of my life—an apocalypse, if you would.

I began to relate to stories in a radical new way: the approach I explained before. I insisted on asking questions: Whose voice is missing in this story? What interpretations are we missing if we accept the story at face value? How are we failing to see the narrative in its complete form? And finally, what are we importing into the story that isn't actually there? This approach is called *nonbinary theology*. These are some of the main components of this theology:

1. God is *always* with the oppressed, focused on their needs, and on alleviating their oppression.
2. Our place as humans is therefore *always* with the oppressed as well.
3. We need to keep listening for the unheard voices and seek to hear their stories.
4. We must always be creative, continuously reimagining the world and our place in it.
5. God rejects our binaries and does not identify with them.
6. As creation is made in the image of the complex Divine, it is also inherently diverse and multifaceted.

In this way, nonbinary theology exists in the spaces in between, rejecting the divisions of us and them that are imposed on humanity by our need to create binaries, whether good/evil, pure/impure, woman/man, or any other binary we create to make sense of our world. From that perspective, let's examine this parable anew:

First, who are the "children of the kingdom"? I bet many of you are quietly thinking that you'd include yourselves in that camp. Why? What gives you the right to make such assumptions about yourselves?

Second, who are the "children of the evil one"? If, for example, you're picturing a certain set of judges in robes, I'd recommend that you stop that nonsense right now. Before we continue, I need to address the unspoken context. My emotions are a maelstrom: Disenchantment, distraction, disconsolation, disempowerment, discouragement, I'm feeling them all, at once. I'm overcome with rage and overwhelmed with fear. These last few days have delivered a one-two punch to my soul, leaving me gasping for air and clutching for stability in a world that seems to be falling apart at the seams. I know many of you share my confusion and anger and are in mourning.

I am frightened about the consequences of these decisions. What will this mean to the people across our country who have now lost access to basic health care—especially for BIPOC people, who are the majority of those who have abortions? What will this mean for anyone who is "different" in public—but especially those BIPOC and LGBTQ+ people who are often the target of hate? As a person who is visibly queer in public—and very intentionally so—should I start wearing a bulletproof vest over my apparently offensive clothing? If I allow myself, I am certain that I will tip over into incapacitation, unable to function because of a fear of the future. That state of fear, of confusion, of disempowerment: That's the *point*. That's the *intent* of these decisions. We cannot allow ourselves to fall into that trap.

We need to remember that Jesus himself says that as soon as you're certain of your own righteousness, you've begun to lose any claim you might have ever had to being a child of the kingdom—and boy, are we *certain* that we are correct about this! Yet, this is not to say that God isn't entirely on the side of the oppressed, the marginalized, and the vulnerable. I'd say that Jesus doesn't actually take a side, because that—to me—implies that (1) Jesus and God have a choice in the matter, and (2) that God would even accept the binary of a choice. Instead, I'd argue that God is always on the side of the oppressed simply because it's who God is, at their very foundations. You could say that Jesus was just . . . born this way, perhaps?

I want y'all to consider where you are importing your own binaries into the text. We see good and evil as binary, absolute opposites of each other. We then strive to provide definitions of *good* and *evil* that are rooted in Scripture and our understanding of Jesus as the liberator of the oppressed. We might even devote our lives to ensuring that we do all we can to bring about good into the world. Yet, as soon as we state that something is good, we are inevitably declaring that something else is bad. This is a dangerous road to walk down, because once we decide that something—or someone—is bad, it is one very short step toward making the equivalence between bad and evil, and suddenly something—or again, someone—represents "the evil one." Now, once we do that, we have no choice but to fight both the idea and its proponents with all our energy, even to the point of defending actions as good that we would never accept from anyone else, and would decry as bad—if not evil. This is empire thinking! For example, this is the kind of thinking we often praise—however unintentionally or reluctantly—when we celebrate July 4 and all it represents.

Let's read the parable again. Did you see that the farmer allows the wheat and the weeds to exist alongside each other, because, as Matthew 13:29 states, "In gathering the weeds you would uproot the wheat along with them"? This is essential! God does not give us permission to decide what is or is not good wheat; instead, we are to live with everyone else in the field of the world, sharing resources. Remember: We are all inextricably interdependent on this fragile earth. We are just as bound up in the structures of the world as anyone else. We are just as likely to harm others as we are to help them. We are deeply dependent for our survival on others, even and especially those we are certain are simply evil.

Did you catch who Jesus says will be doing the reaping, separating the good from the evil? The Son of Man will send his angels to do that work: It's Jesus doing the reaping, not us. It's not our job to decide who's evil, because as soon as we fall prey to that binary, we forget that harming the evil one will damage our own roots as well and even uproot us entirely from the field of the world. This could result in ending our lives or else leaving us adrift, literally rootless, cut off from the soil of God and from the connections we share with everyone else through the complexity of the roots planted deeply in the soil of God's creation.

What, then, is our job? It's both surprisingly simple and unbelievably complex simultaneously. Yes, even living God's desire for the world is nonbinary. If we strive to be the good wheat—and yes, it is a choice, for no one is born good or evil but instead acts in good and evil ways—we must be as Jesus is: focused entirely on the needs of the oppressed and working to heal the world of this same oppression. Note that I said *heal*: No one has ever made soil better by dumping a bunch of poison into it. Anyone who does that has forgotten that we're interdependent in this field, and they've gone and poisoned themselves as well as everyone else. No one benefits from such a Pyrrhic victory.

June 23 is the Feast of John the Baptist, an event I find notable for what John's example can teach us about how to respond to the fear of death, fear for the future, in the face of the empire. John consistently retained hope in the coming of the kingdom of God, and never ceased to call on the empire to repent, even in the face of certain death. Now, I am no John the Baptist! I am, however, called on by God to always hold to hope, having faith in the revolutionary potential of the power of God's love.

Resistance takes many forms, from marching in the streets and political agitation to joining Jesus among the oppressed and vulnerable, offering direct service to all who are in the sights of this cruelty and malice. Yet, resistance also takes the form of retaining hope in the face of what seems like certain defeat, reveling in the joy of being alive and fully living into all we are, keeping our hearts soft and continuing to show love to others, rejecting the urge to become cynical and instead demanding that they can rip our faith, our hope, our joy, our love . . . from our cold, dead hands.

Today I will mourn. You know, I might even mourn for the next week. We all must mourn. Then, we must dust ourselves off, open our hearts to God's love and the joy the Spirit brings, and resist with every fiber of our being. I mean: Hope is *literally* the name of our community; we have no choice but to live into that inheritance.

This work is dangerous and difficult, and may even cost us dearly. It is work that will demand all of our energy, every ounce of our creativity, and every shred of our devotion and perseverance: in other words, all of everything we are. It will require that we give up easy binaries and the easy interpretations of our foundational stories. Finally, it will call us to stop telling stories that hurt us and harm our relationships with each other, the creation, and with God, instead choosing those stories that heal and liberate all of us. It will demand that we cease to make ourselves the hero of the story and instead begin to see the story from the perspective of God: in which we all have the potential to bring something necessary to the field of God's body. What is a weed, anyway, other than simply any plant that we don't want? Even dandelions can be the hero sometimes.

I will be holding all of us in the Light as we navigate these challenges; let us use this to root ourselves ever deeper in the family of this community. Faith, hope, and love abide, and the greatest of these is love: I love you all.

Seeds—*Cooper River Watershed, Lower Delaware River, Late October 2022*

By October of that same year—2022—it became obvious that Circle was going to divide, and each of its constituent communities would go its own way. It was sobering and desperately saddening. Yet, at the same time that this community I had poured myself into for the last year and a half was tearing apart at the seams, the community of people who lived in New Jersey had looked straight into the maelstrom—and decided to simply keep meeting and to figure out who we were now as we grew even closer as a family. We could see the shoots of new life taking root, and hope swelled within me. After a particularly hopeful camping trip where we gathered together as a community, mourned our death, and spoke into being a vision for new birth, I wrote this reflection on Habakkuk 1:1–4; 2:1–4 for the Politics of Scripture.[23] The seed this piece planted in me grew rapidly into a leading to write this very book—and I submitted a proposal within days.

~ ~ ~

What I find most striking—and even disconcerting—about Habakkuk is how timeless its first two chapters sound. The drums of war, beating loudly, threatening imminent invasion. The irrepressible surge of desperation welling up within anyone who is in the path of that inexorable force. The yawning pit in the stomach as it appears that all hope is lost. The overwhelming desire for God's appearance on the scene, bringing a miraculous rescue. The recriminations in the small hours that cause doubt and blame. The righteous certainty that emerges when blame is apportioned, locating the proper shoulders on which to lay it. The recognition that this situation demands societal

23. Christy Randazzo, "The Timeless Power of Hope," Political Theology Network, October 24, 2022, https://politicaltheology.com/the-timeless-power-of-hope/.

transformation, including a call for repentance and a return to a path of justice and compassion. Habakkuk's context is the imminent destruction of Jerusalem by the Babylonian Empire, yet these feelings would just as easily apply to the Russian invasion of Ukraine, the climate crisis, the rise of far-right ideology around the world, and the saber rattling of autocratic states. The emotions it evokes are as present to us now as they would be to Habakkuk's original audience.

On one level, this sense of timelessness is quite fitting, as almost nothing—save a few snippets—is known about the author(s) of this short book. I'd argue that this lack of information actually frees us to engage in an act of creative license. Akin to setting Shakespeare in a modern context, we should feel welcome to locate ourselves in the emotional landscape of this passage. We should allow its complex atmosphere of fear and hope to inspire us as we ourselves face a contemporary world that is both metaphorically and literally on fire.

Habakkuk begins abruptly, as 1:2 immediately jumps into mournful cries for help from the Lord. Notably, each cry for help is immediately followed by an accusation of divine abandonment. Habakkuk is certainly not shy in his demands of the Lord. He not only accuses the Lord of abandoning him and his people when they most require salvation, but he's also shocked and indignant that the Lord requires him to bear witness to the wrongdoing, strife, and contention that exist on all sides (1:3). Habakkuk laments the perverted state of his society (1:4)—in which justice is twisted to serve the powerful—while also lamenting God's demand that, as prophet, he bear witness to such a violent and destructive time.

Habakkuk is reflecting the paradox inherent in the role of prophet: Prophets are compelled to serve as God's witness and voice to God's people; yet prophets are also free to push back on God and demand that God save God's own people. Habakkuk, then, feels it is his duty to demand that God pay attention to the dire state of affairs the Jewish people face. In 2:1 Habakkuk makes explicit what had been only implicitly stated: He is the watchman on the ramparts witnessing the state of the world, relaying that information back to the Lord. Habakkuk serves in a vital dual role as both messenger and translator: bearing and interpreting the message of the Lord for the people, and voicing—to the fullest extent possible—the fears, dreams, despairs, and hopes of the people to God.

I can only imagine Habakkuk's emotional state at this point. He's literally stuck in the middle of a desperate situation: forced to witness the pain and suffering of his people, knowing that the Babylonian armies are likely on their way. At the same time, it seems that the Lord has abandoned Israel, leaving them to their fate. Yet, he stands firm, patient on the ramparts, hopeful for God's deliverance. I can't help but wonder: How does Habakkuk remain committed? I'd argue that it is hope that sustains him: the hope of salvation, the hope of a message from the Lord, the hope of a people who, while long oppressed, have always found God present with them in their most desperate hours. Hope, that ephemeral yet powerful emotion that once gained aids us in moving mountains, and once lost can be lost forever, nearly impossible to replant.

I admit that all this talk of the power of hope can sound extremely naive and cliché. Yet, I'd argue that the loss of hope feels as if a light has gone out of the world. Hopelessness sucks in all light from around it, creating an inescapable gravitational force. Hopelessness clings to our heels, dragging us into a swirling, molasses quagmire. Let's flip the perspective, then, focusing on what hope can achieve. With hope, what depths of suffering can be endured? With hope, what can be created, imagined, overcome? With hope, what reserves of strength and resolve can be tapped? I'd argue that the possibilities are nearly endless.

Why do we often mock hope as naive and unrealistic? Self-styled realists—calling themselves prophets—often dismiss the power of hope and preach the message that a realistic view of the world demands that we allow the ugliness of the world to infect us, for it is only in facing the cold, hard reality of the world that we will survive. Now, I must admit that there is an inherent danger in allowing ourselves to let hope cloud our perception of the world: For example, no amount of time spent consumed by the dream of utopian fantasies and saviors—whether that be God or the newest shiny technological toy—will stop climate change in its tracks. We must also actively participate in our own salvation.

These two components—hope and action—are interconnected, therefore: We have the resolve and courage to act only when we are bolstered with the medicine of hope. At the same time, we must keep our hope from mutating into a cloying, rancid fantasy through maintaining the clarity necessary to see what is actually achievable and necessary. The Lord may not stop the

Babylonians from invading. However, if we insist on holding fast to a spiritual discipline of hopeful witness, we might be capable of rebuilding our world when God moves within the gears of history and the time is right: when Babylon is eventually defeated and we are able to return home.

I'd like to offer a vision of this hope in action, using a scene from the television show *Derry Girls*. The world of this show is the divided town of Derry (also known as Londonderry), Northern Ireland, in the mid-1990s, during the final days of the three-decade-long civil war known as the Troubles. While the Troubles provides the backdrop of the show, *Derry Girls* actually focuses the majority of its attention on telling the coming-of-age story of a group of Northern Irish teens. It's absolutely hilarious in the brutal honesty it offers about the universal experience of the painful awkwardness of being a teenager. However, it is deeply poignant in its portrayal of the fog of despair that often accompanies challenging times of conflict and social upheaval.

In what I consider to be one of the most beautiful scenes in this entire show, we see one of the teens—the eccentric dreamer Orla McCool—dance her way along the medieval walls that still surround the center of Derry. Orla's smile is wide and infectious, and in the fantastical world that seems to exist only in musicals, she dances with people she meets along her journey, including performing an intricate stepdance with a row of schoolchildren. This splash of unbridled joy in the context of the walls provides poignant symbolism in this scene, as they are themselves physical reminders of unstable and violent times in Derry's history.

Orla is seemingly oblivious to the world, deeply immersed in her headphones . . . until she reaches a British Army checkpoint. Orla's smile slips, and she faces the guard directly, stating that she needs to pass. As we see Orla walk through the gate, for a second it seems that her shoulders slump, and the ugliness of the power and violence of the checkpoint will defeat her.

Then she does something magical: She leaps up, clicking her heels, before confidently striding off. This one moment provides an indelible image: of hope in the face of despair, beauty in the ugliness of war, and childlike naivete in the face of brutal reality. Orla isn't weak, or silly, or even oblivious: She knows exactly what world she lives in and refuses to allow it to conquer her hope and her ability to bathe in the beauty of the world around her. These are the spiritual disciplines we need during times of despair: hope, beauty, and an unrelenting resolve to remain open to dreaming new worlds.

Eventually, Habakkuk achieves what he has been desperately hoping for: He hears from the Lord (2:2–3), who offers a vision of a new world, which—according to Jewish tradition—will see the coming of the Messiah, a savior who will free the people of Israel from their despair. The Lord doesn't offer a specific timeline for this salvation—again, this isn't a fantasy—but a promise is offered: Have patience and wait for deliverance, as it is guaranteed to come.

How do we maintain hope in the face of a seemingly unending time of strife, violence, and conflict? Seek out beauty, depend on hope, and dance, even in the face of unending war. Hope does not ignore the struggle, nor does it free us from the scars resulting from our struggles. We will always carry the scars of our trauma with us, and what an amazing thing that is: Scars mean that we've survived to live another day.

So: Live! Choose life!

Epilogue: The Church Is Hope

Passaic River Watershed (New Jersey), November 6, 2024

I can remember every single time that I have ever "lost hope," mainly because it has happened so infrequently to me. This is not for lack of a good enough reason to lose hope, however. In fact, hope is often the last reserve of strength for me, my final defense in the face of impending defeat. Maybe it's a result of my intense stubbornness, but I absolutely refuse to concede hope, no matter the circumstances. I consider hope to be mine to claim or to accede, purely on my own initiative. Try and wrest hope from my grasp, and you will find that I will bring every resource to the fight, including the dirty and underhanded. I consider hope to be my most precious possession.

All of this strong talk is not hyperbole. Every day, before I even rise out of bed, I make a commitment to retain my hope: in the day, in God, in my marriage, in my child, in my career, and in the potential for love and beauty to win the argument against hate and cruelty. I firmly believe that this decision, this continual commitment to hope, is one of the most important spiritual practices that I have ever encountered. It's one of the very few practices that have been able to sustain me through every challenge in my life. My hope is not a greeting-card platitude; it's a tenacious terrier staring despair in the face and—with a smile—saying, "Try and get a piece of me."

Please do not mistake me: I am not claiming to have superhuman powers of hope. It has been tested and tried and stretched and choked, and persevered and healed and flourished—in turn. I've clung to hope as if my life depended on it. There have been days when my hope has been the only reason I dragged myself out of bed in the morning. I don't view hope as a special ability reserved for those with greater spiritual and mental strength. Hope is often the only option left for kids trying to make sense of a world where a parent can treat them as if they are subhuman. Hope is the last reserve for parents who, when looking at their sleeping children, have no clue how they will make it to the next paycheck. Hope is the last line of defense for families dealing with chronic illness.

Hope is the reserve of the dispossessed, the poor, and the marginalized. Hope isn't a luxury when you are faced with the struggle to retain your dignity and all that makes you human. This is a robust, stubborn hope that can overcome all of the voices telling you that you will fail; this is the only hope that will ever sustain "the church" in the face of all of its challenges. I know this because I have experienced it personally. Let me tell two stories of church communities flourishing in Appalachia—one northern, the other southern—that welcomed me with open arms when I was a child and in which I experienced this tenacity of hope.

The Church Is Hope in Appalachia

For the first five years of my life, the people most core to my understanding of family all lived in New York, both in the city and out on Long Island. Then, in the mid-1980s, my grandfather kicked off an exodus from the city, leading what eventually became the *entire* population of the New York City branch of my family to the Endless and Pocono mountain lands—northeast Pennsylvania coal country and the first generation of exurbs.

One of the foundational aspects of understanding the culture of the communities stretched along the ridges—and embedded in the valleys—of the region known as Appalachia is that the majority of these communities depended on the extraction economy for their existence: In other words, these were towns built by (and for) a company that either mined for resources underground (mainly coal), logged the vast interior forests of the Appalachian Mountain chain, or processed either of these materials to feed heavy industry. It is nearly impossible to overstate the significance of these companies and their products on the history of the United States. Without vast forests to provide the wood to lay the foundations for the booming industrial North, and the massive seams of coal—that ran right up the spines of the long ridge valleys snaking in long, parallel tracks across Pennsylvania and West Virginia—to fuel the gaping maws of the steel furnaces, the United States of America—as we know it—simply would not and could not exist. (Whether it should exist as it does is, of course, an extremely valid question . . . and one for another time.)

As a result, however, the communities in this region were extraordinarily vulnerable to the vicissitudes of the market. When there was a strong market for the resources these communities extracted from the land, these communities thrived economically and boomed as people flooded in, seeking work and homes for their families. However, as booms are wont to do, these booms eventually all went bust, with catastrophic consequences for the communities that rooted during the boom times: This is especially the story of this northeastern corner of Pennsylvania. Some branches of my mother's family lived in Forest City, Pennsylvania. I spent my childhood visiting my family—and this town—at least once a month, with sometimes entire months spent at my grandparents' house. While I never lived there, Forest City felt like home, a place where my roots were planted.

Forest City is a town whose initial reason for existence is glaringly obvious: Yes, the lumber magnate whose mills ran the town elected to call his booming lumber town Forest City. Similarly, the steel magnates who found a rich coal seam—a long, thin finger of black—running through this entire region of northeast Pennsylvania, creatively named the town at the top of the valley Carbondale. (*Carbondale*: Do you see what I mean?) These two towns are just miles from each other: Carbondale was the only place to go for miles around if you needed to shop anywhere larger than a corner store.

By contrast, Forest City is tiny, despite—as residents always loved reminding me when I was a child—being a mile long. However, it once held the population to fill the congregations of five Roman Catholic churches—one each for the Irish, Lithuanian, Slovakian, Slovenian, and Polish communities—*five. separate. large. buildings*. And that's not counting the wide diversity of Protestant and Eastern Orthodox churches, both in town and out in the area around. At the height of its boom, over six thousand people called Forest City home.

Then the mine collapsed. Then the Great Depression hit.

Then deindustrialization . . . and then . . .

By the 1980s, only a third of that number remained.

Each of these churches still held Masses and services in their own building.

Each and every Sunday.

At staggered times.

As each community couldn't afford a pastor on their own—thus sharing one.

Yet, they were *committed* to keep their community alive.

Committed to celebrating the uniqueness of their community—its culture, its traditions.

Its life—believe me, they were *alive*: Sunday morning breakfasts, weekly Bible studies, annual festivals—and that's just what each church did on its own. They would regularly do events together and always participated in the town's annual homecoming celebration: Old Home Week. Each summer, parades, events, markets, and the beauty of the area and its people combined to create that most elusive of miracles: the perfect summer week. Yes: The summers, holidays, and weekends of my childhood were spent immersed in the life of communities that had faced devastation, death, decline—and refused to accept defeat, defiantly declaring that they were going to live fully and live in hope. Stubborn, unyielding, perhaps even impractical—and yet, hope nonetheless.

When I was thirteen, we left the New York suburbs and moved to Appalachia—Scottsboro, in northeast Alabama, to be precise—in the last few years before the internet finally connected everyone to everyone else. This beautiful town—nestled along the Tennessee River, tucked in the shadow of Sand Mountain—was (in)famous for the Scottsboro Boys case, in which nine Black kids were falsely accused of raping two white women in 1931. These boys had been hitching train rides across the South and simply happened to arrive in town because the train stopped there. It was extremely easy for some townsfolk to concoct a fantasy in which these boys were somehow responsible for raping two white women. Poor, unemployed drifters, who happened to be Black? This was all the proof needed for the all-white juries, of the hastily prepared trials, to convict each of them. A brazen attempt at legal lynchings, of course. Eventually (years later), the US Supreme Court tossed their sentences and convictions. The last man waited until 1976 for a pardon. One woman later recanted—without consequence, of course.

I should note that I learned the story only years later. This story was not taught in either of the two history classes (US and Alabama) I took while living there, nor did anyone in town ever refer to this history. It wasn't disputed, it was *erased*.

Notably, Sand Mountain is itself well-known to those who are familiar with that uniquely Appalachian, apocalyptic, religious culture known as holiness snake handling, where girls wear their hair down, women wear it up, all of them wear skirts—and everyone took Mark 16:18 at its word. If the Bible says that the disciples of Jesus Christ will go out into the world speaking in tongues, casting out demons, handling deadly snakes, drinking poison, and healing people—they *believe* it. The girls attended the public school, though. None of them ever spoke to me—the Catholic *Yankee* with the weird, Italian last name—the entire time I lived there.

I bear the proud marks of Sicilians: olive complexion and hair that reflects the personalities of our grandmothers—untamable and unbreakable. In the early 1990s we'd still rub the ashes off of our foreheads in the car, driving home from Ash Wednesday. Suffice it to say: It was obvious that my family were Yankees *and* Roman Catholics, and thus we stuck out wherever we went. The first renaissance of the Ku Klux Klan—in the 1920s—was built on the pillars of white supremacy, anti-Semitism, and anti-Catholicism. My first year living there, I unknowingly befriended the nephew of the Grand . . . something of the KKK—dragon? goblin? giant? titan? sentinel? Seriously, all of their titles were "Grand," even if they were just the treasurer of their tiny mountain town's local racist club—or "Christian fraternal organization."

We attended the one Catholic Church in town. At that time, Scottsboro proper ended *miles* before the actual town limit—hills and cotton and small factories and green (so *green*), occasionally dotted with homes—trailer and otherwise. At that time, the town boundary ran close to the church building—the outskirts of town. Two percent of the population of Alabama was Roman Catholic, while the church boasted less than one hundred souls.

The church was (and still is) named after St. Jude.

St. Jude is the patron saint of lost causes and desperate situations.

The irony and humor of the name did not escape anyone who attended there, and the community actually took it on as a badge of honor, a declaration of our fervent commitment to building community in a place that, from all evidence, viewed us with deep skepticism. Yet, every single Sunday the church held an extremely popular breakfast that brought the entire community together over the gloppy, creamy wonderfulness that is biscuits and gravy. At St. Jude's I experienced firsthand the power of food to weave a community into a family: This tiny community, clinging to the edges of town and culture, gathered as one family over coffee and then brought this joy with them into worship—literally, as we'd walk, chatting loudly, across the parking lot from the hall to the church building, carrying our laughter through the doors toward our seats. Everything I ever needed to learn about the importance of building church community through nurturing close relationships I learned from St. Jude's. We didn't *have hope* for our community; instead, we simply lived *as community* and expressed our hopes for the community through rolling up our shirtsleeves and getting to work embodying the community we wanted to exist in the world. In other words, we didn't *have* hope, we *lived* hope.

The Church Is Hope Wherever You Are

Not to sound too dramatic, but this is also the only hope that I can retain in Quakerism. I'm not seeking to be alarmist. I don't foresee or forecast the imminent doom of Quakerism: neither its constituent parts nor its place as a force for change in the world. Yet, according to demographic projections, many parts of North American and European Quakerism are facing a numerical crisis. Endowments are stretching past breaking point, and some meetings are faced with the unenviable choice of what bills to pay. We are not alone in this; nearly every denomination in the Christian community is facing similar challenges. It might seem to be a foolhardy gesture to have hope in the future of Quakerism or even Western Christianity.

Yet, I retain hope. This is the only choice I have. Then again, this is the only choice we ever have. The determination to retain hope is the only method we have to keep our faith communities alive and healthy. If we rest complacent, we sign the death warrant of the church. Every moment we rest in the confidence that the church is fine is a moment we have lost hope in the church. Every moment we commit ourselves to building the community of God in the world is a moment we have hope in the church. If this sounds exhausting, it is and should be: Simply put, this is the most important task we will ever be faced with. Building community is our task, and hope is the main resource God has provided for us to fulfill it.

This all only makes sense, however, if we restructure our understanding of church and of hope. I used to think that church meant a building or even an institution. I've searched for the perfect church home for decades, sojourning from the Roman Catholic Church through the Anglican Communion, with a pause for healing with an Anglican lay Franciscan Order, to Quakerism, and finally as a member of this family of people I know as my community—whatever we are, in the liminal hybridity that is Woven Faith Community. Every time I felt as if I had found "it"—the place, the church—I've been disappointed. That's because the church isn't a building, or attendance numbers, or even our institutions. These are all ephemera.

The church isn't a place; it's hope itself. The church is our stubborn determination to root our lives in the God who so loved God's creation that God stared complete hopelessness in the face and still retained hope; this happened not just once, but still happens every single moment. God demonstrates hope in us through a gritty determination and commitment to remain in relationship with us. We demonstrate hope in God by committing ourselves every day to remain in relationship with God and with each other.

Our church communities are the relationships that help us to best meet God and give us the strength to maintain hope amid the challenges of life. Everything serves that end: theology, liturgy, testimonies, even business method. If a community is not fostering hope and committed relationships, it will eventually pass away. We can't fret about the growth or decline of denominations, for the act of fretting takes away our energies from having the active hope that is the only true lifeblood of a community. Our responsibility is to remain committed to doing the hard work of active, vital hope. If we hope, our communities will be strong and vital, because it is the act of hope itself that weaves us together as a community.

It's often said of Convinced Friends that we feel immediately at home in Quakerism. One of the gifts of my long and varied journey is that it has given me this very specific perspective: There was a time when I felt at home in each and every community I have ever been a part of. I was never deluding myself: Each community was right for me at that specific moment in time. At this time in my life, I have hope that Woven Faith Community is where I am supposed to express my Quaker testimony. I can't worry about where I am going to need to be tomorrow, or whether I'm going to eventually move—I mean, what's more Quakerly than obedience to Divine leading?

Today I have hope, and that *must* be enough.

This morning, I woke early to drive to one of the schools I teach for, because life still goes on, classes need teaching, students need to learn, and regardless of the outcome of an election, I am a teacher and I have a responsibility to keep faith in the value of that task. I am also a member of a community, of a family, of a commitment to each other that remains. Finally, I am a writer and a poet, sacred tasks that—over these last few months—have come to mean more to me than they ever did before. If the election last night taught me anything, it's that we each have a responsibility to each other *to be who we are*. I cannot be fully myself when others are not fully themselves, yes, but this is like unto it: Others cannot be fully themselves when I am not fully myself.

It's now time to get to work. We have a monumental task ahead of us, and while we shouldn't begin when we're not ready, we also can't allow the mire to swallow us and douse the light of Divine Love that courses through our veins. Nothing can do that to us but ourselves, for that love is as close to our hearts—and as central to our being—as our own blood. We are followers of a man who lived a life that centered peace, and justice, and compassion, in the face of occupation and oppression and ostentatious, overwhelming violence—who refused to accept the world as hate had made it and demanded a new world. And they killed him for it.

Yet, the power of his witness ripples through the ages, touching each of our lives deeply and profoundly. We know what is right and true, and we must live into that rightness, and truth: that God loves us all—completely, and that we must respond in kind.

We can do no other.

We are not new to this whole apocalypse thing. We are a people who have survived and who are still here, preaching the gospel of infinite love for all—and using words only when necessary. The world desperately needs witnesses to that love, testimony of the power of hope to sustain us, and sanctuaries—refuges—where the vulnerable and the lost can find a home, root, and begin to heal. That is our task as church: That is who we are, that is what we are made to do. We are people who stare the power of hate and the state in the face and say: Bring it on.

BIBLIOGRAPHY

Anderson, Paul. "Continuing Revelation—Gospel or Heresy?" In *Good and Evil: Quaker Perspectives*, edited by Jackie Leach Scully and Pink Dandelion. Ashgate, 2007.

Anderson, Paul, Christy Randazzo, and Lonnie Valentine, eds. *Quakers and the Future of Peacemaking*. Quakers and the Disciplines 8. Full Media Services, 2024.

Bailie, Gil. *Violence Unveiled: Humanity at the Crossroads*. Crossroad, 1995.

Battle, Michael. *Blessed Are the Peacemakers: A Christian Spirituality of Nonviolence*. Mercer University Press, 2004.

Battle, Michael. *Reconciliation: The Ubuntu Theology of Desmond Tutu*. Pilgrim, 1997.

Battle, Michael. *Ubuntu: I in You and You in Me*. Seabury Books, 2009.

Bauer, Jerald C. "Puritan Mysticism and the Development of Liberalism." *Church History* 19, no. 3 (1950): 151–70.

Beals, Corwynn. "Evil: The Presence of Absence." In *Good and Evil: Quaker Perspectives*, edited by Jackie Leach Scully and Pink Dandelion. Ashgate, 2007.

Benatar, Solomon R., Abdallah S. Daar, and Peter A. Singer. "Global Health Ethics: The Rationale for Mutual Caring." *International Affairs* 79, no. 1 (2003): 107–38.

Blunden, Jessica, and T. Boyer, eds. "State of the Climate in 2020." *Bulletin of the American Meteorological Society* 102, no. 8 (2021). https://ametsoc.net/sotc2020/State_of_the_Climate_in_2020_LowRes96.pdf

Bock, Cherice. "Quakers and Creation Care: Potentials and Pitfalls for an Ecotheology of Friends." In *Quakers, Creation Care and Sustainability*, edited by Cherice Bock and Stephen Potthoff, Quakers and the Disciplines 6, 69–95. Full Media Services, 2019.

Bock, Cherice, and Christy Randazzo. *Quakers, Ecology, and the Light*. Brill Research Perspectives in Quaker Studies. Brill, 2023.

Boesak, Allan. *Black and Reformed: Apartheid, Liberation, and the Calvinist Tradition*. Orbis Books, 1986.

Bonhoeffer, Dietrich. *Discipleship*. Fortress, 2003.

Bonhoeffer, Dietrich. *A Testament to Freedom*. Edited by Geffrey B. Kelly and E. Barton Nelson. HarperOne, 1995.

Boulding, Elise. *Building a Global Civic Culture: Education for an Interdependent World*. Teachers College Press, 1988.
Boulding, Elise. *Children's Rights and the Wheel of Life*. Transaction, 1979.
Boulding, Elise. *Cultures of Peace: The Hidden Side of History*. Syracuse University Press, 2000.
Boulding, Elise. *One Small Plot of Heaven: Reflections on Family Life by a Quaker Sociologist*. Pendle Hill, 1989.
Boulding, Elise. *The Underside of History: A View of Women Through Time*. Halsted, 1976.
Boulding, Elise. *Women in the Twentieth Century World*. Halsted, 1977.
Brain, W. Russell. *Man, Society, and Religion*. Swarthmore, 1944.
Braithwaite, William C. *Spiritual Guidance in the Experience of the Society of Friends*. Headley Brothers, 1909.
Brinton, Howard. *Friends for 300 Years: The History and Beliefs of the Society of Friends Since George Fox Started the Quaker Movement*. Sowers, 1972.
Brinton, Howard. *The Religious Philosophy of Quakerism: The Beliefs of Fox, Barclay and Penn as Based on the Gospel of John*. Pendle Hill, 1973.
Brown, A. Barratt. *Democratic Leadership*. Allen & Unwin, 1938.
Buber, Martin. *I and Thou*. T&T Clark, 1987.
Cadbury, Henry J. *Quakerism and Early Christianity*. Allen & Unwin, 1957.
Calhoun, Craig. "Morality, Identity, and Historical Explanation: Charles Taylor on the Sources of the Self." *Sociological Theory* 9, no. 2 (1991): 232–63.
Carter, Charles F. *On Having a Sense of All Conditions*. Swarthmore, 1971.
Central and Southern Africa Yearly Meeting. *Living Adventurously: Quaker Faith and Practice*. Central and Southern Africa Yearly Meeting, 2009. https://www.quakers.co.za/wp-content/uploads/2014/04/Living-Adventurously.pdf.
Collier, Howard E. *Towards a New Manner of Living*. Swarthmore, 1936.
Cone, James. *A Black Theology of Liberation*. Orbis Books, 1990.
Congar, Yves. *I Believe in the Holy Spirit*. Seabury Books, 1983.
Creasey, Maurice A. *Bearing, or Friends and the New Reformation*. Friends Home Service, 1969.
Daly, Gabriel. "Forgiveness and Community." In *Reconciling Memories*, edited by Alan D. Falconer and Joseph Liechty. Columba, 1998.
Dandelion, Pink. "The Creation of Coherence: The 'Quaker Double Culture' and the 'Absolute Perhaps.'" In *The Quaker Condition: The Sociology of a Liberal Religion*, edited by Pink Dandelion and Peter Collins. Cambridge Scholars, 2008.
Dandelion, Pink. *An Introduction to Quakerism*. Cambridge University Press, 2007.
Dandelion, Pink. *The Liturgies of Quakerism*. Ashgate, 2005.
Dandelion, Pink. *A Sociological Analysis of the Theology of the Quakers: The Silent Revolution*. Edwin Mellen, 1996.
Davey, Ray. *A Channel of Peace: The Story of the Corrymeela Community*. Marshall Pickering, 1993.

Davie, Martin. *British Quaker Theology Since 1895*. Edwin Mellen, 1997.
Davis, Christine A. M. *Minding the Future*. Quaker Books, 2008.
Delio, Ilia. *Clare of Assisi: A Heart Full of Love*. St. Anthony Messenger, 2007.
Delio, Ilia. *Franciscan Prayer*. St. Anthony Messenger, 2004.
Den Uyl, Douglas J., and Douglas B. Rasmussen. "The Myth of Atomism." *The Review of Metaphysics* 59, no. 4 (2006): 841–68.
Doncaster, Hugh. *God in Every Man*. Allen & Unwin, 1963.
Dunstan, Edgar G. *Quakers and the Religious Quest*. Allen & Unwin, 1956.
Eccles, Peter J. *The Presence in the Midst: Reflections on Discernment*. Quaker Books, 2009.
Eddington, Arthur Stanley. *Science and the Unseen World*. Allen & Unwin, 1929.
Elowsky, Joel C., ed., *John 1–10*. Ancient Christian Commentary on Scripture New Testament 4A. InterVarsity, 2006.
Enloe, Cynthia. *Bananas, Beaches, and Bases: Making Feminist Sense of International Politics*. 2nd ed. University of California Press, 2014.
Fairn, R. Duncan. *Quakerism: A Faith for Ordinary Men*. Allen & Unwin, 1951.
Farmer, Paul. *Pathologies of Power: Health, Human Rights, and the New War on the Poor*. University of California Press, 2005.
Fell, Margaret. *An Epistle to Convinced Friends*. Quaker Historical Press, 1656. http://www.qhpress.org/texts/oldqwhp/mf-e-3.htm.
Fisher, Simon. *Spirited Living: Waging Conflict, Building Peace*. Quaker Books, 2004.
Fosdick, Harry E. *Rufus Jones Speaks to Our Time*. Macmillan, 1951.
Fox, George. "Epistle 200." George Fox's Epistles, 1831. https://qbi.earlham.edu/gfe/e200-206.htm#e200.
Fox, George. *The Journal of George Fox*. Edited by John L. Nickalls. Philadelphia Yearly Meeting of Friends, 1997.
Friesen, Duane K. "Encourage Grassroots Peacemaking Groups and Voluntary Associations." In *Just Peacemaking: Ten Practices for Abolishing War*, edited by Glen Stassen. Pilgrim, 1998.
Garrow, David. *Bearing the Cross: Martin Luther King, Jr., and the Southern Christian Leadership Conference*. W. Morrow, 1986.
Gillman, Harvey. *A Minority of One: A Journey with Friends*. Quaker Home Service, 1988.
Glover, T. R. *The Nature and Purpose of a Christian Society*. Headley Brothers, 1912.
Gorman, George H. *The Amazing Fact of Quaker Worship*. Friends Home Service Committee, 1973.
Graham, John W. *The Quaker Ministry*. Swarthmore, 1925.
Grant, Rhiannon. *Theology from Listening: Finding the Core of Liberal Quaker Theological Thought*. Brill Quaker Studies 3.2. Brill, 2020.
Greenwood, John Omerod. *Signs of Life: Art and Religious Experience*. Friends Home Service Committee, 1978.
Grubb, Edward. *Authority and the Light Within*. James Clarke, 1909.

Grubb, Edward. *The Historic and Inward Christ: A Study in Quaker Thought*. Headley Brothers, 1914.

Gwyn, Douglas. *Apocalypse of the Word: The Life and Message of George Fox*. Friends United, 1986.

Gwyn, Douglas. *The Covenant Crucified: Quakers and the Rise of Capitalism*. Quaker Books, 2006.

Harvey, John W. *The Salt and the Leaven*. Allen & Unwin, 1947.

Harvey, Margaret M. *The Law of Liberty*. Allen & Unwin, 1942.

Hauerwas, Stanley. *A Community of Character: Towards a Constructive Christian Social Ethic*. University of Notre Dame Press, 1981.

Hauerwas, Stanley. *The Hauerwas Reader*. Edited by John Berkman and Michael Cartwright. Duke University Press, 2001.

Hauerwas, Stanley. *The Peaceable Kingdom: A Primer in Christian Ethics*. University of Notre Dame Press, 1983.

Hauerwas, Stanley, and William H. Willimon. *Resident Aliens: Life in the Christian Colony*. Abingdon, 1989.

Heathfield, Margaret. *Being Together: Our Corporate Life in the Religious Society of Friends*. Quaker Home Service, 1994.

Held, Virginia. "Feminist Transformations of Moral Theory." *Philosophy and Phenomenological Research* 50, supplement (1990): 321–44.

Hetherington, Ralph. "A Theology of Quaker Universalism." *Quaker Universalist Fellowship*, no. 5 (1985): 15–22.

Hill, Christopher. *The World Turned Upside Down: Radical Ideas During the English Revolution*. Penguin, 1984.

Holdsworth, Christopher. *Steps in a Large Room: A Quaker Explores the Monastic Tradition*. Quaker Home Service, 1985.

Holmes, Barbara A., and Susan R. Holmes-Winfield. "Sex, Stones and Power Games: A Woman Caught in the Intersection of Law and Religion (John 7:53–8:11)." In *Pregnant Passion: Gender, Sex and Violence in the Bible*, edited by Cheryl A. Kirk-Duggan. Society of Biblical Literature, 2003.

Hopkins, Gerard Manley. "God's Grandeur." 1877. https://poets.org/poem/gods-grandeur.

Hughes, John A. *The Light of Christ in a Pagan World*. Allen & Unwin, 1940.

Jantzen, Grace M. "Choose Life! Early Quaker Women and Violence in Modernity." *Quaker Studies* 9, no. 2 (2005): 137–55.

Jeffery, George B. *Christ, Yesterday and Today*. Allen & Unwin, 1934.

Jones, Rufus. *The Nature and Authority of Conscience*. Swarthmore, 1920.

Jones, Rufus. *The New Quest*. Macmillan, 1928.

Jones, Rufus. *New Studies in Mystical Religion*. Macmillan, 1927.

Jones, Rufus. *A Service of Love in War Time: American Friends Relief Work in Europe, 1917–1919*. Macmillan, 1920.

Jones, Rufus. *Social Law in the Spiritual World: Studies in Human and Divine Inter-Relationship*. John C. Winston, 1904.
Jones, Rufus. *The Testimony of the Soul*. Macmillan, 1936.
Jones, Rufus. *The World Within*. Macmillan, 1918.
Jones, Serene. *Trauma and Grace: Theology in a Ruptured World*. Westminster John Knox, 2009.
Julian of Norwich. *Revelations of Divine Love*. Penguin Books, 1998.
Katongele, Emmanuel, and Chris Rice. *Reconciling All Things: A Christian Vision for Justice, Peace and Healing*. IVP Books, 2008.
Kim, Jean K. *Woman and Nation: An Intercontextual Reading of the Gospel of John from a Postcolonial Feminist Perspective*. Brill Academic, 2004.
Kinahan, Timothy. *A More Excellent Way: A Vision for Northern Ireland*. Corrymeela, 1998.
Kruse, Michael. "The Escalator Ride That Changed America." *Politico Magazine*, June 14, 2019. https://www.politico.com/magazine/story/2019/06/14/donald-trump-campaign-announcement-tower-escalator-oral-history-227148/.
Lacey, Paul. *The Unequal World We Inhabit: Quaker Response to Terrorism and Fundamentalism*. Quaker Books, 2010.
Lampe, G. W. H. *God as Spirit*. The Bampton Lectures 1976. Clarendon, 1977.
Littleboy, William. *The Day of Our Visitation*. Headley Brothers, 1917.
London Yearly Meeting. *Report of the Proceedings of the Conference of Members of the Society of Friends, Held, by Direction of the Yearly Meeting, in Manchester from the Eleventh to the Fifteenth of Eleventh Month, 1895*. 3rd ed. Headley Brothers, 1896.
MacMurray, John. *Search for Reality in Religion*. Allen & Unwin, 1965.
McCreary, Alf. *Corrymeela: The Search for Peace*. Christian Journals, 1975.
McCreary, Alf. *In War and Peace: The Story of Corrymeela*. Brehon, 2007.
McFague, Sallie. *The Body of God: An Ecological Theology*. Fortress, 1993.
McFague, Sallie. *Life Abundant: Rethinking Theology and Economy for a Planet in Peril*. Fortress, 2001.
McFague, Sallie. *Models of God: Theology for an Ecological, Nuclear Age*. Fortress, 1987.
McMaster, Johnston. *A Passion for Justice: Social Ethics in the Celtic Tradition*. Dunedin Academic, 2008.
Min, Anselm Kyongsuk. "Solidarity of Others in the Power of the Holy Spirit: Pneumatology in a Divided World." In *Advents of the Spirit: An Introduction to the Current Study of Pneumatology*, edited by Bradford D. Hinze and D. Lyle Dabney. Marquette University Press, 2001.
Morrow, John. *On The Road of Reconciliation: A Brief Memoir*. Columba, 2003.
Mott, Lucretia. "Not Christianity, But Priestcraft." 1854. Speaking While Female. https://speakingwhilefemale.co/religion-mott/.

Muers, Rachel. *Testimony: Quakerism and Theological Ethics*. SCM, 2015.
Nelson-Pallmeyer, Jack. *Saving Christianity from Empire*. Continuum, 2005.
New Jersey Climate Change Resource Center. "Sea Level Rise in New Jersey: Projections and Impacts." Rutgers University, May 2020. https://njclimateresourcecenter.rutgers.edu/climate_change_101/sea-level-rise-in-new-jersey-projections-and-impacts/#:~:text=For%20example%2C%20according%20to%20a,feet%20between%202000%20and%202050.
NOAA. "What Is a Watershed?" National Ocean Service, June 16, 2024. https://oceanservice.noaa.gov/facts/watershed.html.
NOAA National Centers for Environmental Information. "2023 Was the Warmest Year in the Modern Temperature Record." Climate.gov, January 17, 2024. https://www.climate.gov/news-features/featured-images/2023-was-warmest-year-modern-temperature-record#:~:text=Details,decade%2520(2014%E2%80%932023).
O'Day, Gail R. "John." In *The Woman's Bible Commentary*, edited by Carol A. Newsom and Sharon H. Ringe. Westminster John Knox, 1998.
Outler, Albert C., ed. *John Wesley*. Oxford University Press, 1964.
Pato, Luke Lungile. "African Theologies." In *Doing Theology in Context: South African Perspectives*, edited by John W. de Gruchy and Charles Villa-Vicencio. Orbis Books, 1994.
Peters, Richard S. *Reason, Morality, and Religion*. Swarthmore, 1972.
Polder, Kristianna. "Margaret Fell, Mother of the New Jerusalem." In *New Critical Studies of Quaker Women, 1650–1800*, edited by Michelle Lise Tarter and Catie Gill. Oxford University Press, 2018.
Priestland, Gerald. *Reasonable Uncertainty: A Quaker Approach to Doctrine*. Quaker Books, 1982.
Punshon, John. *Testimony and Tradition: Some Aspects of Quaker Spirituality*. Quaker Home Service, 1990.
Rae, Murray. "Remnant People: The Ecclesia as Sign of Reconciliation." In *The Theology of Reconciliation*, edited by Colin E. Gunton. T&T Clark, 2003.
Randazzo, Christy. "Affirmation Mysticism: The Activist Theology of Rufus Jones." *Quaker Religious Thought*, no. 133 (2019), article 3. https://digitalcommons.georgefox.edu/cgi/viewcontent.cgi?article=2401&context=qrt.
Randazzo, Christy. "Christian AND Universalist? Charting Liberal Quaker Theological Developments Through the Swarthmore Lectures." *Quaker* Religious Thought, no. 131 (2018), article 4. https://digitalcommons.georgefox.edu/cgi/viewcontent.cgi?article=2383&context=qrt.
Randazzo, Christy. "The Complex Hybridity of Ham Sok-Heon." *Quaker Religious Thought*, no. 129 (2017): 18–24.
Randazzo, Christy. "'The Divine Light of Creation': Liberal Quaker Metaphors of Divine/Creation Interdependence." In *Quakers, Creation Care and Sustainability*, edited by Cherice Bock and Stephen Potthoff, Quakers and the Disciplines 6, 96–114. Full Media Services, 2019.

Randazzo, Christy. "An Ever-Branching River: The Beautiful Watersheds of the Quaker Theological Ecosystem." *Quaker Studies* 29, no. 1 (Winter 2025).

Randazzo, Christy. "Let Love Be the First Motion." Political Theology Network, April 19, 2021. https://politicaltheology.com/let-love-be-the-first-motion/.

Randazzo, Christy. "Liberal Quaker Pneumatology." In *The Quaker World*, edited by Wess Daniels and Rhiannon Grant. Routledge, 2022.

Randazzo, Christy. *Liberal Quaker Reconciliation Theology*. Brill Research Perspectives in Quaker Studies. Brill, 2020.

Randazzo, Christy. "The Sleepers Must Awaken." Political Theology Network, March 23, 2020. https://politicaltheology.com/the-sleepers-must-awaken/.

Randazzo, Christy. "The Timeless Power of Hope." Political Theology Network, October 24, 2022. https://politicaltheology.com/the-timeless-power-of-hope/.

Randazzo, Christy. "The Tree Is Always Known By Its Fruit." Political Theology Network, September 2, 2024. https://politicaltheology.com/the-tree-is-always-known-by-its-fruit/.

Randazzo, Christy. "True Vines and True Branches." Political Theology Network, April 22, 2024. https://politicaltheology.com/true-vines-and-true-branches/.

Randazzo, Christy, and David Russell. "The Inner Light and the Light of God: Islamic and Quaker Mysticism in Dialogue." In *Quakers and Mysticism: Comparative and Syncretic Approaches to Spirituality*, edited by Jon R. Kershner. Palgrave Macmillan, 2019.

Randazzo, Daniel (Christy). "The Interdependent Light: A Quaker Theology of Reconciliation." PhD diss., University of Birmingham, 2018.

Ruston, Roger. *Human Rights and the Image of God*. SCM, 2004.

Rutter, Michael. *A Measure of Our Values: Goals and Dilemmas in the Upbringing of Children*. Friends Home Service Committee, 1983.

Schoolman, Morton. "The Moral Sentiments of Neoliberalism." *Political Theory* 15, no. 2 (1987): 205–24.

Schreiter, Robert J. *Reconciliation: Mission and Ministry in a Changing Social Order*. Orbis Books, 1992.

Schwab, Lukas, Nadja Gebhardt, Hans-Christoph Friederich, and Christoph Nikendei. "Climate Change Related Depression, Anxiety and Stress Symptoms Perceived by Medical Students." *International Journal of Environmental Research and Public Health* 19, no. 15 (2022).

Schweiker, William. "A Preface to Ethics: Global Dynamics and the Integrity of Life." *Journal of Religious Ethics* 32, no. 1 (2004): 13–37.

Scott, Janet. *What Canst Thou Say? Towards a Quaker Theology*. Swarthmore, 1980.

Scott, Richenda C. *Tradition and Experience*. Allen & Unwin, 1964.

Scruton, Bruce. "'We Are All in Trouble.' New Jersey Tops List of States Warming up the Fastest." *New Jersey Herald*, August 30, 2021. https://www.njherald.com/story/news/2021/08/30/nj-weather-tops-list-of-states-global-warming/5615695001/.

Scully, Jackie Leach. "Quakers and Ethics." In *The Oxford Handbook of Quaker Studies*, edited by Stephen W. Angell and Pink Dandelion. Oxford University Press, 2013.

Scully, Jackie Leach. "Virtuous Friends: Morality and Quaker Identity." In *The Quaker Condition: The Sociology of a Liberal Religion*, ed. Pink Dandelion and Peter Collins. Cambridge Scholars, 2008.

Sender, R., S. Fuchs, and R. Milo. "Revised Estimates for the Number of Human and Bacteria Cells in the Body." *PLoS Biology* 14, no. 8 (2016): e1002533. doi.org/10.1371/journal.pbio.1002533.

Sigurdson, Ola. "Is the Trinity a Practical Doctrine?" In *The Concept of God in Global Dialogue*, edited by Werner G. Jeanrond and Aasulv Lande. Orbis Books, 2005.

Silcock, Harry T. *Christ and the World's Unrest*. Swarthmore, 1927.

Smith, R. Drew. "Ecclesiastical Racism and the Politics of Confession." In *Race and Reconciliation in South Africa: A Multicultural Dialogue in Comparative Perspective*, edited by William E. Van Vugt and G. Daan Cloete. Lexington Books, 2000.

Spencer, Carole Dale. "'Quakers in Theological Context." In *The Oxford Handbook of Quaker Studies*, edited by Stephen W. Angell and Pink Dandelion. Oxford University Press, 2013.

Stevens, David. *The Land of Unlikeness: Explorations into Reconciliation*. Columba, 2004.

Stevens, David. *The Place Called Reconciliation: Texts to Explore*. Corrymeela, 2008.

Sullivan, Walter Hjelt. "Earth Quaker Action Team: Reclaiming the Lamb's War for Justice and Sustainability in the Twenty-First Century." In *Quakers, Creation Care, and Sustainability*, edited by Cherice Bock and Stephen Potthoff. Quakers and the Disciplines 6. Friends Association for Higher Education, 2019.

Thelle, Notto R. "Relation, Awareness and Energy." In *The Concept of God in Global Dialogue*, edited by Werner G. Jeanrond and Aasulv Lande. Orbis Books, 2005.

Thomas, David. *Christ Divided: Liberalism, Ecumenism, and Race in South Africa*. Unisa, 2002.

Thurman, Howard. *Jesus and the Disinherited*. Abingdon-Cokesbury, 1949.

Thurman, Howard. *The Luminous Darkness*. Friends United, 1989.

Trevett, Christine. *Previous Convictions and End-of-the-Millenium Quakerism*. Quaker Books, 1997.

Trump, Donald. "Presidential Announcement Speech." *Time*, June 16, 2015. https://time.com/3923128/donald-trump-announcement-speech/.

Tutu, Desmond. *No Future Without Forgiveness*. Image Books, Doubleday, 2000.

Ullmann, Richard. *Tolerance and the Intolerable*. Allen & Unwin, 1961.

Van Der Heijden, Marcel G. A., and Thomas R. Horton. "Socialism in Soil? The importance of Mycorrhizal Fungal Networks for Facilitation in Natural Ecosystems." *Journal of Ecology* 97, no. 6 (2009): 1139–50.

Villa-Vicencio, Charles. "Christianity and Human Rights." *Journal of Law and Religion* 14, no. 2 (2000): 579–600.

Wildwood, Alex. *A Faith to Call Our Own: Quaker Tradition in the Light of Contemporary Movements of the Spirit*. Quaker Home Service, 1999.

Williams, Rowan. *The Wound of Knowledge: Christian Spirituality from the New Testament to Saint John of the Cross*. Cowley, 1990.

Wilson, Lloyd Lee. *Essays on the Quaker Vision of Gospel Order*. Celo Valley Books, 1993.

Wilson, William E. *Our Response to God*. Allen & Unwin, 1935.

Wohlleben, Peter. *The Hidden Life of Trees: What They Feel, How They Communicate—Discoveries from a Secret World*. Translated by Jane Billinghurst. Greystone Books, 2016.

Wood, Herbert G. *Quakerism and the Future of the Church*. Swarthmore, 1920.

Woodard, Colin. *American Nations: A History of the Eleven Rival Regional Cultures of North America*. Penguin Books, 2011.

Wright, Frank. "Reconciling the Histories of Protestant and Catholic in Northern Ireland." In *Reconciling Memories*, edited by Alan D. Falconer and Joseph Liechty. Dublin: Columba, 1998.

Yearly Meeting of the Religious Society of Friends (Quakers) in Britain. *Quaker Faith and Practice*. Britain Yearly Meeting, 1994.

INDEX OF STORIES

INDEX OF BIBLE REFERENCES

INDEX OF SUBJECTS AND AUTHORS